Jane Doe January

Jane Doe January

MY TWENTY-YEAR
SEARCH FOR
TRUTH AND JUSTICE

Emily Winslow

WILLIAM MORROW
An Imprint of HarperCollins*Publishers*

HarperCollins books may be purchased for educational, business, or sales promotional use. For information please e-mail the Special Markets Department at SPsales@harpercollins.com.

FIRST EDITION

Designed by Jessica Shatan Heslin/Studio Shatan, Inc.

Library of Congress Cataloging-in-Publication Data has been applied for.

ISBN 978-0-06-243480-7

16 17 18 19 20   OV/RRD   10 9 8 7 6 5 4 3 2 1

For John Hughes,
much missed

PART I

———

Remembering

1

SEPTEMBER 2013

Relief is first. After twenty-one years, the man has at last been identified. Tabs fill my browser: news articles describing his arrest in New York by a Fugitive Task Force at the request of Pennsylvania police. Google's image search has called up many different faces, but I know his immediately. His chubby cheeks make me flinch. I find his Facebook page, but don't dare friend him to see what he's posted, even though I'm desperate for information.

Jealousy is second. The other victim is going to get it all: a solemn courtroom, a sympathetic jury, an avenging judge. For more than twenty years, that's what I've wanted: to get to say what happened, to be who he's punished for. Now she gets the detectives who need her to prove their case; she gets the attorneys who need her to perform on the stand. She matters. I'm still the beggar I've been for two decades, calling the police every couple of years to ask them to look again; always talking to new detectives because none of them stay; always having to explain who I am, explain the case, because no one remembers, except for me. And her. And him.

This is good news. This is terrible news. This is everything I've wanted, but for someone else.

He's been arrested for what he did to her. I want him charged for what he did to me.

I practice, just in case.

I pace; I talk to myself. If I get to court, if I get my chance, I want to tell everything in an orderly way. I want to get it right.

In 1992, I was a junior at Carnegie Mellon University's elite drama conservatory in Pittsburgh, Pennsylvania. It was an intense program, the goal of which was to turn out actors who could transform. Being "safe" was looked down on. Freshmen and sophomores were forbidden from playing characters with which they were comfortable. No elegant, witty Restoration ladies or innocent ingénues for me anymore. In acting class, in voice and speech class, in movement class, I was challenged to play against type: be physical, be sexual, be angry. I accepted the challenge, but clung to church-going and Bible study in my personal life as a counterweight. I was proud to have made it into the program. I was proud at the end of each of the first four semesters to make it through "the cut." More than thirty young actors had been admitted to the program in the fall of 1989. Four years later, after aggressive cuts and a handful of students ditching the program to go straight to New York, only thirteen of our original class would graduate.

In our third year, we were past the cut. We were also supposed to have been sufficiently stretched by the experiences of our first two years to be given back our comfortable roles that we would now play better, deeper, and with real choice. Underclassmen looked up to us.

I lived in a little studio apartment off campus, in Shadyside, the most posh of Pittsburgh's college neighborhoods, full of restaurants and shops. I had worked at the nearby Victoria's Secret briefly over Christmas break, as holiday help, enjoying the over-the-top femininity of the job. All my life I've vacillated between enjoying and eschewing dress-up; I was then on a dressy upswing, wearing makeup and girly clothes daily. Classes were going to start up again that week in January. I had two monologues to memorize. I needed to do laundry, but had no change for my building's coin-operated machines. I went out to get some.

It was early evening on a Sunday. I saw a man watch me exit the building, and was wary. The fancy ice-cream shop on the corner was open and I got quarters for the washer and dryer. People were happy in there, chatting and choosing flavors. Outside, the man was still there, still hanging around. I hesitated. He started walking toward my building, not behind me, but from the side. That seemed to make it okay; it's not as though he were following me. He'd started from farther away than me, which timed him to reach the building just after me. I wanted to make the door click shut behind me, but it had a pneumatic closer and moved slowly. I couldn't pull it any faster. He caught it.

Again, I hesitated. I sort of knew the woman who lived in the other apartment on my floor. I could knock; safety in numbers. But he passed me and went up the stairs, clearly on his own way, again not following me. He passed my apartment door, and trotted up more stairs toward the next floor.

I knew he wasn't the man who lived up there, but I assumed he was a friend. This was a college town. Confident nonresident visitors were normal to me, even if they weren't common in this particular building, which was more full of yuppies than students.

I passed, without knocking, the apartment of the woman I sort of knew. I unlocked my door. He sprang from the stairwell behind my shoulder, pushing me inside my apartment, covering my mouth. He shut the door and pressed me up against the wall by my face. He asked me, "Do you wanna die?"

"Do you wanna die?" was the phrase that made detectives sit up straighter when they interviewed me in the hospital later. An attacker had said the same to another student three days before, in nearby Oakland. She, the detectives told me, had escaped before the man could do what he wanted to do.

I did not escape. He had me for exactly as long as he wanted me, which, it turns out, wasn't that long. He seemed to have a mental checklist of foreplay that he cycled through efficiently: *Do this, now do this . . .* I had never done any of it before. I had only ever kissed, and not even that since high school, except for onstage. I was waiting for love and marriage.

Later, my attempts to describe him to the police were pathetic. *He was big,* I said. *He had a childish face and voice.* That vague "big" could have meant any number of things, and at first they brought me a tall man, a jogger they'd found nearby. He looked terrified. At the hospital, a tall detective had towered over me and asked, "Was he as big as *me*?" I had never meant tall. I'd meant fat, broad, strong, heavy, powerful, and terrifying.

I did what he said, but I begged him to please stop. He persevered through token touches of all the "bases": kissing, hands and mouth above the waist, hands and mouth below the waist, him to me then me to him. He didn't linger at any of those places, just claimed each intimacy as if he were winning points for it and moved on to the next.

I balked at the fucking. As much as I wanted to live, I screamed. He had to put his hand over my mouth, over my nose and mouth together, and push down hard. I couldn't breathe. He told me he would move the hand if I promised to stop screaming. I nodded, desperately. Anything for a breath. His hand moved; I sucked air and screamed again, unstoppably, overriding any logical sense of self-preservation. He had to smother me again, longer this time. He taught me how much I want air, how much more important it is than anything. I nodded again, promising, begging. I was able to mean it. He released my face. I didn't scream anymore.

He positioned my feet on his shoulders, my knees squished up against my chest, and pushed. I told people later that this part took a long time. I know now that it was actually a pretty standard amount of time, but to me then it took surprisingly forever for him to finish. While he was doing it, something splashed from his face onto mine: either a shower of sweat from his forehead, or maybe he was crying. Maybe it was tears.

I remember all of this easily, having told it so many times back when it happened. But some details have faded; for example, I realize I've forgotten the name of the street I'd lived on then, and have to look it up in an archived news report. I reread the poems I'd written then and which I haven't looked at in years. There's a lot that haunted me then which surprises me now.

I've forgotten that he nipped at my legs with his teeth; the detectives had perked up with interest when I mentioned that, but he'd done it too lightly to leave forensically useful bite marks. I've forgotten that he pulled my shoes off, which was different from the way he'd left so much of the rest of my clothing on, shoved out of the way but still connected to me. I'd wondered after if shoe leather could take fingerprints.

I've forgotten that I'd tried to push him away with my hands. He'd wanted me limp and had to tell me, over and over, to put my hands on the floor, but I kept pushing against his shoulders, trying to force some small extra distance between us while he worked toward getting done. He'd repeated it, over and over, annoyed and commanding—"Put your hands on the floor"—so I must have kept them there, or kept putting them back.

That phrase had stuck with me after, bothering me when I washed my hands or even just looked at them. "New memories," I'd written a few months later. "Wouldn't that be nice? To think of, say, my hands, and think of someone nice instead of him. But wouldn't it be even better to look at my hands and see my hands, to think of my body and think of myself? Must my hands, my body, always make me think of a man, even if someday a nice one?"

My mind is a jumble of details coming back again and again to the smothering: his hands pulling at the buttons down the front of my dress; his hands pulling down my leggings and tights; his hand pushing down hard on my face, the back of my head pressed into ratty renter's carpeting. It's not his mouth or his body or sweat or tears that I think of; it's his hands and my hands. Lots and lots of hands.

The drama department was surprisingly patient with me after it happened. Actually, it's to be expected that creative people would be sensitive, but I found their generosity unexpected given how readily they cut from the program those who don't keep up. I was allowed to miss the first few weeks of the semester entirely, and, after my return, was fully excused from "rhythm," a demanding physical class that could reduce participants to tears even under normal circumstances. I attended the rest of my classes, but was allowed to slip away anytime I needed to, without consequence. I was even allowed, if I wanted, to take a friend out with me.

I made rules for myself. I wanted to accept the support I'd been offered, but not become dependent on it. I wanted to grieve and rage and whatever else I needed to go through, but didn't want to get stuck there. I was a little afraid of being hurt again, but mostly afraid that I had been fundamentally changed for the worse. I didn't want to permanently become (as I wrote then) "timid and fearful, faithless and cynical, frigid, hysterical, angry and bitter and tired, weak, crazy." I didn't want to become any of those, but I felt it a real danger that I would become all of them. So, I made rules.

The first was that I would let myself be a mess for one year. After that, I had to get it together. The second was that I would lean on my friends, my generous, sweet friends, only during the day. I would go ahead, tug someone's arm to bring them aside with me, or make a phone call asking for company on the rare daylight occasions that we weren't already together in class or rehearsal (we were heavily scheduled). The caveat was that I would never allow myself to wake someone up. At nighttime I had to look after myself. That gave me a bit of self-respect.

I slept surprisingly well, and in the whole "be a mess" year I only had to act on that second rule, the no-nighttime-neediness one, once. The police had taken my clothes away for evidence the night of the rape, and weeks or maybe a month or two later they returned them to me, in a tall, thick paper bag with numbers scribbled on it in heavy marker.

I was living with friends, previous graduates of the drama department, in my own room in their newlywed apartment, where I would end up staying for the whole semester. I had all of my things in my one room, including then this awful bag. I couldn't sleep. My friends were just on the other side of the wall, in bed.

I was desperate to talk, but had promised myself to get through my nights on my own. To make it possible to sleep, I wrote down what I wished I could tell someone. I could call someone in the morning, I reasoned, and could read from my notes like a script if necessary. This is what I wrote:

The bag broods in the corner
sitting on its haunches
squat, over two feet tall
with my body inside
my coat
pretty little thing
used to be my mother's
old-fashioned high neck mink collar
that had been covering my low-cut neckline that evening—I swear!
The detective persuaded the lab not to cut it up for evidence
The dress had soaked up enough, he told them
so that he could bring the coat back to me
stained but in one piece
one whole piece
like me
alive but blotched
the coat that was taken away from me that night
the body-shaped thing I haven't seen since
the dead me
who I used to be
sitting stuffed in a bag

The next morning, I read it and was satisfied. I didn't need to call anyone. After that, I wrote as much as I talked.

I never wore the coat, or any other clothes from that night, again. I did wear the shoes, even though he'd pulled them off my feet. They were my favorites. It seemed very important to deliberately decide that just because something had been touched by him, that didn't automatically make that thing garbage.

My first flashback happened outside next to the statue of inventor George Westinghouse, just a few weeks after I'd returned to the drama department. It had started during a class, and I took my friend Allen out with me. When we were far enough away from everyone else, I explained to him what was happening. I knew in my mind where and when I was; I knew I was safe and on campus; but my emotions and my body were reacting as if I were back in my studio apartment, on that awful January Sunday. My heart raced and my breathing was shallow. I was terrified, though I logically knew that nothing bad was currently happening and that I had nothing to be afraid of. The mismatch of my knowledge of reality versus my feelings both emotional and physical was terrifying. I honestly thought that I had lost my mind.

These flashbacks ended up happening a lot for about eighteen months, six months beyond my self-imposed deadline for self-sufficiency. I got used to it. When they happened, I leaned on the men in my class more than the women. The women were just as loving and kind to me, but they felt they understood my experience to a certain degree, while the men were just horrified and in awe. The women tried to relate to my experience, generously, which made me feel possessive. *It's mine,* I wanted to say, hoarding it. The men treated me gingerly, like an alien creature, which felt safer somehow. I was still trying to figure out how I felt about everything, and appreciated freedom from other people's interpretations, however genuinely well meant.

Acting school is touchy-feely. We were used to hugging one another in greeting, massaging one another as part of class, even kissing onstage, all as a matter of course. We played opposite one another in a round robin of romantic parts, and there was a lot of mutual attraction. The atmosphere was a soup of feelings. It was the best possible place for me to be.

My friends of both genders were physically affectionate and emotionally articulate, and we had few boundaries. That was just how we were taught. Our bodies and our inner lives were the tools we used in the classroom and on the stage, so they were normal topics of discussion, both with and among the faculty and with each other. Sometimes—often—the personal aspects of the work, and of the criticism, were overwhelming. But, after the attack, the department's routine public handling of normally private topics, and the habitual physical closeness, became gifts.

My religious chastity, which was no secret, put me out of the running for being anyone's girlfriend, and in the middle of all that openness was the one bright line. Though it was difficult to abstain—I was desperately worried that putting off happy sex could give the rape further power over me—it freed the men to be generous with me, without any confusion over what their platonic affection might signify, and allowed the women to not mind if their boyfriends looked after me. I was desperate to not become afraid of men, and I looked to my classmates as examples of "good men" who would override the blot on my experience. In particular, I was able to experiment with relearning how to feel attraction, without worrying that anything would actually happen. No one in my class would have considered crossing that line.

Light shone gorgeously on the fine blond hairs of John's arm, and I got to kiss Aaron in a scene in acting class. Bradley took me up to Mount Washington to look at the city skyline with him and cry. He squeezed me against his chest. "I had all those little lights," I wrote afterward about the city view, "one for every hundred tears. How sad it would have been if I had had only the tears."

For one of my first roles after coming back, I was Clytemnestra the queen, playing literally bloody Greek tragedy. I felt finally able to key in on some difficult and complex emotions due to my recent experience; but the director was uncomfortable with my delivery of a monologue that coupled sex and rage, so it was cut. For my character's murder, however, there was no reprieve.

The character Orestes was directed to stand over me with a knife while I begged for my life, a scene we repeated over and over so that the Greek chorus could be blocked in behind us. There was no safe-word for me to signal that I was actually distressed, not just acting, but my friend read me well. Still posing his face in grim determination, still bearing down on me with a pointy phallic object as he was required to do, he crossed his eyes to crack me up. He had to press his lips together to keep silent, and so did I, but we both giggled inside while we acted out my murder, and guffawed when it was over.

Orestes had been played by the only black man in our admittedly small class. The man who had raped me was also black. I'm white. I know that my experience after the rape is what it is in part because of biases that reward my race and class and religion. I was the perfect victim, not in the sense of attracting harm, but in the sense of the world being indignant on my behalf.

Everyone was angry, and it was the best gift they could have given me. Because they were so angry, I didn't have to be. Up on Mount Washington, while Bradley held me, he whispered in my ear what he wanted to do to the man, a torture-filled fantasy of revenge. I didn't have to prove that what had happened had hurt; that it was wrong; that it was significant; that I was not at fault. I think self-destruction can become necessary if a pain is not understood by others. You have to show people that it's so bad that you want to die. You have to make them understand if they don't already. Luckily, my pain had been understood. I was freed by the anger of my friends from having to prove anything by demonstrating anger myself.

That said, I was angry. I'd genuinely forgotten about that until now, when I found it in the poems I wrote then: wanting to stab my mother's cousin with a steak knife when he innocently put his arm around my shoulders for a photo, and later wanting to strangle a pigeon. Even inanimate objects weren't spared. When my tights caught on the head of a screw in a window seat, I "plunged my finger in and ground the screw down . . . I hoped I was hurting it."

Sometimes I felt suicidal, but I wasn't actually going to do it. I had a rule for that, too: you can kill yourself tomorrow if you still need to then. I just had to say it every day, tomorrow, too, to keep putting it off.

Though all the kindness and affection around me were platonic, there was one person I was madly in love with. He was my dearest friend, and might have returned my feelings in part, but lack of sex was a deal breaker for him. I wallowed in unrequited longing, which was a wonderful distraction from grief and rage.

After seeing him on a date with someone else, I wrote about stars and how, no matter how special they are, they're invisible when there's something brighter around. Even when feeling ashamed of myself for not being good enough, I wanted to think of myself as something sparkly, if inadequate: "I'm not who you want but, however far I may be from your desires, I am in my own place a sun. Please be at least flattered by this fire loving you. Though I may seem to you smaller than a penny and common in the pin-dot sky, I am a fire and I do love you."

It felt so wonderfully normal. In college, you're supposed to suffer from youthful heartbreak. Crying over the sweet friend who didn't love me was a nice change from crying over the bad man who'd held me down and cracked me open.

I traveled to Europe with my mother over the summer, just as we had planned before the attack: lazy long walks in the Black Forest and in the Alps and along Venetian canals, visiting family and friends and familiar places. She let me pick which way we'd go every time a path gave a choice; the only German phrase I still know from that trip is *diesen Weg*—"this way"—because I said it over and over every day.

I returned for senior year refreshed. I got a new apartment, living on my own like before, but in a different neighborhood. I worried about doing well with my work and getting good roles and pleasing my teachers. I enjoyed the tight corsets and swishy skirts of period costumes, acting in the epic nine-hour *Nicholas Nickleby* and in a funny and elegant production of *Tartuffe*. Mingled in with the trauma, from which I still suffered in various ways but worked hard to start coping with less obviously, were ordinary college thoughts, the typical acting-school vanity and insecurity that we all shared. We were always looking at ourselves. The mirrored walls of the dance studios made this easy but also too obvious. I wrote, "The windows are better. When the lights on inside reflect my transparent silhouette off the glass night, I can pretend I'm bored, gazing at the tennis courts, when really I'm watching myself."

I was terrified from the rape; and also terrified by worry that I wasn't good enough—at performing, at being pretty, at being liked—just like most everyone else.

It's easy for actors to get into the mind-set of always seeing ourselves as if from the outside, always thinking of how others are viewing us. I tried to balance that with a moratorium on photos in my daily life, only allowing them for performances and special events. As a result, most of my college pictures are of me in costume, in shows or backstage or at cast parties. In almost all of them, even after the rape, I'm smiling.

There's a temptation to regard the hidden and tragic as the "true," and the presented and happy as the "fake," but I don't find that to be accurate. All of it was true. I was broken and sad and angry and weak and scared and in love and ambitious and hardworking and proud of myself and really into the fun wigs and costumes we got to wear. I mentally compared it to British taps, where there are separate faucets for the hot and the cold. Unlike in normal single taps, where increasing the cold makes the hot less hot, and adding hot makes the cold less cold, the sinks I'd used abroad kept the two apart. Things were apart in me. Happy feelings didn't cancel out the terrible ones; nor did the bad mitigate the good. Every feeling was just itself. They rushed side by side, each of them strong on their own and unaffected by the other. All of them were powerful in their own ways.

In November 1992, less than a year after my rape, another woman was attacked, again in Shadyside, like me.

The new victim had answered her door to a man with a clipboard in his hand. I had a clipboard job in Pittsburgh one college Christmas, raising money for some environmental cause. People had always opened their doors to me. Some of them had even invited me in. If I'd made my quota for the evening, I would stay in out of the cold and snow, sipping hot chocolate with a random, hospitable family until it was time to be picked up. Opening the door to clipboard people was a standard thing to do.

This new victim heard her clipboard man out and declined to give and tried to close the door. He'd stuck his foot in, though, and pushed himself through, and lifted her up by her neck.

It's the DNA that he left in her that gets him arrested in 2013, twenty-one years later, and which has the potential to lead to the solution of my case, too.

2

I used to keep the names of all the detectives I've ever spoken with in the back of an address book. Years later, when I transferred my collection of addresses to a digital record, I made the deliberate decision not to copy the names of the police before I threw the book away. What did it matter? If the pattern of turnover held, none of them worked in the Sex Assault Unit anymore.

For years I followed cases in Pittsburgh similar to mine. The one that overshadowed all the rest in the news was the East End rapist, who got a lot of press when he was caught in 2007. Keith Wood was ultimately convicted for raping four women in 2000 and 2001. When his name came up in one of my searches, I wondered if he could have been my guy. I wasn't the only one asking that question.

The victim of a 1988 rape contacted the police in 2011 to ask if Wood could have been her attacker. She was lucky to reach Detective Aprill-Noelle Campbell, who pulled her case file and sent her rape kit to be analyzed. "Rape kits" are the evidence packs collected after assaults, full of potential bits of the man, and comparison bits of the victim. The DNA results from her kit matched not Wood, but another man, in California, who was then arrested and confessed. He's in prison now.

I, too, had called the Pittsburgh police, reaching Detective Dan Honan, in hope of similar success. I came close to getting my kit in the lab queue, but it never quite got there.

The policy of the lab had once been to analyze DNA only when there was a suspect to compare it to; otherwise there was nothing to test against, as there was not yet a reference database of criminal DNA as there is now. Now DNA analysis is routinely performed for current cases, but for the old cases, they don't have the time or workforce to tackle them all. Individual old cases are carefully chosen. Honan didn't think that the East End rapist fit my attack profile. I was not a priority.

It's also the general policy of the Sex Assault Unit to leave victims alone. I assume that there are people who appreciate that, who want to move on and forget, and would find check-in contact from the police to be unwelcome and traumatic. I, on the other hand, felt abandoned. I called every few years, and each time there were new detectives, no one whose name I recognized. None of them had heard of me either, or of the early-nineties Shadyside rapes. I would have to explain myself and, to their credit, the automatic response was always to treat me very, very carefully, as if there were a soap bubble around me that they had to be mindful not to pop. Every member of the Pittsburgh police who has dealt with me has always been respectful and kind in manner to me. Still, nothing progressed. There were present cases that needed more urgent attention. I had moved overseas, to my British husband's home city. It had happened a long time ago.

In April 2013, a friend of the woman who'd opened the door to the man with the clipboard also called the Pittsburgh police to follow up. She, like the lucky woman above, reached Detective Campbell, and the woman's evidence kit was analyzed. It matched the DNA of Arthur Fryar, from a sample taken for a 2002 drug conviction in New York. He was arrested on September 12, at 6 A.M. at his home in Brooklyn.

That rape had taken place in the same year as mine, only blocks from my apartment. This one they were willing to run my kit for.

Though I had thrown away the names of all of the previous detectives, I remembered one without having it written down: Detective Valenta. He was the one who had questioned me in the hospital the night it happened.

In 2013, I find him via his LinkedIn profile. I discover that his first name is William, that he's become an assistant dean at the University of Pittsburgh's business school, and that before retirement from the force he'd been promoted all the way to commander. I e-mail to let him know about the arrest and possible link with my case.

He replies kindly, goes to police headquarters to review my file, speaks to the lieutenant of Major Crimes on my behalf, and replies again. We exchange family photos. His youngest and my oldest are near in age.

We e-mail almost daily. He explains the forensic and bureaucratic processes to me. I tell him what I remember about the original investigation, and he puts names and backstory to the figures I describe.

He'd heard of my case over the police radio that night in 1992. While regular police responded to my 911 call by coming to my apartment, taking my clothes as evidence, and escorting me to the hospital, he and another detective had driven around the surrounding streets looking for the man.

At the hospital, the nurses had fussed over me, clearly upset but trying to put on good cheer. They'd blushed and giggled when Detective Valenta arrived, because he looked just like you would cast a movie's young leading detective to look. I remember thinking that their reaction was sweet. I was in shock, I assume.

Valenta had apologized for having to ask me, but, he'd explained, every touch would become a separate charge. I had to answer yes or no for every sexual act he could reel off. Two decades later, I ask him if he'd had a checklist for that, or if he'd just improvised such a long, weary catalog. He says that he'd done a hundred sex assault interviews by then, five years into the job. He hadn't needed a checklist.

I finally feel that I, who'd failed to win the lottery of being assigned to Detective Aprill-Noelle Campbell with her knack for cold cases, at last have a real ally.

I look to the trial of Pittsburgh's East End rapist for some hints of what to expect, if all goes as I hope it to. One of the more descriptive articles details the "impact statements" that victims had presented at sentencing. They describe lasting physical injury, career effects, repeated suicide attempts, sexual fears, PTSD, and ongoing depression.

I feel threatened by these stories. I feel like a slacker. What kind of victim am I? Getting past what happened should be a victory, but I feel like I'm letting my side down. It doesn't seem fair to measure the badness of what my attacker did in an inverse ratio to how I've coped. It seems that the better I've done, the more I've been able to thrive, the more he'll then be excused, the more that what he did to me will be downgraded in significance.

I want to take the stand to tell what he did in my apartment, even if it means facing a defense lawyer who'll ask what I'd worn that night. Impact statements, on the other hand, seem to require talking about what I've done since. I don't want to be the one on trial.

I honestly can't figure out in what exact ways I'm different because of this. How do I know what I would have been like otherwise? Am

I wary, when I walk at night or sleep alone, because of this, or just because it's sensible to be? I can't tell if my fascination with crime, reading all of the serial-killer books in my hometown library, is a memory from my high school years, before the rape, or from when I came back home to live with my parents for grad school, after.

A friend of mine thinks that I left acting because of the rape. I don't know if that's true. I think I was getting sick of acting before it happened. I remember feeling exhausted by how vague and tricky it was to try to improve, how personal and immediate the criticisms were. It was exciting, too, of course, and deep and meaningful and playful. But if I don't like being on display as an inherent aspect of my job, well, that could be the rape, or it could just be common sense.

Some friends think it's a wonder that I'm functional at all. They're surprised to learn that this happened to me, because they expect someone to whom this has happened to be less optimistic, less out-going. They don't know that this has probably happened to a lot of other people they know, who just haven't mentioned it yet, and who are still versions of their earlier selves afterward. I'm glad that rape is now popularly understood to be a serious and violent crime, not just a "mistake" or "misunderstanding" or "bad date." But popular under-standing can go too far in the other direction, and put expectations on victims to be not just hurt but permanently broken.

What if the rape has made me more empathetic, more honest, more open to the wide spectrum of acceptable feelings? It's made me a better writer, which is now my job. Am I supposed to thank him for that? I want to thank myself for that, and my friends. I want for him to be judged for what he did, not for how I reacted.

I don't want to have to say that he ruined my life. I don't want to consider my life ruined.

My husband, Gavin, is protective about keeping this about me, not about him. He wants to know how I feel and what he can do for me. He won't divulge how he feels about it, I think even to himself. He would consider that unseemly and self-indulgent. He can't sleep and admits that he's stressed. I ask him what about, and he says, "Nothing."

I haven't told our boys, ages eight and twelve, but perhaps they know something's up. I'm being impatient, and easily frustrated by interruptions; I'm distracted, sensitive, panicky. The twelve-year-old looks over my shoulder. I'm writing an e-mail about "detectives" and have tabs open about "extradition" and "DNA." He assumes it's research for my next novel. I let him think that.

Euphemisms help.

I try to avoid saying "rape." That word upsets people. It's too personal. It doesn't help that I live in England now, not just England but *Cambridge,* and everyone here is so fucking polite and formal and circumspect.

When I tell Gavin about the latest updates, I refer to the subject breezily as "that whole Pittsburgh thing." That's for my sake, not his.

I pick friends at random, whoever happens to be standing close to me but out of earshot of kids, to tell about the arrest and prosecution, but I imply that I'm a "witness." I say, in hope, that I'm going to testify in a cold case now reopened, and they think that I saw something, which I did. I saw him doing things to me. I'm not outright lying, just circling the truth. They ask, gingerly, if it happened to a friend. I finally say, "No, me." I point to my middle, just under my rib cage. "Me."

Talking about it now is harder than it was then. Then, the information had been urgent, and was a needed explanation. "I won't be in class for a few weeks," I'd had to explain. "I'm a little messed up right now," I'd had to excuse. Now there's no context. The information drops with a thud. My friends now are as kind as my friends then. The difference is that now there's no call to action, no necessary assistance they can offer. I don't need a place to stay, or help getting things out of that apartment, or someone to walk with me while I have a flashback. I don't know what I want in return for telling now, but I do want people to know. I need to be able to talk about what's happening with the case, and for that to be understood they need to know about the crime.

Back then, I saw a counselor for just a few sessions. She concluded that I was handling it in a healthy way and could move on without her; I agreed. I had enormous support and no guilt. Talking it out with people who loved me felt much more satisfying and healing than telling a paid stranger. At the end of the first year, when I had promised myself that I would stop being a full-time victim, I tried again, at the university's counseling center. That was a disaster. I told my randomly assigned therapist, straightforwardly, that I had been raped; my friends had been a great support; but I wanted to start weaning myself from relying on them so much. He'd leaned back and said, smugly, "Well, we both know that this isn't *really* about the rape. We can talk and try to figure out why you're really here." I walked out.

I've made a counseling appointment for later this week, with a chaplain, John Hughes, who I also consider a friend. His being in an official capacity means that I can make an appointment and that it won't be selfish and awful of me to talk mostly about myself; his being a friend means that he knows that I'm not just this, not just a mess, not just a falling-apart person, and also that he'll genuinely care. I already matter to him.

I don't know what to say to him. It seems awfully self-indulgent to just narrate what happened, without some goal, some dilemma or present decision to make. I've been trying out ways to begin, but none feel right. Do I start with that night? Or step back to first set the scene? Just cut to now, and my anxiety as I hope and wait to get my name added to the charges against the man? I want that more than anything. I feel an urge toward seeing this through, thoroughly. My friends wish for me to be spared having to travel, spared returning to the scene, spared a trial and having to testify, but I want it all.

I end up telling John everything, starting with what acting school is like, so that he understands the people who took care of me after. Without those bookends, the attack would be just a sordid action sequence; with them, it's a story. He makes us tea and listens carefully. He offers to connect me with a woman he knows who is an excellent counselor, but I don't want a stranger. I want to talk again with him. He seems surprised, and maybe flattered. His schedule is full up with services and students, then somehow now full with me, too. He makes room for me.

In New York, Detective Aprill Campbell has traveled from Pittsburgh to ask Arthur Fryar if he's remorseful, and if he wants to avoid a trial. She says that he can show that by telling her something: What had he said to both of the women in Shadyside?

"Their legs," he admits, matching exactly what the detective is looking for. "I liked their legs. I told them they had nice legs."

I'm told that that's in my file. I'm sure it is, but I don't remember it myself. At the time, I had apparently remembered it well enough to tell the police, but it's not one of the things that had then played again and again in my mind. It had been of little interest to me, not shocking or distressing, just a throwaway remark. Now it's one of the things solving my case.

I wonder about him remembering that so readily. It doesn't sound like he was recalling that we'd had legs he liked, but recalling specifically that he had *told* us that he liked them. Maybe saying that was his thing. Maybe he says that to his girlfriend.

Yes, he has a girlfriend. Detective Campbell talked to her. I think I'm supposed to feel sorry for her, but I'm disgusted, horrified, and sick at the thought. *How can she let him touch her?* It's shocking to me. I wonder, briefly, if she looks like me.

Detective Campbell tells me that Fryar assured his girlfriend not of his innocence, but that the statute of limitations had passed.

Statutes of limitations have a long history, even as far back as ancient Greece. The power of accusation can be abused and must be controlled. In the United States, many felonies have relatively short time periods in which a charge can be brought against someone; Rhode Island, for example, has one of the shortest limitations on charging someone with rape: just three years. Pennsylvania in 1992 allowed only five years; now they allow twelve.

One reason for statutes of limitations is concern for evidence. As time passes, witness memories fade and physical proofs (receipts for an alibi, for example) are thrown away. It would be unfair to wait to charge someone who might have been able to defend themselves at the time but no longer can, through no fault of their own. With technological advances, however, new forms of evidence, such as DNA analysis, better stand the test of time.

Another reason for limitation is the idea that someone who has committed only a long-ago crime, and not a recent one, could be considered reformed and of more good to society as an active citizen than a prisoner. I dislike that reason. Acknowledgment of the weight of the crime—and punishment is that acknowledgment—seems more important.

In the case of stranger rape, the delay of prosecution is often not a delay of accusation, which is what statutes of limitations are designed to prevent, but a delay of identification. That crucial difference has inspired several states to try to get around their current limitations. There are two common tactics: no-name warrants (charging, for example, "John Doe, unknown male, whose DNA profile has the following genetic locations . . . ") and amending the old statutes with new DNA exceptions.

In 2004, Pennsylvania took the second route. They added a law that allows new DNA matches, if they identify previously unsuspected persons, to reopen expired cases for a single fresh year. This, and only this, is what can reopen my case. In the absence of a DNA match to trigger the law, even a full confession won't be prosecutable.

The hospital visit right after the rape had been my first-ever gynecological exam, and the rape kit had added to the ordeal. I'd been combed and swabbed and plucked, humiliatingly and painfully, in the hope of one day bringing proof to court. But my evidence is not a sure thing. One of the samples from my kit, my blood, has already been found inadequate, either gone off or used up from when the kit was tested back in '92.

It hadn't been tested for DNA, of course. They had tested for blood type, enzyme markers, and secretor status of the attacker, characteristics far more general than a DNA identification. They had been as thorough on my behalf as the technology of the time recommended. Unfortunately, my kit might be in better shape for proper DNA analysis now if it had been, back then, left untouched.

Pittsburgh has sent my local police in England a collection kit for a "buccal swab" from the inside of my cheek. Unlike blood samples, which require temperature control, the swab only needs a little silica pack to see it through being shipped back across the Atlantic. When the Pittsburgh lab gets my fresh exemplar, they can try to untangle my DNA from the man's in the 1992 samples swabbed from inside me and cut from my underwear.

The sergeant looking after me here in Cambridge is a cheerful, chatty woman who told me earlier that she's working only nights this week. I show up at the police station at 10:30 P.M. and have to ask for her through a yellow phone attached to the outside wall. I've just come from a book club meeting that was discussing one of my novels, and have an enormous bouquet from them in my arms, orange roses mixed with buds that look like little strawberries. My laptop bag hangs heavily and awkwardly. I'm worried about being late for our babysitter. A man loiters on the street corner, making me nervous.

I think asking for a DNA test is code for "this is a sexual assault case." Earlier in the day I had dropped by to make sure I knew the correct entrance for later. The man at the front counter had been perfectly fine and friendly, but when I asked about entry after 10 P.M. he had just indicated that the station would be closed. I persisted, saying that the sergeant I needed to see is working nights, and then at last added that "I need to do a DNA test." That triggered an immediate softness, and the instruction to later use the yellow telephone.

The same happens with the man on the other end of the yellow phone. I ask for Sergeant Judith Hiley, and he tries to ring her. No answer. He tries a different number; no answer, and he seems like he's about to give up. I tell him that I'm there to take a DNA test, and, immediately, he swings into action, sending someone around the station to find her. I will get to see her tonight.

Sergeant Hiley brings me inside and then through, into a tiny room. I see no other people in the station, not one, not even in a corridor. Opening the UPS envelope from Pittsburgh feels like Christmas. Besides two swab kits (in case one goes wrong) there are instructions, a prepaid return label, and a prizelike fabric patch that says PITTSBURGH POLICE.

Sergeant Hiley says that the swabs are different from the British kind; they're also, I note, different from any I've seen on TV. They look like pregnancy tests. We lean in over the instructions and read them aloud to be sure we'll get it right. I'm to rub it seven times against the inside of my cheek, pulling only forward toward the lips, not rubbing back and forth. I think I've done it right. She seals it and marks the date carefully as "October the 4th" rather than using the usual numeric shorthand. The Brits do that day-month, opposite of Americans, and she worries it would be read as April 10th instead of 4th October if she did it her normal way.

It's the weekend, so the package won't even start flying until Monday.

I wait.

I feel stalled. The swab has arrived and I've been told that the lab manager in Pittsburgh is "excited" to receive it and that it's been made "a priority." Somehow this adds up to weeks before I can expect results. I'm impatient, and can't concentrate. An extradition hearing, to authorize moving Fryar from New York, where he was arrested, to Pennsylvania, where he'll be tried, was scheduled to have happened yesterday. Once he arrives, his charges will be read against him. They won't include mine. I don't count yet.

I feel guilty for continuing to see John the chaplain to talk about nothing happening, but he says that I'm welcome. He works for the Cambridge University college at which my young sons sing as boy sopranos with the college men. I have no relationship of my own with the college, so I worry that John may get into trouble for spending so much time on me. He cheerfully insists, always suggesting the next time with his calendar out. I asked him for help just the first time; he's never made me ask again.

The college makes an effort to embrace choir families, and the whole beautiful place feels open to me: the cloister court, the candlelit chapel, the practical rehearsal room lined with shelves of repertoire, the big green lawn where the boys battle with autumn chestnuts (which are called conkers here) and play soccer (which is called football) until they're called in for practice. The resulting music is extraordinary. It makes me happy. Sometimes it's so lovely I could cry.

I talk with John a lot. Random memories bubble up and pop. Not memories of the rape itself, but of ripples that radiated out from it:

In the hospital. The doctor gave me two pills: one for right then, and one for twelve hours later. She didn't tell me what they were but said, with intense gravity, that I *really really* should take them. I figured out later, after terrible cramps and queasiness, that they were the morning-after pill. My friends who'd come to the hospital had prayed in the waiting area, and I wore a gold cross around my neck. I assume that the doctor didn't tell me what the pills were out of concern that I might refuse them. I probably would have. I'm grateful now.

Going back to that apartment exactly once, to pick up my things. There were clouds of black fingerprint powder on the walls and door. Even the inside of my sink was dark and smeared, where the forensic people had washed their hands, and my pretty scented soap had dried dirty.

Some people ask me about forgiveness (notably not the chaplain, for which I'm grateful). It's something people want me to say yes to, but I'm not clear what's meant.

The parable of forgiveness in Matthew 18 has to do with forgiveness of debt. It comes down to canceling a debt and walking away from it. But when I ask these people, so keen for me to forgive, if they think that Arthur Fryar shouldn't go to prison, they're appalled. Of course, they insist, he must. I'm not sure how one can demand forgiveness and punishment in the same breath. Isn't the definition of forgiveness release from punishment?

I think they mean forgiveness as an internal position, something like a feeling. They want, for my sake, for me to be free of thinking of him at all. They want, for their sakes, for me to follow the religious script.

What I feel is that I would like for him to be sentenced long enough that he will surely die in prison, which I think is the opposite of forgiveness. What I also feel is pity for him, because I know he's worse off than me. I can't imagine how anyone can bear that kind of guilt. Well, the guilt that I think he ought to feel. I can pity him for that potential guilt, or pity him for being too broken to feel guilt, which I think would make him too broken to feel most anything else. Perhaps pity comes close to forgiveness. Pity is at least kind, if also condescending.

Detective Campbell has told me that Arthur Fryar claims to have lived in fear of capture these past two decades, and that he wants forgiveness from us, the two women he's admitted to. Again, I don't know what this means. Perhaps his best-case scenario is that we tell him that it's all right, it didn't hurt, we didn't mind. Impossible.

Next-best may be assurance that it was bad then, but all right now. I could almost offer that. I am happy now. He didn't break anything in me that didn't eventually heal. If that comforts him in prison, in the years he'll while away before he dies there, I don't mind.

Maybe that not-minding if he finds peace in prison counts as a kind of forgiveness, or at least indifference.

The date of the extradition hearing passes with no news. I ask Detective Campbell about it, and she scrambles to get information about a mysterious new New York court date that has appeared on the docket for a month from now.

It turns out that Arthur Fryar is fighting extradition, which means that he's denying his identity, the only thing an extradition hearing tries to prove. By doing so, he's inherently denying that he's Arthur Fryar, the man whose DNA has matched, an absurd argument that will be disproved but it will take time. Detective Campbell has never seen this before. This delay helps me, gives my evidence a chance to catch up. I'd been desperately worried that the other woman's case would surge ahead without me. The prosecution is slow motion now, like the lab. So long as court and forensics keep pace with one another, and keep inching forward together, it's not so bad having to wait.

This complication helps me in other ways, too. I feel like there's this huge machine, a machine made of dozens of people, acting out anger for me. Not that they feel angry; I don't think they do; but they're acting out what anger demands. The Pittsburgh police are gathering photos and fingerprints from a previous arrest to prove Arthur Fryar's identity. The district attorney is drafting a Governor's Warrant to force him to face what he's done. I don't have to demand anything.

It's nice inside the machine. The parts are working without my help. I think it's significant that in criminal cases there is no plaintiff. I'm not suing Arthur Fryar; if my evidence comes through, the state will prosecute him on my behalf for his offenses not only against me and the other woman but against society.

Some people think that I'm serene because I'm good. Really, I'm serene because other people are doing the ugly things for me. The ugly things need doing. I'm ready to act out anger if I have to, to be loud if I have to, to be demanding and pushy and forceful, but it's not needed. The machine grinds on.

I tell John what Arthur Fryar wants from me. He flinches when I say it, which I appreciate. He says that Fryar has no right to ask me for forgiveness. Fryar can ask God, but not me. Fryar's not allowed to ask me for anything.

John, so formal in the chapel and so domestic in his college office, is another hardworking part of the good machine.

Some people think it's surprising that I talk to him, of all people. I think he finds it a surprise, too. People assume that I would be uncomfortable talking to a man, but I don't mind men. I mind the one man.

The other reason for surprise, I suppose, is his age. He's young. Not too young; not in his twenties anymore; but, still, he's in his early thirties, about ten years younger than me.

I did marvel, when I hit forty, that I had aged significantly past many of the authority figures in my life: my agent and editor, the kids' teachers and coaches, various doctors and pastors. It bothered me for about a year. Now I feel like we're all in this together, all of us over-thirty grown-ups.

The undergraduates at the college—even the organ scholars, who have so much authority in the choir—look impossibly young to me. When I think about 1992, the males in my college class are "men" because I was their peer and we all felt grown-up at the time. But these undergraduates here in Cambridge, born so long after me, are kids. That's how young I used to be. *I was your age when it happened,* I think. Or maybe a little older, because I took a gap year before that was fashionable to do.

I realize, suddenly, that most of them weren't even born when it happened. In three months, it will be twenty-two years since that night. I was twenty-two then. It will be exactly double my life.

I've been assuming that the evidence will work. I've felt impatient, having to delay celebrating an official DNA match, but my anxiety has been only over waiting, not over the possible outcome.

Suddenly, at twelve days since the lab got my exemplar, I wobble. That the old evidence may be useless seems not just possible, but almost certain. I imagine that the police just don't want to tell me. The machine will drop me and move on. Legally, I'll be separated from the case, from the "real" victims. It's been years since the fast breathing, the sudden tears, and oppressive dread. These symptoms feel strange, old-fashioned, and self-indulgent. Who has a panic attack over something that *might* happen?

I shift my fantasy of good news to a fantasy of bad news. It's still a fantasy, a wished-for thing, because any news is better than limbo. Once I know, I'll be allowed to react and to tell. If the evidence fails, people will comfort me. While I wait, I'm just alone.

John's office in the college is like roof guttering for my feelings; it's where I can route my upset to do the least damage. It's a large but cozy-feeling room, full of well-worn furniture and books, with tea-making things and a large grandfather clock that I use to pace myself, to be sure that I've finished putting myself back together when it's time to go pick up my boys from rehearsal. I'm allowed to take off my shoes and curl my feet under me on the couch. He has only toilet paper for tears, no tissues. I tell him that that's okay; it's the same in our house; it's the kind of thing we always forget to buy. This is the first time I've cried in front of him. I didn't even cry when I told him exactly what had happened back then. I don't know what's come over me; I don't know why this reaction took five weeks to coalesce. I tug against the little dashed lines in the paper, separating the roll into streamers that I then fold and dab against my face.

Another day, after rehearsal, I'm supposed to walk my sons to a friend's book-launch party. I think that I've pulled myself together, but a comment sets me off. I'm able to hide it: I'm the last parent at pickup; it's dark; I cry silently. I ask the boys to just play on the grass for about ten minutes while I sit on the steps; I promise that I'll get it together and we'll go to the party then.

Our twelve-year-old, S., goes back into the rehearsal room instead, I assume for a cup of water. But he asks the organ scholar, Ben, if he can use his phone, and calls Gavin. "Dad?" S. says, right in front of Ben. "Can you pick us up and take us home? Mom's crying."

I don't mind that he phoned Gavin or that we're going to miss my friend's party. I do mind that he said, in front of Ben, that I'm in tears. I'd worked hard to hide it. He's blown my cover.

It's because of that that I have to explain. I've already told some people at the college, just a few, like the choir secretary and John. John has asked me over and over, "Let me tell Mark, please," meaning the Director of Music. "Let me tell the organ scholars," I suppose in order to make sense of the simmering and probably odd-seeming distress that I'm failing to keep completely hidden. I always said no.

After the crying incident, I agree at last that he can tell, but insist that he has to be precise. If he says that I'm going through vague "difficult, personal things," they'll think that Gavin and I are getting divorced. If he says that I'm going to court, they'll think that we're being sued. I instruct him, "If you're going to tell them anything, you have to tell them that it's rape. You have to use that word. You have to explain that it was more than twenty years ago and that the police have caught him now."

So the adults have to be spoon-fed specifications, while with my boys I dance around details. They're already used to a certain amount of inappropriate crime-talk around the house, because of the detective novels I write. The boys even came along once on a jaunty family outing to help me choose exactly where a fictional corpse would be dumped out in the fens. So long as I frame things from the police or courtroom point of view, they handle it. There's a big difference between a protagonist being hurt and a protagonist who is trying to fix things. I'm genuinely both, both victim then and now potentially avenger, so all I have to do is choose carefully how I say things in front of them.

Not much later, I get the chance to carefully say a little more.

It's a rare moment to be shepherding just one child on the bus; usually I have both. But W., our eight-year-old, is at kung fu with his dad, so S. and I have the journey to ourselves. We wait for the big, red, double-decker behemoth that still delights me eight years after moving to England.

S.'s eyes roam the Park-and-Ride waiting room, reading everything, including a newspaper headline about a local "home invasion." I quickly scan the text, enough to glean that it's about a robbery without murder or torture; scary but not extreme. I grab my chance: "Hey, did you know that something like that once happened to me?"

Something like that means something frightening, something criminal, something that didn't, though, kill me.

He looks more closely at the article, reading all of the words.

I clarify, "Not exactly like that, but close. It was a long, long time ago, when I was in college. You know the police I've been talking to? Well, they found the man who did it and I get to help put him in prison. It's really good news."

He nods. He already knows that something is going on, so I hope that this explanation answers a question rather than raising more.

"Like in Phoenix Wright," he says, meaning the courtroom video game he plays.

"Exactly. I might get to go to court, if the evidence comes through. The lab is working on it."

"What's the evidence?"

Semen. The evidence is semen.

"I'm not going to tell you."

He shrugs. "Okay."

My friends with daughters tell me that it's only sons who let things go that easily, who take huge news at face value and move on.

"Don't tell your brother," I add. "He's too young." W. only gets to know that I might get to help put away a bad guy, like superheroes do. That's the kind of story that makes them happy.

I keep Valenta updated. I tell him about Fryar fighting extradition. He replies, "Arthur has come to the realization that he will likely be spending the rest of his life in a prison in Pennsylvania, so I am not surprised to hear that he is doing everything that he can to delay the process."

Valenta's confidence in the coming punishment comforts me. His use of Fryar's first name, however, jars me. That "the bad man" is now "Arthur Fryar," no longer some nameless villain, is strange enough. Hearing the first name alone is actually shocking, as if he's a normal person, a person who might be greeted or phoned or e-mailed, a person with peers and school friends and coworkers. "Hey, Arthur!" someone might say, in a casual, happy way. It doesn't fit.

I think about Valenta's assessment, that "Arthur," who had previously been compliant to Detective Campbell's demands in interrogation, is now fighting, and so ridiculously, because he's scared. *Good,* I think. Honestly, he reminds me of me.

When he'd first gotten me down on the floor, I'd been afraid for my life. Placating him had been my priority, and I'd obeyed, even tried to please. But when it got to the worse part, I'd screamed anyway, even at the cost of being smothered for it. It wasn't rational. It wasn't worth my life to struggle so futilely, but I'd done it anyway; I'd had to.

This sudden reversal of his, this about-face from admission and remorse to futile denial of even his own identity? That's him screaming.

3

The phrase "going through the motions" is usually derisive, but I'm coming to appreciate having motions to go through, via the legal and religious systems around me.

If the lab takes too many more weeks with my evidence, even if there is a match, the legal processes will begin without me. I'll become an afterthought. Though we were equally harmed in 1992, the November victim will become the real invitee; I, Jane Doe January, will be merely the tagalong "+1." I don't think the police or the district attorney understand that. They must think: So long as the charges are added eventually, so long as Fryar is sentenced for me in the end, what does it matter if I'm not included in the original charges and preliminary hearing? But it matters a lot. Justice, for me, is about more than the sentencing. There's a process here, a ritual, and I want my place in all of it.

As for religious ritual, the brief, ceremonial evensongs on Thurs-

days and Saturdays in the college chapel are more comforting to me
now than our casual Sunday-morning church in town, which has
been leaning more toward glib American-style instruction lately,
with less humility, less awe, more how-to-live-your-life formula.
I'm far too old to put up with being told what to do.

In contrast, the chapel's formal recitations and extravagant music
console me. The services are Church-of-England Protestant—the
equivalent of American Episcopal—but as elaborate as Catholic
mass. Their tight structure holds me up from the outside, and asks
in return only for some standing, then sitting, now stand again and
say together a few scripted words. There's no sermon; I appreciate
the break from being hectored. There's just assurance, order, beauty.

Some chapel services are crowded, but a lot of them are attended
by only a handful of chorister parents. We all know each other and
each other's kids. The room is arranged with stalls along the two
long sides, so that the two halves of the choir face each other. The
parents are split in half, too, each of us sitting to face our own children. I've grown used to the way each parent across from me looks
when they're listening: rapt, amazed, grateful, humble; and the way
that some boys glance around, as they file in, to look for their parents' faces, and how those boys shine when they find them.

Membership in the choir has no expectation of belief; some
families are devout, some nominal, and some explicitly nonreli-
gious. I think I would have disparaged such an arrangement when
I was younger, but my ideals have slackened. I'm coming to see the
tenets of my faith as aspirational rather than foundational. We try;
we listen; we consider; we reach. We're going through the motions.
I mean that in a lovely way. The motions are literally lovely.

I apologize for talking about it, but talk about it anyway. There
never seems to be a right time, a private time. I told friends while
at a cocktail party. All of our kids were in the same room with us,

far enough away so that they wouldn't hear, but right there. There wasn't any other chance. Everyone I know I see only in the context of other things, either important things that we're supposed to be focusing on, or kid things that we're supposed to keep happy and light. I feel guilty for being more than just the one facet of myself that I'm there for.

Sometimes it's overwhelming to look at the world and notice that everyone in it is a whole person, the center of their own universe of experiences and concerns. Just to be able to function, we have to reduce people to their roles in our lives, even ourselves to our role of any given moment. The occasional glimpse of the complicated wholeness behind each role is humbling.

Stephen Hawking has suggested that the Big Bang could have been caused by the intersection of two universes, a bump that set off the explosion of a new universe. Sometimes I feel like human interactions and relationships are bumps like that, that we're all so enormous with pasts and desires and faults and ambitions that our little meetings have larger, occasionally explosive, effects.

I teach W. that when he asks his brother for help, with his schoolwork or with a video game or with music, he isn't getting a help robot; he's getting his brother, a whole person, who may not give exactly or only what's being asked for, but that what he gives is a gift to be appreciated as it is. Just saying that out loud rattles me, reminds me of how guilty I sometimes feel for being a whole person, for being complicated and chatty and inquisitive and emotional and brash. I'm never just a writer, or just a mother, or just a child-delivery system bringing my sons to their various activities, though I feel sometimes that I should be and apologize for being more.

I'm never as productive as I want to be, or as good at anything as I want to be, and now, so distracted by this case, I'm only worse. I suppose I should be as gentle with myself as I ask my children to be with each other. I suppose that being a universe of a person is what makes me however good a writer or mother or wife or friend that I manage to be, even if that full universe distracts me and others, and slows things down.

I tell myself: *Efficiency isn't the highest good*. I blink at the words. I know that they're true, but they honestly surprise me.

It's mid-November, two months since the arrest, and the date of the second extradition hearing passes. All I can find online is that, just like last time, there's a new New York court date set for a month away, at which time Pennsylvania can try again. Even though in the meantime Fryar stays in jail, the delay is maddening. It's also ultimately good for my case. The lab, it turns out, is going to take months, not weeks, despite my evidence being bumped ahead of everything except murder.

All I want is to catch up to the other case, to charge him together with the other known victim once he's extradited. I would hate for her to get to put him in prison and all I later get to do is add years to the sentence, years that, depending on the lengths assigned, he may never even live to serve. If we charge together, I can be part of putting him away. I can metaphorically shut the cell door on his pleading face. All his delay is accomplishing is creation of that chance.

His fighting of the extradition also means that, despite his smug and faux-remorseful admissions when he thought that the statute of limitations protected him, he's probably going to fight the charges when he does at last get to Pennsylvania court, which could get ugly. Part of me dreads the potential cross-examination. Part of me thinks, *Bring it on*.

Most of the people around me are careful not to ask how the case is going, which I know is meant to be polite but makes me feel instead like they're ashamed of me.

The American detectives look after me. They communicate effusively. Detective Campbell sends me an e-mail with the words "I PROMISE" in all caps. Valenta sends me an e-mail asking "Any updates???" with three question marks. It's as if we're teenagers, an age when every emotion is huge and requires punctuation to reflect that. I feel allowed to feel big things with them. It's as if they feel big things, too. It's as if it didn't happen to just me; it was an offense against all of us. We all want that chance to shut Fryar's cell door. We all want our hands pushing on it when it clicks.

Thanksgiving Day at home in the States is just an ordinary Thursday here. Gavin has just come back from business in California, and we're in a café, getting coffee into him, while our boys are off rehearsing. He asks me, shyly, about the rape: "Have you been reliving it, since the arrest?"

I hesitate. I've been thinking about it; not sure if that's "reliving" it. I worry that maybe he's sensed something off about me, something not present, maybe something in sex or parenting that I've been doing badly. I answer cautiously: "Kind of."

He says, quickly, relieved to blurt it out: "I have." He didn't know me then, but before we got married he read the poems I'd written then and we talked about it. I wonder what pictures those words add up to in his mind, how he imagines my apartment, how he imagines younger me. He probably doesn't know that my hair was bobbed that year, not long like it is now. I'd forgotten that myself until just recently.

He looks worried, and sad.

"Why don't you talk to John?" I suggest. "He's really nice." John is friends with both of us, both me and Gavin, though he knows me better because I'm more often at choir.

Gavin shakes his head. "I can't do that and look after your feelings at the same time." I think he's worried that starting is easy and stopping may be hard.

We compromise. He agrees to see John when I finally go away for the hearing. I've decided that I'm going to go, whether my evidence is ready or not, whether or not I get to testify. We still don't know if it's imminent or weeks away, but, whenever it will be, Gavin will get to stay behind and take over being the sad one, the one who needs listening to.

It's like when S. goes away, even just for a day, and W. gets to be the "big kid" of the house. W.'s personality shifts; he takes on a temporary confidence and sense of responsibility that then evaporate away when the usual order resumes. When I go to Pittsburgh, Gavin will get to have feelings about this, briefly. It will get to be his pain, his worry, his turn.

December. Arthur Fryar's still in Rikers Island, New York City's infamous jail, waiting on a midmonth hearing. I'm told that if he continues to fight the extradition, he'll get six more weeks there, at least. I look up how the jail celebrates Christmas. An old news article describes a program that provides the inmates with gift-wrapped socks, and a more recent article gives the recipe for the jail's special holiday carrot cake, featuring ingredients such as "3 gallons vegetable oil" and "25 pounds flour," noting that each batch "makes 25 loaves."

Cambridge does the season prettily. S. sings treble in a sold-out *Messiah,* and plays timpani in a paid, black-tie gig of Rutter's *Gloria.* W. sings the college Christmas services and squeaks "Away in a Manger" on his cello at home. Because the university term ends very early and most of the students will go home, all of these concerts and services glut the beginning of the month. By the time the holiday actually arrives, we'll be sick of carols.

It's during this run of getting our sons to and from rehearsals and performances that my evidence, after more than twenty years in a freezer, manages to produce a DNA profile that's then matched with Arthur Fryar in the FBI database. I get the news while walking home one evening under twinkly white lights; Detective Honan had called our home phone, and Gavin phones me. That week's music seems to punctuate the breakthrough: *Hallelujah. Gloria.*

It was Detective Honan who had called, not Detective Campbell, because she's attached to the other victim. She's kept me abreast of developments in her case; now that I have a case of my own, I'll deal more with Honan, the detective I'd randomly been matched with more than a year ago, when I'd tried to get this started.

The match starts my clock ticking: the police have an exception to the statute of limitations of exactly one year, starting now, to "commence" the prosecution. I'm not sure whether charging Fryar counts as "commencing," or if we have to actually get into court within that year. Assuming that my case will be linked with the other, which matched back in August, we'll be "commenced" by summer at the latest, whatever the definition is. All his delaying has been an attempt to run out the clock, but the measures available to him simply won't stretch far enough.

I casually e-mail Detective Honan that it would be nice if Fryar's officially charged for me in time for my birthday. Honan replies that they still have to wait for the complete lab report, so it won't be that fast. I double-take, surprised that he knows when my birthday is. Gavin laughs and says, "Of course he does. It must be at the top of some page in your file."

I wonder how the current detectives picture me, having just the old case notes, and recent phone calls and e-mails. They know such personal things, yet hardly anything else. Does my file have a photo from back then? Do they know what I look like now? Have they seen my website or looked at the picture above the bio in one of my books? They probably don't even know that I write. Valenta does, but I don't think the new ones do. What do they see in their minds when they think of me? Is their imagined me a twenty-two-year-old student or an almost forty-four-year-old mother? To be honest, in my own mind I'm both.

I'm sick of waiting, and I piss Detective Campbell off. I can tell that she's annoyed with my repeated requests for an explanation of the rescheduled hearings. I am demanding, but only of information that already exists. I can be patient for information that's still being created, but, once something is known, I want to know it, too. It's maddening that New York won't be more open about what's going on with the extradition hearings, and maddening that Campbell won't dog them.

New York is far away from me now, but still feels like a kind of home. It was "the city" when I grew up nearby, close enough to take the train to after school (or instead of school); it's where I interned as a grad student and worked on my thesis; it's where I got my first magazine work. My sister lives there, my college and camp friends, too, and my agent, and editor. It's my editor, Randall, who helps me. He agrees to attend this third extradition hearing and tell me what happens. He asks me what I want to know.

Everything, I think. *What's it like to be in the same room with him? Is he awful? Or does he seem normal? From his manner do you think he's ashamed, or cocky, or resentful? Do you think he fully appreciates that this is about what he did then, or is he only able to chafe at what's happening to him now? What's his lawyer like? He knows Fryar's guilty, right? And the judge? Why is she putting up with his ridiculous claims? Is the girlfriend there? Tell me the story.*

I don't phrase it like that. I compose a normal-sounding reply about wanting to know Fryar's legal grounds for fighting the extradition, to know the process, the decision.

Randall is sweetly anxious about doing everything right. He even wears a tie. He reports that he was "very overdressed . . . Pretty sure most people thought I was a lawyer just sitting in the wrong section."

In the end, Fryar didn't even show up.

It's a good thing that Randall did go. As before, the Pittsburgh police are unable to get any information out of New York. Because of Randall, I'm able to report to them that Pennsylvania's Governor's Warrant demanding extradition has been served and that Fryar will be arraigned on it in front of the local supreme court in three days, on the nineteenth. This warrant is an upgrade of the original extradition request from the Court of Common Pleas. Hopefully it will be enough to move him.

The other reason it's good that Randall went is because it was kind of him, and his willingness comforts me apart from any practical effect his action also has. For all that I have dozens of connections in and around New York, most of whom know the situation, I had felt embarrassed to ask anyone. He's someone that I'd told only recently, and that freshness had made me feel able to bring it up.

Meanwhile, Honan is drafting my charges so that they'll be ready to send as soon as the final lab report is complete. I've learned to phone Honan. While Detective Campbell's e-mail replies are detailed and long, generously full of information, Honan's are spare. But, I've discovered that he's friendly and even sweet on the phone. My call about the hearing interrupts him, and we chat. I ask him what my charges specifically are, forcing him to translate from legalese to normal words: breasts, fingering, blowjob. He stammers, clearly preferring the official acronyms and euphemisms.

I ask him why the smothering isn't being charged as an assault on its own. He tells me that it's the forcible aspect of the highest charge, the "forcible rape," not a charge itself. I don't like this. The smothering was a big deal. I check with Valenta, but he agrees with Honan: it's an aspect of the rape.

I don't mean to set them up against each other, but, when Honan gets back to me and says he'll double-check, I tell him that there's no longer any need; Valenta agrees with him, so I'm on board. I think I've hurt Honan's feelings. Valenta's got no power in the current investigation, but I trust him more than anyone else in Pittsburgh. He was kind to me in the hospital. He's kind to me now, answering any e-mails quickly, even checking in if he doesn't hear for a while. He cares.

I'm so grateful to him for his commitment and transparency that it's jarring to realize that he technically failed. This was his case and he didn't solve it, not then and not now. DNA did that, and he didn't have the technology or the database in 1992. In fact, if he had ever suspected Fryar, even vaguely, we wouldn't be able to be in court now. The theory of the law that overrides statutes of limitations for DNA is that if the police knew enough back then to suspect someone, then they've had their shot at finding evidence, non-DNA evidence that should have been findable so close to the crime itself. Game over.

What I'm grateful for from Valenta is not the resolution, which he never gave to me. I'm grateful that he was kind to me, that night and now; that he was indignant on my behalf; that he took care with my case for the short time that it was his. Long before the police got near Fryar, there were chances to believe me, to take me seriously, to declare that I was right to tell what had happened, and that the man was terrible to have done it. There was the chance to call this thing a crime, a genuine crime. All of that was done for me then, and it's just as important as what's happening now. More than twenty years before the Pittsburgh police caught Arthur Fryar, they put the weight of their authority behind my version of events. They wrote down my words and kept them safe; they took my evidence and kept it frozen.

Detective Valenta did that. This is, profoundly, his case.

Perhaps because of the holidays and end-of-year, the court date set for the nineteenth becomes the thirtieth, then December 31. At this point I don't know if Fryar ever really did fight the extradition, or if New York is just disorganized. At home in Cambridge, we celebrate Christmas twice, once for the kids on the day, and again a week later for my unwell mother-in-law, who is recovering from heart surgery.

The day of New Year's Eve, Detective Campbell tells me that, at last, prisoner transport is being arranged. A new date—January 13—has appeared on New York's docket, but she assures me that it's not a new hearing; it's a status conference and deadline by which Pennsylvania must have picked him up. I wait, ready to fly at a few days' notice. Once Fryar arrives in Pittsburgh, the hearing has to happen within thirteen days.

Even though the lab has matched my evidence, he can't actually be charged for me until they've officially confirmed the match. They may or may not finish this in time for my charge to catch up with the other victim's; but, even if I can't yet testify, I'm going.

Urgent things have been completed: I've finished a revision of my next novel and am in a lull while others are reading it. I've dug up our tax numbers and handed them in to our UK accountant, barely making the deadline for her to be able to turn those numbers into finished returns. Gavin puts off the business trips he's supposed to be booking. We brainstorm childcare options depending on what date the hearing may fall.

I dry-clean an outfit for court. I plan to dress carefully: makeup, blow-dry, well-fitting clothes. I want to present myself flatteringly, aware that onlookers will mentally rate whether I was worth it. I assume they'll wonder why he bothered. I'm middle-aged now, and fat from indulgence and babies and sedentary work. I was pretty then. Not special, but the perfectly serviceable prettiness of being young. I'm grateful for the victim protection policies that will prevent me from being photographed, drawn, or described in this context. I'm open about what happened, and about what's happening now, but only on my own terms, in my own words.

This year, the anniversary, January 12, is on a Sunday, just as it was then. I don't mention it to anyone on the day, but it always feels strange to me when that happens. It's like an eclipse, or that time when I was in middle school and all the planets lined up, or like the tick-over to the year 2000. It doesn't mean anything, not really, but it feels like it should mean something. It means something to me.

I check New York's online "inmate lookup" every day, hoping to see that Pennsylvania has picked him up. I don't know how the physical extradition process works except that Detective Campbell has said that "two sheriffs" have been sent to New York do it. The word "sheriff" makes me crack a smile. It sounds very Wild West.

When I Google for extradition services and processes, the top hits are independent companies. They advertise that they are "cost effective," "available 7 days a week," and that their vehicles are equipped with little segregation cells for the violent, mentally ill, and juvenile, and for keeping the sexes apart. One has the cheerful slogan "No Where to Run" and branded hats, coffee mugs, and teddy bears for sale. Another company's YouTube video, with a background soundtrack of the theme song from the reality show *Cops,* promises "consistent, reliable, timely handling of your prisoners." I find my impatience placated by the language used, word choices classing Arthur Fryar in the way of a zoo animal or object. He doesn't need to get to Pittsburgh to start being punished.

When I finally see the change, see him listed as, as far as New York's concerned, "released," it's late at night, after we've had some guests over to watch a long movie. I have trouble falling asleep. I've done the journey between the New York area and Pittsburgh many, many times, to visit my sister at college, then later to go to college there myself. The drive with my parents used to take about seven hours, with a stopover at the state's halfway point in a town that exists for only that purpose, made up of motels and restaurants and shops selling Pennsylvania-themed souvenirs. Taking the Amtrak train was a bit of a longer trip, blissfully zoning out listening to musical-theater tapes on my Walkman. I loved those journeys, those elongated transition times, and it's uncomfortable to now share the route with Fryar.

By the time I wake up, I figure he must have gotten there.

The confirmation report from the lab comes in a few days later, and he's charged for me. My hearing is added to the docket for the same day as the other victim's, already scheduled. I'm told on Friday that I'll be testifying Thursday, just six days away.

I realize that I'd been wishing so hard for the hearing because I felt that I needed a new and significant development to justify continuing to talk about my ongoing panic and distress. But, instead of the upcoming trip reinforcing my upset, it makes me giddy. Detective Honan tells me that Fryar will be there, and that I'll have to point him out. He assures me casually that Fryar will be "shackled." That cheers me immeasurably. I'm bouncy and talk too fast. This lasts about twenty-four hours, through all my preparation and organization of travel details. Even as I'm in this state I recognize that my manner is oversized, inappropriate, and probably the climb before a fall.

My plans shape up. Valenta makes arrangements to be there on the day and offers me a ride to court. I explain breezily that my hotel is near, so I'll just walk. He e-mails back to say that he'll meet me at the hotel and walk with me.

That's what does it. That's the trigger that makes me understand, like a sudden view over the edge of a cliff, that this is serious and probably difficult and that I'll need support. Everything in me shifts back to emotional again, this time somber-emotional instead of panicky.

I've felt this shift before, at the hospital twenty-two years ago. It was when I was being interviewed by the detectives, and I was frustrated by the time. Classes were starting up for the semester in just two days, and I had planned to spend the evening memorizing the monologues that were due. I'd been lazy all Christmas and hadn't even started; I needed that evening if I was going to get it done; the evidence collection and questioning and gyn exam were all getting in my way. I'd had work to do. It was either Valenta or the other detective, the tall, blond one, who'd interrupted my frantic worrying to say, gently but seriously and a little sadly, "You're not going back to school on Tuesday."

I remember that punch-in-the-gut feeling, the realization that this is bigger than I'd let myself perceive. Valenta now making sure that I have someone to walk to court with, well, it hits me like that.

Back when it happened, my parents and my sister and my high school friends had wanted to visit. They wanted to look after me. I didn't let them. My top priority had been to keep normal anything that could be kept normal. People from other spheres of my life suddenly appearing in my college town would not have been normal. It would have rocked a very delicate balance. I made my parents wait for a performance as an excuse to come, because they always came for performances. Taking cast pictures is normal; applause is normal. Waiting, and so keeping my world steady, was a greater comfort than upending my world just to give me a hug a few weeks sooner.

Discrete worlds is why I won't let Gavin come with me to Pittsburgh. Besides one of us needing to stay home with the kids, I don't want to bring any part of my present life back there. I'll be passing from one world into another and out again. It's an expedition, made easier by my uncontaminated world here at home staying the same and very far away.

Deliberately going alone confuses people, but it's what I want. One of the most liberating things about the aftermath of the rape had been that I was asked, repeatedly, "What do you want?" I'd felt then, for the first time in my life, that that question was genuinely open-ended. Before that, I'd always assumed that there was a right answer to figure out and hew as closely to as possible. After, for about a year, I was allowed anything. I could want to be alone or want company, feel desire or be frigid, want to rage or want to forgive. Anything was acceptable. It's a trick I still use, in the privacy of my own mind, to figure myself out: I ask myself what I want as if I'm allowed to want anything. I don't always do what I want, but it's interesting information to have.

I want to book a hotel. This is strange, because I have friends I can stay with, really nice friends who I like and miss and can trust, but I don't want to have to compose myself and be social and explain things at the end of each day. I don't want to worry about how crying or just shutting myself in my room might upset someone.

I want to see my police file. I'm curious about my past self, as if she's another person.

I don't want to visit my old apartment building. I'm not scared of it, just not interested. I passed by it once, years ago, during a brief visit shortly after getting married, on our way to going out to lunch with friends. It didn't affect me.

I want to learn what it's like to see Arthur Fryar in person. I might panic or cry or get angry. Or, I might not recognize him. He might just seem like an old man, unconnected to what he did then. I don't know if I'll be fragile or stony or indifferent. I'm curious about my future self, the me just about to be.

I want to know how Arthur Fryar will react to me. Will he recognize me? If he does, will he regret or gloat? Will he lower his eyes, or laugh at me?

This wondering is different from my writing a novel, where I have to decide everything: what happens, and how each character will react. I don't get to choose this. I have to discover it.

4

My story is already in the *Pittsburgh Post-Gazette* the day I arrive. I'm not named, only referred to as a woman from the United Kingdom.

The hotel distracts me with little luxuries. I've come a day early, in case of weather delaying the flights, and I stay inside, viewing the snow-covered streets outside only through windows. I feel swaddled by the building, and safe.

I already call Valenta "Bill." I decide that I'll address Detectives Campbell and Honan as Aprill and Dan. I want to be peers here. Really, though, I don't get to talk to them much at all. They haven't offered their cell-phone numbers, or checked to see if my plane got in as expected. Bill is indignant over their apparent lack of care.

Bill is different from Aprill and Dan. He's older (though not old), retired from the job, not swamped with other just-as or more-than upsetting cases. The real difference, though, is that he was there when it happened. Not in the apartment, of course, but "it" is bigger than just the crime itself. "It" includes the hospital and the investigation and finishing college and having flashbacks. Bill was with me that night, when I was still in shock, when I was still bleeding, and the case was his. Aprill and Dan care about my case in a generic human way, and in an efficient police way, but it can't be personal for them. It's personal for Bill.

I almost wonder as much about how I'll react seeing him as I do about how I'll react seeing Arthur Fryar. All of the other people who were "there then" were also in my life before and after. The friends who went through it with me went through other things with me, too, good things, or things that were about them not me. I can see them and there's lots to remember; "it" is only one of them. With Bill, "it" is all there is.

He meets me in the hotel lobby the night before the hearing, with his wife, Jane. They find me instantly because of my pink coat. I've braced myself for the greeting, not sure how to touch. In Cambridge, there would be European cheek kisses, which even after eight years still make me uncomfortable. I'm happier with simple hugs, but I've had to practice not hugging in greeting since moving to England, especially with university people. It's just not done. So when Bill reaches for a hug I reflexively balk, out of English habit. He smoothly switches to a handshake.

He's made us reservations at a nearby restaurant with attentive waitstaff and a coat check. Despite the fancy surroundings, the conversation is informal and profoundly American in a way that I recognize deeply and have missed. We three talk about our kids and our jobs, and lightly swear in passing, not rudely just simply, words like "bullshit." I sip from Bill's martini, falling back into the casual familiarity I grew up with. He banters with the waiter. The accents! Not strong Pittsburghese, but a generic East-Coastishness. I feel at home.

The conversation alternates between chitchat and case talk. He's

upset about the new detectives being so aloof to me, and upset
with himself over not having been available to me for these twenty-
two years. But it's understandable: he left the Sex Assault Unit just
months after my case, switching to Internal Affairs because it was
daywork only and he was starting college at night. He eventually
moved to Vice, then became a commander, before retiring from
police work for a new career in academic administration. Aprill
remembers him from her early police years as "the boss."

She and Dan seem to find it baffling that Bill's so kind to me,
that he cares after all these years. Dan had even told Bill that
he was surprised at the thoroughness of Bill's case notes. Bill
rolls his eyes recollecting that, and wonders if he could help
change things over there, make things better. He says, wistfully,
"Maybe . . . " Jane, glad to be past the life stage of being a cop's
wife, says, "No, Bill. We've talked about this." She's a newly promoted vice president at Pittsburgh Plate Glass, and they both
have to travel a lot, taking turns to ensure someone will always
be home. They need a controllable schedule for the kids' sakes.
That's when we switch to telling funny stories about times we
were left at home by our traveling parents, and what we got
away with. When my parents left me for a couple weeks at seventeen, I adopted a kitten. Bill was naughtier, throwing crazy
parties while his parents were gone. He steam-cleaned the house
before they got home, to the delight of his doting Italian mom
and the justified suspicion of his cop dad.

His wife says to me, right in the middle of other things, "I want
you to know that I'm okay with this." She means that she doesn't
mind Bill caring about me and helping me. I'm glad that she
doesn't mind, because I need him tomorrow. Every time he's said
that he can be with me for this part or for that, I've looked down
at my lap and said "Yes, please" or "Good" or, once, "I need you to
stay for the whole time. I need you to not leave." I think he feels

that need, too. When he talked about how "some cases stay with you," his eyes had gotten shiny.

When we get our coats, while we wind scarves around our necks and tug on gloves for the brief dash across the street back to the hotel, I thank him again for prioritizing the hearing over a university event that he's supposed to attend at the same time. I'm just relieved that the hearing didn't fall a few weeks later, when he'll be representing the university in Prague and China. He says, without hesitation, "I would have changed the trip if it did."

I wake up early, because of the time difference, and find a marathon of *Law & Order* reruns on the hotel room TV. The pattern of each episode is familiar and comforting as it hums in the background, driving toward a resolution every hour. It's what I would watch anyway, even if I weren't going to court, but being headed to court makes watching it seem funny. I drink an entire pot of room-service decaf. I get my shoes shined. I have till noon, when Bill and I will walk to court together, through the blade-cold winter air. England doesn't typically get to these temperatures, and the chill feels like childhood to me.

The hearing is not in the historic courthouse near the hotel. It's a few blocks away, in the municipal court, a run-down building awkwardly shaped to look like a police badge from above. Bill and I have been instructed to meet the other detectives in front of the "broken elevators." They're easy to find once we're through the oversensitive metal detector and past the chipper, already bored security lady; there are no working elevators to trick us.

Everyone knows Bill. He's greeted by passing uniformed cops, security, and press. Newspaper journalists are there, and TV cameras. They're only allowed to film my feet. I'm glad for the whim that had led me to use the hotel's shoe-polishing service.

The unpleasant building is pretty much just rooms off a single

long hallway, a corridor that's quickly filled by the line for today's hearings. Everyone is scheduled for a twelve thirty start and
will just wait their turn. Accusers, accused, and witnesses for lesser
cases all stand together in that line. For us, a more sensitive case,
Fryar is in a holding pen. Dan Honan and Aprill Campbell arrive
and we go upstairs to meet the assistant district attorney (ADA)
from the Crimes Against Persons Unit (shortened in conversation
to "Crimes Persons") who'll be prosecuting our case. His name is
Kevin. I'm told that this case was fought over in the DA's office.
Everyone wanted it.

On our way up the stairs, the detectives tell me that "Georgia" is
already here. I figure out that they mean the other victim, from November the same year as me. It's the first time I've heard her name.
She's with her husband, and two women: we've each been assigned
an advocate from Pittsburgh Action Against Rape.

Georgia has the first prep session with the prosecutor, so Bill,
Dan, my advocate, and I continue to hang out in the hallway. Dan's
brought my file for me to see, at my request. I blip over all the paperwork from this year to get to the real stuff, the notes from that
night, pages and pages in Bill's neat handwriting, and then pages
and pages in single-spaced typing. I mutter, "Holy crap! Holy crap!"
over and over. There's a lot I haven't bothered to remember. There's
nothing that contradicts what I do recall; it's just stuff that's news
to me.

Apparently I'd had a conversation with Fryar before he went
upstairs and waited in the stairway next to my door. Bill had transcribed my recounting of it like a play. I feel faint and have to sit.
Dan gets me water. I don't cry once the entire day, but my hands
shake.

Our turn comes with Kevin the ADA. We're led into a back
office with a pin-the-tail-on-the-donkey game taped to the door.
The goal of the hearing, it's explained to me, is not to prove Fryar's

guilt but simply to demonstrate that there's a reasonable case for it, to persuade the judge to "bind over" the case for an actual trial later. We go over procedure and review my testimony.

I'm worried about vocabulary. I have to be very specific in my descriptions, to clearly match the charges. My concern is what words to use. I feel ridiculous using clinical terms, and rude using slang terms. We brainstorm phrasings, me and these three men I barely know.

As we exit, Bill holds the door for the advocate to go out first. I follow her, then hang back, noticing that Bill has waited in the office to listen to something Kevin is saying. I wait, too. For the entire day, I don't let myself get more than three feet away from Bill except to go to the bathroom. When he's in front of me, I follow closely. When he's behind me, my head swivels back, over and over, to make sure he's still there.

More hallway. I bore my victim advocate with pictures of my kids; she's a good sport about it. While she and I flip through images on my iPad, Bill chats with Dan; shoptalk, I suppose. I don't listen, but I keep Bill in the corner of my eye. He's just a foot or two in front of me, leaning on the railing that surrounds the opening overlooking the line for court below. Sometimes he shifts position and my eyes flick up, making sure he doesn't go anywhere. Once he walks a couple yards away to the men's room and I almost panic; then I see that he's left his coat on the rail and I know he's coming back.

Georgia and I tell "how I met my husband" stories and it's all very social, very chatty. She observes what we have in common, that we were both performers then, that we both subsequently had sons; I point out that we lived so close; she says that we have *him* in common and I, caught up in the camaraderie, joke that he has "great taste." Everyone laughs, then looks around a little nervously. She and I are grenades of emotion with loose pins; they don't know when we're going to go off.

I feel faint again. Bill gets me vending-machine crackers and a sports drink. Dan goes to the bathroom.

Dan's wife has apparently been waiting downstairs for just this opportunity. She's suddenly up here, introducing herself, trying to tell the victims from the advocates, distributing hugs and hellos. She'd told Dan that she wanted to come today, and he'd said no. But she had to, she explains to me. She had to see me.

She says that this case has gotten to him, that it means the world to him that the lab came through, that the extradition finally happened, and that I've come all this way. I'm amazed. He'd never shown those feelings to me. She and I hug, three times, by the time Dan comes out of the bathroom. He sees her and freezes. I call out, "We've already hugged three times! She's great." She gazes proudly at him and tells us all that he got a new suit for this. Dan looks down, embarrassed. She follows his eyes and says, "He got those cuffs hemmed just yesterday." She tells me that she had English tea and an English muffin for breakfast, in honor of me.

We're called into court.

The room is downstairs, very plain, just rows of stackable chairs lined up to face a high area at the front, for the judge and two assistants. The judge looks youngish and is wholly bald, leaning back in his big swivel chair like a throne. He looks powerful and a little bored, reminds me of Lex Luthor, and chews gum the entire time.

I sit between Bill and my victim advocate. Dan's wife sits behind us and holds my handbag for me for when I testify. She pokes her head between me and the advocate and points to the screened-off area in the corner to the right of the judge. That's where Fryar is. "Do you know what that's called? That sort of cubby where they keep the criminal?" she asks. Bill and the advocate and I all demur. She whispers, fiercely, "I call it the *cubby of shame!*"

There are glimpses of Fryar, huddling with his defense attorney, flashes of his bright jail uniform, but no tug in my gut. I'm not afraid of him; I'm curious about him; I'm curious about my reaction to him. He's old now, old-old, not adult-old like me. "Across the room" feels very far away, safely so. We've swapped: now he's the one who has to defend himself.

It's decided to go chronologically, January before November, so, after a group swearing-in, I testify first. There's no seat or box or fancy setup. We go up together to stand before the judge, with our backs to the rest of the room. We stand in a line: me, Bill, Dan, Kevin the prosecutor, the defense attorney, and the defendant. Aprill's attached to the other woman's case, not mine, so she stays seated. Kevin positions himself, kind of leaning, to block me from having to see Fryar while I speak.

It's all fine. I'm glad we practiced. I'm glad we carefully chose the words to use. It's just like it was in the pin-the-tail-on-the-donkey office, except that when it's over there's cross-examination.

The defense attorney's questions try to pin me down to a physical description that he'll later be able to dispute. Our case is based on DNA, not eyewitness identification, so, though I do in fact recognize Fryar, this whole road is just an unnecessary diversion to try to catch me out. I don't fall for it. I'd read advice about this very thing, about defense attorneys prying for nonessential details, the kind of details that aren't really the point so the witness won't have prepared for them, in hope of mining a contradiction. It's important not to let the natural social form of at least trying to answer direct questions prompt me to guess at anything I'm not absolutely certain of.

I say "I don't know" to most things. *Did he have a beard? Was his hair gray or dark?* That's not what I remember. I remember his round cheeks, his babyish face. I remember him as "big." That's what I'd told the police, because he'd seemed huge to me. He'd been powerful. I worry now that that could be used against me, because I can see in court, clearly, that he's not. I'd been warned that he'd lost weight in jail, but it's not just that. He's taller than me, yes, but shorter than my detectives and lawyer. I literally cannot even see him when he's behind them.

The defense attorney points out that it was evening and asks if it was dark in my apartment. *I don't know.* Was a light on? *I don't know.* "Well," he says in a folksy, skeptical tone, "was there really any opportunity to get a good look at his face?"

Something fills me up. My voice hardens, solidifies from the quivering, careful tone of the rest of my testimony, and I bellow at him, "Yes, while it was bobbing up and down in front of mine *while he was fucking me!*"

No more questions. We return to our seats. I glance at the two newspaper reporters nervously.

I sit through the rest of it and hate every moment. Dan's next, clarifying how the case was investigated these recent months. The defense attorney fishes around for information about the original investigation, asking if that detective is still with the police, or even still alive. I nudge Bill with my elbow and we all titter.

Then there's Georgia, and Aprill, and the criminalist from the lab. I thought I'd be asked to step out when the other victim speaks, but I never am; it turns out that, officially, we're still two separate cases, so I'm as welcome in the room as anyone else. The only time Fryar has any apparent interest or animation at all is when Aprill recounts her interrogation of him in New York; he's leaning in to talk to his lawyer and seems agitated about what Aprill's claiming he said. It doesn't matter. I close my eyes. I whisper to Bill that as soon as we're allowed I want to get out of there.

Predictably, probable cause is considered established and the case bound over for trial. The defense requests that the $400,000 bail be lowered. Kevin requests that it be raised. Lex Luthor casually doubles it, to $400,000 for each victim.

We all stand and mill in the aftermath, debriefing before facing the hallway. There's a cameraman out there. I'm torn between wanting to get away and wanting to hide in this room forever. Kevin tells me and Georgia that we did a good job; I'm assured that my outburst was on point and did no harm; there's lots of verbal back-patting and smug nods over the bail rise.

The arraignment—where the accused will be formally told the charges against him and asked for his plea—and pretrial conference (neither of which requires me) are scheduled together for March 13, at which time a trial date will be set. Aprill, who had slipped out into the hall, comes back and tells us, her face stuck half between shock and laughter, that Dan's wife is out there berating the defense attorney. She hadn't liked how he'd treated me on the stand.

The hallway is long. I try to walk normally but it's hard to do while a huge video camera dogs my feet. Bill puts his hand on my back to push me along faster. When we get outside the air is full of swirls of falling snow.

Bill and I leave the others and walk to a café, in a glass atrium from which I can watch the pretty weather. I worry that between the cash register and table I'll drop my cup of tea from my shaking hands.

Back at the hotel, in the lobby between the elevators, I thank Bill again, and ask him to thank his wife for lending him to me. He says that she's never seen this side of his work before, she's never met a victim from one of his cases, and that last night's dinner meant something to her. I jump up to hug him around the neck, and he hugs back. He says, "This was good. This was . . . this was good for me, too." He chokes up, and cries.

I leave this home, and return to my other one.

This sense of moving between homes started when I was in Pittsburgh as a freshman in college in 1989. Going back to my parents' house in New Jersey for Thanksgiving had been, of course, "going home." Then, strangely, returning to my dorm four days later had also become "going home." Since then, New England and Silicon Valley have also become home, and, eight years ago, England, too.

I want Cambridge; I want my kids; I want Gavin. I get back to the house at 8 A.M. after flying all night, and he's arranged for a friend to look after the boys so that I can sleep all morning and he can lie next to me.

The images that stay with me are specific, physical things: Bill's martini, the broken elevators, the judge chewing gum. Most of all, I remember standing in that line before the judge, with Bill, Dan, and Kevin between me and Fryar. They're so big, and Fryar is so insignificant, that I couldn't see him behind them, either literally in the courtroom or figuratively now. Everyone good seems much more important.

5

An etiquette guide for dealing with me after the hearing:

1. Ask me how it went.

2. Probe the bits that are interesting.

3. Laugh at the bits that are funny.

Very few friends here seem to be able to manage this, despite my efforts to make it easy for them. I call it "the prosecution" or "the hearing," or even just "my recent trip," only rarely referencing the crime itself. I smile, and tell bite-sized anecdotes that have black humor or mini story arcs. None of that appears to be enough.

A lot of my friends won't ask me about it at all, even though I e-mailed them from the airport to say how it went. I think they don't want to "bring it up" when they see me, but I'm already thinking about it. It's already "up." If they would just ask me then I could share it out. I think they reason that I'll introduce the subject if I want to talk about it, but that's a lot to put on me. I already introduced it by e-mailing them. Making the traumatized person beg, over and over again, for every individual interaction, is a bit much.

A small few of my friends do ask about it, generally, but leave the interesting bits just lying there. Don't they want to know what I shouted at the defense attorney? I tell them that I shut him down and the next words out of their mouths aren't "What did you say???" I feel hurt, angry, and sarcastic, thinking meanly, *How do such incurious people get to adulthood without dying of boredom?* At least my kids cheer me on over my small outburst on the stand. I even tell them that I used a swear word, but not which one. They think that that's awesome.

Literally only one person asks for everything. It's Alice, the choir's administrative assistant. She's the only one in the first week who acts the least bit interested in what's happened. She knows how to ask, and then ask for more, making me feel more welcome in her office than I do anywhere else in Cambridge besides my home. Even she, though, can't laugh at the judge's gum chewing, or at Dan's wife's sweet interference, or at the camera following my feet out of the courthouse. Instead, she looks like she's going to cry the whole time we talk.

My accent has suddenly shifted back to broad American after an eight-year slide toward posh mid-Atlantic. I have to consciously stop myself from saying "crap" and "goddamn."

Ben, the senior organ scholar, who's just an undergraduate but had been told about the hearing in case my kids acted out or brought it up while I was gone, has a terrified, tight smile every time he sees me in passing now, as if I might be contagious or explosive.

This is my thank-you note to everyone at Carnegie Mellon University Drama in 1992: It would have killed me if I'd had to go through it here at Cambridge. Thank you for being goddamn human beings when I needed you.

The second week gets better.

John the chaplain suggests that perhaps not every friend here, not even every good friend, is up to the task of acknowledging the case, never mind actually discussing it. Though that's exactly what I've just described to him, said back to me in different words, I fight it. I decide to prove it wrong. Surely we're all just people, *even the British,* I add in my mind, only half seriously, annoyed by the tightly controlled self-sufficiency all around me. I just need to figure out where the winder is that makes them go. I'd tried being open myself, as an invitation to their natural compassion and curiosity, but that didn't work for most.

Being a week away from it helps all of us; me, too. I'm a word person, and I'd been unwilling to accept their kind body language, their sad expressions, as communication. I'd wanted them to talk. I'd been unwilling to repeat myself in person, having already explained things in e-mail, but they were nervous, and needed a push. We'd been at a standoff, them waiting for words from me as much as I was waiting for them to talk. I give in. They answer with generosity and relief. I make an appointment to gloat to John that he was wrong, and that my friends function as they're supposed to. They just needed a little help.

I draft a script for them that I'll e-mail out before the trial:

1. Before I go, wish me good luck.

2. When I come back, welcome me home.

3. If you're willing to talk about it, please do. I want you to.

———

While the Americans tend to respond to my story by saying "wow" and "Jesus Christ," the British literally say "crikey" and "blimey" to me, which makes me laugh.

Even now, with people at last willing to talk, it's hard to tell the difference between someone faking interest out of kindness over their own discomfort, and someone feeling embarrassed that their genuine interest might be prurient. The ones who ask questions and help me along to tell it are my favorites, whatever their motivation.

It's funny to me that even those who talk to me about it don't talk to each other. There appears to be a huge taboo against "gossiping" about me. (I hate the word "gossip." It makes being interested in people sound ugly.) Back in Pittsburgh when it happened, a spontaneous phone tree had been put into action within a day to make sure that all of my class knew as quickly as possible. Ours was a small, intimate department and we took it for granted that everyone would have to know, would both need to and want to. I was grateful; it spared me having to explain individually, and mobilized people to look after me. The reticence here may be a difference between the British and Americans, or between middle age and college age, or between academics and actors. Most likely, I think, is that, at this stage of life, we're not a group, except within our immediate families. There's no "us," only individuals attached to me by spokes, even if they're also attached individually to each other.

There are two words that come out of people's mouths a lot: "brave" and "closure."

I'm not brave to be doing this. Testifying would be brave for someone who doesn't want it, but I do. There's nothing "brave" about doing exactly what one wants to do, even if it's awful, even if the defense attorney jabs and jabs, with questions like pointed sticks. If Fryar pleads guilty and takes the trial away from me, I'll feel robbed.

"Closure" is too vague. It's not sharp enough or physical enough for what I'm after. "Vengeance" isn't quite right either; I'd feel guilty about that. "Justice" is too impersonal. I guess what I want is just really specific: I want him sentenced long enough to guarantee that he'll die in prison. Mental gymnastics just aren't satisfying. I want something to happen in the actual world, not just in my head.

Bill warned me that putting a bad guy in prison is great but it's still just . . . putting a bad guy in prison; it doesn't change anything that happened. I'm fine with that. If this were a murder case, I would agree with his caution about expectations. That kind of loss is unfixable. This, though, is really, really fixable, not so much by the man being in prison as by the cooperation of all those who are pulling together to put him there. They do undo what happened, they do, at least the part of what happened that makes the world seem dangerous and unfair, and the part that makes me worry that I'm just weak and overreacting. Those are big parts.

It feels great to see what he did to me called "felonies" in the official charges. I take a screenshot of the docket so that I can look at it whenever I want: five felonies and three misdemeanors, all mine; Georgia has four felonies and one misdemeanor. Calling them crimes, specifically felonies, the worst kind of crimes, means that I'm not crazy to be so affected, not lazy for being so distracted. It's difficult to shake the feeling that my weakness is a fault, but the serious charges show that he's the bad person, not me.

I'm glad that the people around me know now.

All of my friends knew then, too, but my "everyone" has grown by a lot in twenty-two years. It wasn't until the arrest that I had a reason to tell the new people.

I worry, though, that people will read my novels differently now and, when coming across any sexual or violent scene, look for me there, look for the rape seeping in. It *is* there, I admit it, but the truth is that I'm everywhere in my books. I'm in the investigators and witnesses and even the baddies as much as the victims. My rape is there, but so is my upper-middle-class New Jersey childhood, my dad's decision to ditch a law career to design board games, my mother's roots in wartime Germany, my training as a performer, my grad school work in art history and curatorship, my faith, my doubt, my travels, my happy marriage, my motherhood. The rape is not a secret. It's a fact from my life, like my eighties adolescence and my Gen-X twenties. I'm made of a lot of things.

I've been asked, and I've wondered myself, why it is that, even in my fiction, I choose to write about terrible things. Wouldn't I rather spend my energy on stories that aren't violent and awful? But crime stories are not only, or even mostly, about the crime itself. They're a little about what came before the crime, and mostly about what comes after. What comes after can still be pretty terrible, but, like growing old, it beats the alternative profoundly. That there is an after, maybe even a long after in which the crime lingers but isn't the only thing in the world, is itself a comfort.

There was a lot after the rape itself, even just immediately after. I wrote about the 911 operator who snapped at me to "Stop crying!"; about having to give my clothes to the police and so changing in the crook of my closet door for privacy in my one-room apartment; about the hospital, busy with nurses and uniformed police and plainclothes detectives, all of them with their own forms that required the same information over and over. I'd left blood, right through my blue sweatpants, on chairs all over the emergency room, at all those different desks, only realizing it later when they finally put me in an exam room with a toilet.

I wrote about the nurses being distraught over me, trying to cover their upset with efficiency but not quite managing it. I wrote about the doctor telling me that I'd done well to keep my head, that my control and sensible thinking had saved my life:

"But . . ." I blubbered, tears falling into my mouth. "But that's my *acting problem*!" I blurted, because my teachers always told me that I never let myself get carried away enough, that I'm too cautious and watchful, too much in control.

I wasn't even joking when I said that to the doctor, then I realized it was funny and laughed to spit out the tears.

Just hours before, lying on the carpet next to my big white couch, not able to breathe, not allowed to scream, trying so hard to keep my hands on the floor, I'd fantasized a scene like this: cops, a hospital, being dressed. Being alive. I'd never wanted anything in the world as much as I'd wanted to get up off my floor, and print blood on waiting room chairs, and have a doctor stick her hand up me, and to tell jokes to nervous nurses who weren't sure if they should laugh or not but ultimately leaned to the side of humoring me.

My friends came out to take me home. The nurses pointed to a jar of candy canes on the sign-out desk: Merry Christmas.

I don't much like candy canes, but it's like when someone offers to buy me popcorn at the movies: Even if I'm not hungry I sometimes take it, just to accept the kindness. Just to be spoiled by the gesture.

I hope those kind, emotional nurses and good doctor know how much they meant to me; and Bill, too, for his gentle, purposeful questioning, and the friends who took me home to live with them so I'd never have to live in that apartment ever again. Now it's John and Alice who listen, and Gavin who accepts all of my moods and strangeness without question. There's a lot of *after*, most of it good after, years and years and years.

PART II

Opening the Gift

6

I choose an old photograph to send to the detectives and the prosecutor. Except for Bill, they didn't know me then. I want them to know who I was when it happened.

I dismiss my backstage and performance photos, which doesn't leave a lot. There are pictures from vacation with my mother that summer. That doesn't feel right either. Vacation is another kind of costume, not representative of the normal me.

Graduation was just eighteen months after the crime. It was a special event, not a normal day, but it was the culmination of all of my normal days there. Pittsburgh is a college town. Bill, Dan, Aprill, and Kevin the ADA will understand that kind of photo. They'll remember their own graduations, their school and college days; maybe, if they have kids, they'll think of them.

Most of my pictures from that day are group shots, and we're all facing in different directions, because there were so many cameras held by so many parents. In my favorite one, I'm smiling straight on, and my friend Aaron has his arm around my shoulders. The red tassels on our mortarboards are midswing from us turning our heads.

I write, "I've attached a pic of me from back then. Well, 18 months later. I graduated on time."

I let the message sit for a while instead of sending. The last sentence takes on a huge importance to me. I did it, despite the interruption forced on me: *I graduated on time,* from one of the most challenging conservatories in the country, despite not going back to school that Tuesday, despite three weeks off and dropping one class and sometimes, only rarely and when absolutely necessary, walking out for flashbacks or tears. Everyone in Pittsburgh knows the department's reputation. Everyone in theater knows it. They were kind to me, but I wasn't graduated out of kindness or pity. In the picture, the ribbon and medal representing university honors, and the white cords representing college honors, are clearly visible.

I hit my marks back then, and I can't help but compare that with now. I'm keeping up the whole parenting thing pretty well, and the whole personal life thing, but I've backed out of various commitments: judging a contest, hosting a lecture. I'm behind on finishing my current book. I'm late, I'm revising poorly, and it upsets me terribly. There's an unspoken equation in my head: *If I can finish this, then I'm okay.* Which means, of course, that not finishing makes me not okay. I try to work, but I fail, again and again. I'm told to take my time, but I don't think my publisher or agent really means it. Or, they mean it, but their indulgence will have consequences nonetheless.

I don't think that I was a better person back then, more persistent, more talented, more able. It's just that the structure of school, with all of the little built-in goals along the way, makes it easier to succeed. I toy with the idea of going back in to get another degree, just to hide in a system, to collect little approvals in the form of grades, but I know that I don't really want assignments and exams again.

My kids' educations structure my days. It's soothing to to-and-fro them, to fuss over handwriting and algebra. S. will be a teenager soon, and measures his height against mine every morning, hoping for that last inch that will make him taller than me. W. still clings, pretends to be a cat, and reads *Captain Underpants* and *Calvin and Hobbes* every day.

I show them the photo that I've chosen, though I don't tell them what it's for. "Look," I say.

They recognize me, which is nice, considering the number of years between then and now. "Who's that guy?" they want to know; I explain that Aaron was a friend in my class. They move on, not surprised by or particularly interested in the picture. They know that I have degrees.

I keep looking at it.

It's easier to feel proud of oneself from a distance.

I'd gotten to hold my case file while we'd waited in the municipal court hallway for the hearing to begin. The folder they keep the papers in is twenty-two years old and looks it. My various contact addresses from over the years are scrawled on the outside of it.

Dan has scanned Bill's handwritten notes from that night for me, at my request. Now I can read them at my leisure. It's horrifying to do so, but some things must be gone through, not around.

I remember all of the main things, but little details have fallen through the sieve over time. Bill had caught them all that night, in pages of neat, rounded printing, as I'd narrated, without editing, within an hour after it happened. Each rediscovered detail is immediately familiar, and shocking, too, in how suddenly it slots into place.

According to Bill's notes, I had begged: "[Can] we find something else to make you happy?" Meaning that I'd asked if I could finish him off by going back to one of the things he'd already made me do, instead of him doing the new thing that I really, really, really didn't want him to do. I had remembered that months ago, but had doubted myself.

The memory had been too much like a scene I'd written in a novel. One of my characters had tried to negotiate with her abuser this same way. When I prepared my testimony, I left it out, thinking that I was mistakenly conflating my own experiences with my books.

It's a given that I use observations and experiences from my own life in my books, but in this instance I hadn't just used a memory to influence a scene; I'd handed over the attempted negotiation completely, until it became just a scene and not, I'd repeatedly told myself, a memory. This unnerves me, and makes me want to excise all young women from my books, certainly from the one that I'm currently working on. I write far too many girls who lash out, I realize. It's repetitive, and lazy, and feels far too outside of my conscious control.

The line from the case notes that stands out most to me is something I'd apparently pleaded to Fryar:

"If I'm very good, will you not kill me?"

I make a list of all of our relative ages. It helps me to sort us out.

In January 1992, I was twenty-two. Bill was thirty. Fryar was almost forty.

Dan was twenty-seven then, working as a private investigator. Aprill was twenty-one, finishing college. That makes Dan older than me, and Aprill my peer, sharing the same high school graduation year. I'd thought of them as younger than me, much younger, I think because they're doing now what Bill was doing more than twenty years ago. They had seemed to me, both over the phone and even at the hearing, like a whole generation after us.

Turns out that we're all within a decade, all of us good guys: Aprill's forty-three, I'm forty-four, Dan's forty-nine, and Bill's fifty-two. We're all seventies kids. Well, Bill was a seventies teen. When we were learning to walk and talk, playing board games and listening to records, Fryar was already a grown man.

He's almost sixty-two now. There's little about him online, not further education, not jobs. There was a mention at the hearing of his having once been in the military, which seems right to me. He'd been good at cornering me, good at physically controlling me. At the hearing, he'd kept himself in check, not betraying emotions or even interest.

He'd been a child of the fifties, a teen of the sixties, in Beacon, New York, a now-touristy city upstate that, back then, simmered with racial tensions culminating in riots in the seventies.

Online, he lists his high school graduation year as 1972, when he would have been twenty. I suppose he must have had to repeat grades, or something had kept him out for a year or two, or maybe he'd started late or maybe his family had moved around. If he joined the military right out of high school, that could have put him in Vietnam.

Kevin, the prosecutor, is the baby among us. He's only thirty-five, so back when it happened he was just turning thirteen. That seems very young compared to who I was then, a college junior. If we'd grown up in the same town, I could have once been his babysitter.

But, with regard to my own children, thirteen seems nearly adult. S.'s treble voice is peaking; it will be gone within the year, but what a year it is, full of solos and concerts. It's hard to explain to most Americans that the British chorister system isn't historical reenactment or cosplay; it's a still-living tradition that seems extraordinary from the outside, but is, within its own rarefied world, just normal. These boys are singing in the places of all those who came before them, and will be replaced by eager new boys when they go. The leaving of boy trebles is unpredictable, and each new inch of height gives a hint that there may not be much time left. When their voices finally change, it's not just the end of choir; it's the end of childhood. They're suddenly tall, hairy, oily, responsible, cocky, ambitious. One puts a boy into choir, and gets an almost-man out the other end.

Google Images' search results for "Arthur Fryar" have changed. The change reminds me of the way my memories shift, different aspects rising in priority at different times.

I can no longer find the pictures that had looked so immediately familiar. His profile pic is still up on Facebook, but there's little else of him around the Web now. I'm glad that I'd screenshot what there was five months ago.

I have three pictures. Two are of him younger, the way he was in 1992: plump with big round cheeks. One shows him more recently, same as before but with very gray hair. From time in jail now, he's less fat, and he's possibly shrunk a bit from age, so in court he looked comparatively slight as well as old.

At the hearing, even though I'm a "Jane Doe" to the public, I'd had to confirm my real name to the judge, even spelling it. I hadn't realized that Fryar would be allowed to know it. His right to face his accuser trumped my anonymity. All these years I've just been that girl from that Sunday to him; now he has access to everything online about me, which, for professional reasons, is quite a lot. I wonder if he's Googled me like I did him. I don't like him knowing who I am. I hadn't considered that finally finding out who he is would inherently involve an even trade.

Bill's notes refer to us as A. and V.: "actor" and "victim." I know that some people hate the term "victim" and prefer to be called a "survivor" instead, but I don't mind the word. He did hurt me. I was a victim of that. It bothers me to euphemize it.

The first time I'd heard the word "actor" used to refer to the man, it had surprised me. The police who came to my apartment had asked me: "Did you know the actor, ma'am?" (I was just twenty-two and already "ma'am.") I was a drama student, so that word meant to me not just generic famous people, but specifically my friends, and neither definition made sense, nor the definition that implied that it was all pretend.

I'd thought, *But this really happened. He wasn't acting.* That's not what they'd meant, of course. They were using it like "perp" for "perpetrator," meaning "the one who did it." He'd taken action. He *did;* I'd been *done to.*

One of the best things about getting a trial is that I will get to act: not act like "pretend" but act as in *do.* I get to be the actor, accusing and testifying, and he has to hold still, and be the victim of the process.

A friend I told about the prosecution was keen to get me to agree that the main point of the trial is to protect potential future victims, for which he commended me. He was troubled about aspects such as "punishment," "vengeance," and even "justice" as impractical and unseemly. But there's an immense difference between being pinned on my back on the floor of my college apartment and standing up in court. It's my right to get to do that, whether it saves anyone else or not. It's a gift, from the police and the district attorney and the state of Pennsylvania. I matter just as much as each potential future victim who may be spared.

One of the most powerful things a writer gets to do is to decide where stories start and end. I think this friend of mine believes that this story ended when Fryar left my apartment, and so that there's nothing more to be done for me; that's why he's thinking only of future others. I say that the story doesn't end till court, with me on my feet.

The arraignment and pretrial conference are happening today and I get the upsetting news that Kevin the ADA has been moved to

Homicide. The new prosecutor, Evan, seems to be even younger. He's been a lawyer for less than five years.

I don't want to start from scratch. I've already done the short version of testifying, with Kevin at the hearing. I wanted to build on that for trial—which I've been told will have me on the stand for longer—not have to explain it all over again to someone new. Kevin knows me now. At least, he was in the hallway and courtroom and pin-the-tail-on-the-donkey office with me for a few cumulative hours. You can learn a lot about a person just by physically being in the same room. He heard my outburst to the defense attorney, and approved of it. He e-mailed me answers to my questions afterward, and even sent me transcripts of similar trials. I wanted him to stay on. I don't think it's too much to ask that the person who's going to be asking me desperately intimate questions in a public proceeding actually meet me first.

Kevin hasn't e-mailed to tell me. Evan hasn't e-mailed to introduce himself. I only found this out because I e-mailed April, and she only knew because she'd run into Kevin in court.

The time difference means that it will probably be evening here before the meeting to decide the trial date ends in Pittsburgh. Friends who noted today in their calendars have started to e-mail and visit, being wonderful. Everyone wants to know when the trial will be.

I notice that I throw around the word "everyone" in what obviously can't be a literal way. I love that word and I don't want to change it to something more accurate. There's a level of "enough" that's so satisfying and safe that it might as well be "all." There are enough people who know everything (another hyperbolic word, which here means "everything that matters") that it feels like "everyone" here cares.

That's a relief, because the Pittsburgh end of things is suddenly frustrating again. The switch of prosecutors has thrown me. If I hadn't asked, I wouldn't even know about it yet. I'm waiting to see if I get told the results of the meeting by tonight, and if I don't I'll push tomorrow morning. Aprill thinks it's her case, and Dan thinks it's his case, and Evan probably thinks it's his, but it's mine, mine and Georgia's. It's our case, us two, and they damn well should tell us what's going on. They might be waiting for news from the meeting today before reaching out, but the change in ADA is big enough news on its own to have warranted contact.

I decide not to e-mail the picture of young, graduating me after all. There's no point, not when the new prosecutor hasn't even met now-me. I feel distant from Aprill and Dan again, as if mine is not nearly an interesting enough case to matter. Bill doesn't need the photo; he knew me then. Then I think that I might send it to Bill anyway, because he only knew me from the hospital, and I was probably a mess.

My husband, Gavin, is in court himself today, testifying as an expert witness in a patent dispute in Texas. He's not a party to the dispute, so there's no winning or losing at stake for him personally, but it's a responsibility that he takes seriously and he believes in the side he's on. He's never been in court before, and neither have I, not even for jury duty. This year is a first for both of us.

I'm envious of the amount of prep he's been given: months of interaction with the lawyers, and, now, during the trial, debriefing and more prep every evening and morning. For my hearing, I'd been given less than a half hour.

Gavin gets the company attorneys in Texas to use some magical lawyerly access to find out for me the time that Fryar's arraignment has been scheduled for in Pittsburgh so that I'll know when I can start hoping for news. Goodness knows that the Pennsylvania lawyers actually working on Fryar's case haven't bothered to tell me exactly when today it's happening.

I wonder if, perhaps, like my friends here after the hearing, Kevin and Evan do care, and just haven't gotten so far as to let me know. Perhaps they're like Dan, who needed his wife to let me in on him giving a damn. Maybe the world is full of secret caring, and I have to pry it out.

Finally, before the day is done, Kevin and Aprill both e-mail, without prompting from me. I'm immediately placated.

It's a familiar pattern. I vacillate between two states, *waiting* and *having,* and there's little gradient between the two. *Waiting* isn't a sea that gradually approaches a beach; it's a wet pit with vertical walls. Nearing resolution makes little difference to how it feels to be swimming in the waiting. There is only in, or out. In is agony; out is happy; the transition is sudden.

Now I'm pleased, magnanimous. Kevin's been prosecuting a throat slashing, then a bar shooting, back-to-back. Of course he hasn't had time to tell me about Evan, and it was kind of him to follow up with me when it isn't even his case anymore.

Besides the new prosecutor, he tells me, there's a new defense attorney. Fryar must have spent his last on the private defense for the hearing; he has a public defender now, a woman. I can't help but think that this may be safer for me, that a woman won't go after me on the stand in the same way that that man did, all folksy and fake-ignorant just to make a case. She will go after me, but I assume differently. Surely a woman won't be able to stomach accusing me that I don't really remember, right? Maybe she'll try to go after the evidence and the police, not me.

The assigned judge disappoints me a little. I look up some recent sentences she's given in similar cases, and she seems lenient. Gavin points out that even if Fryar does get out of prison someday, maybe that'll be even more punishing. Maybe being put out on the street in his eighties, after twenty years of highly supervised and regimented prison life, will be harder than just staying in. I perk up at the idea that even getting out might hurt Fryar and I nod, even though we're on the phone and Gavin can't see me.

He's just come off the stand in Texas, and is calling me from outside the courtroom. He sounds wired, like he's had way too much coffee. He's just been cross-examined and it's the end of the day there. He'll get some food and an hour's nap, then go back with the lawyers into the "war room," a pair of hotel conference rooms that they've commandeered, to prep for cross-examining the other side's expert tomorrow and for closing arguments.

I look up flights. Kevin's told me that my trial is set to begin June 3, which is right up against the end of S.'s choir trip to a festival in Switzerland, which I'm chaperoning.

I worry that I might be asked to step down from the trip, because of the proximity of the trial, if anyone thinks that I'll be perhaps too emotional or affected to focus on the kids. I have to ask the Director of Music about skipping the bus trip that will take the choir from London City Airport back to Cambridge, so that I can go straight on to Pittsburgh instead, and I worry over what his reply might be. He quickly assures me that the adult-to-kids ratio for the bus leg is fine even without me, because when he's not conducting he can count as a chaperone. He doesn't acknowledge the trial at all, though I'd explained that that was the reason for my travel plans.

The mother of the trip's youngest chorister only wonders how I'll manage to pack enough nice clothes for both Switzerland and Pittsburgh at once, and brainstorms with me a schedule of hotel dry cleaning: half near the end of our time in Basel and half on my arrival in the States. The choir admin insists that I must splurge on an upgrade to business class for the long Pittsburgh journey. People pounce upon the practical, and take it for granted that I'll be my usual self. I get to keep Switzerland, and I hug it close with both hands.

British tact, which had hurt me so much when I came back from the hearing, is now working in my favor.

7

I get to Skype with my new ADA and he talks to me for more than an hour, with video on so that it's more like really meeting each other. Evan's just thirty years old. He's sweet and friendly, and so clean-shaven that he looks like he can't even grow a beard. He's worked in the district attorney's office for four years, after a three-year internship. He prosecutes mostly rapes and child abuse.

I tell him that I like information. He gives it to me.

He explains the possible sentence ranges ahead and what can affect the outcome. There's a Pennsylvania chart of recommended sentence lengths that the judge will use, with crimes listed down the page in decreasing order of their severity, each defined by a number called an Offense Gravity Score. My three biggest charges each have a score of twelve, near to murder, which is rated fourteen.

The crimes have recommended minimum/maximum sentences stated in months. Just the quick calculation of dividing by twelve distances the impact of those time spans, makes them feel less like real years.

Besides choosing sentences within those ranges, the judge will have further leeway to decide if the sentences for each charge should be served consecutively, which could add up to a lot, or concurrently, which means overlapping the accumulated sentences: say, serving multiple ten-year sentences in a single decade. The judge we've been assigned is a sex-crimes specialist who's tried a lot of similar cases, and I can see from past results reported in the newspapers that she habitually prefers middle-of-the-road sentence lengths. Our only hope for significant prison time is to raise Fryar's Prior Record Score (PRS).

The PRS reflects convictions for crimes committed before the crimes on trial took place. In 1977, in Orange County, New York, Fryar was convicted for second-degree rape. He served the maximum seven years, in Sing Sing. I look on a map, finding the county, the prison, and his high school town, Beacon, all upstate. These map dots cluster around my old musical-theater summer camp. In the early eighties, while I was a young teenager knitting and paddle boating between rehearsals, dancing badly in the choruses of musicals and acting well in the plays, he was in prison just two hours away.

Evan is waiting for details of this conviction before he can officially raise Fryar's PRS from zero to, we hope, four. A higher PRS will bump his crimes into a different category of recommended sentences, longer ones. But, as with the extradition, New York is making communication difficult. Pennsylvania has to purchase this information. The process takes time.

The other thing that Evan is waiting for is the possibility of a guilty plea. I still don't think it's in Fryar's nature to make one; he fought even just the extradition, which the detectives tell me they've never seen anyone do before. But our case is solid and Evan tells me that the defense attorney has brought up the possibility. It would be in Fryar's favor to do it, to admit it all, act sorry, and try to get an easier sentence. If he does plead, the process changes dramatically for me.

If Fryar continues to fight and we go to trial, my job will be to testify to what he did. I'm ready for that. If he pleads, he will still go to prison, just as with a jury conviction, but his admission will override any need for my testimony. All that will be left for me to do is to give my "impact statement," in hope of influencing sentencing. That's not what I want. Testimony is about what he did; an impact statement is about me.

I shouldn't have to display my grief. It's demeaning. It tells the man, "Look how powerful and significant you are. Look how fundamentally you changed my life." I shouldn't be forced to tell him that, and certainly not in public. I shouldn't have to give that to him.

Evan knows what I want, but Fryar has the right to plead. Evan could refuse to negotiate a plea (that is, Fryar could dangle a plea as a possibility if Evan will go low enough for him with an offered sentence), but a general plea, which is an unconditional admission of guilt that leaves the sentence up to the judge, can't be rejected. Evan tries to see the good side of the possibility. Even with as great a case as we have, it takes just one juror to scupper things, while a plea is a guarantee.

I mentally shrug. Another good thing, I know, is that a plea would prove, to anyone wondering, that he really did do it. I can see how in some cases this would be a significant plus; in this one, though, it's irrelevant. No one is on the fence about what really happened.

The last possible good I had hoped for was allocution, which is the recounting of the crime by the defendant, in support of a guilty plea. Some jurisdictions insist on it. If I could hear what he did from his point of view, perhaps even learn why and when he chose me, and which specific memories were significant enough to him that he's held on to them, that might be a worthy trade-off, to lose my testimony. But Aprill has told me that Allegheny County has no such requirement attached to a plea, just that he agree to his charges. I'm never going to know.

Maybe to prepare me, but probably just to placate me, Evan talks about testifying, just in case.

It will be very different from Gavin's experience prepping for trial as an expert witness. I had assumed that the reason witnesses in civil trials are so much more thoroughly prepared than those in criminal trials is just money; a private company has a lot more to spend than government prosecutors do. But, Evan tells me, that isn't the only reason. Eyewitnesses and expert witnesses serve different purposes. Experts are there to analyze and present considered opinions; preparation makes them appear responsible. Eyewitnesses, on the other hand, are to answer questions simply and directly, from their memories. Too much preparation can seem distancing or even dishonest. Criminal-trial juries want to hear eyewitness testimony that's being pulled from memory right in front of them, not that's been memorized, even if what's memorized had come out of memory first.

As with Kevin at the hearing, with Evan too everything physical will have to be spelled out. Each charge is very specific about which body part was exactly where. The foreplay bits sound terribly silly when described so precisely.

Evan tells me that the main difference between testimony at trial and testimony at the hearing is that trial testimony will be stretched out. Instead of allowing me a continuous narrative, he'll interrupt to dig for details. I'm fine with that. I want to tell everything.

But he says that he'll also have to ask me how I felt then, each step of the way. That's what juries want to know: not just what Fryar did but how I felt about it as it happened. The jury will want to know what it meant to me. *Prurient bastards.*

No, I don't mean the individuals, who haven't even been chosen yet; I mean the collective organism *jury* that apparently requires that I be a perfect little broken princess if they're going to reward me with a conviction. I say this as someone who comes pretty close to being that version of so-called perfect: a devout and sober virgin when it happened, now a married mother. But if I say he *fucked* me, then forget it, apparently. While Evan sympathizes with my raised-voice response to the defense attorney at the hearing, he says that I mustn't swear at trial. Juries don't like it. I have to make an idiot of myself and say, precisely, "He put his penis into my vagina," as if anyone can say that without sounding like a goddamn idiot. It's fucking ridiculous.

As for pressing me for how I felt, I think Evan's worried that I won't show emotion on the stand. I know that that won't be a problem; I almost fainted at the hearing. But I can see that my disdain for the impact statement has made him worry. I start to think that maybe I need to display even now, on the phone, how upset I am (but without swearing!); that I should, to reassure him, make a show of grief and fragility (but not anger!). I don't, but in the end I'm worrying that I should have. Maybe I shouldn't have put on makeup for this call. Maybe I shouldn't have been polite and chipper. Maybe I shouldn't have my hair touched up just before trial, or buy new clothes. If people think that I'm too lucky, or too happy, or too strong, they might decide that what Fryar did is irrelevant. They might think that I don't need anything, that I don't need him punished.

That's what the impact statement is for. They're going to make me beg for it.

Gavin had said he was going to watch just one more show and then go upstairs. My Skype with Evan went longer than I expected, so I assume that Gavin's in bed. He's not, though. He's waited up for me.

I tell him that I need to write an e-mail and will join him soon.

I attach my graduation picture to a thank-you note to Evan. He should know how young I was then. Then I worry more, that that happy, proud smile will just add to him thinking that what happened didn't matter. I worry that he won't understand.

Gavin fusses in the kitchen, tidying dishes and doting on the cats. I can't concentrate with him so near. That's one of the reasons I don't want him to accompany me to trial. Everyone else who's there for me, Bill and Dan and Aprill and Evan, are all people I define purely in relation to the prosecution. Gavin, though, is three-dimensional to me. I can't reduce him to just my support system. I would worry about how hard it is for him to listen to me tell these things. I'd want to look after him, or feel guilty that I couldn't.

I resist the urge to shoo him upstairs now, and let him continue to hover. I don't need his company—any company—right at this moment, but I need it in general and now is when it's here. I finish up the e-mail and hit send.

He doesn't ask about the call; he just walks up with me, and lies down with me. I tell him bits in the dark, about the Prior Record Score and the likelihood of a guilty plea. We talk about hotels and airplane tickets, and about how *something* will happen in court on June 3—which is still two months away—whether it's the start of a trial or a formal admission of guilt.

It's perfect that Gavin's court case happened when it did, just now, just before my own. It gives him a vocabulary with which to talk about my case, and something to compare it to. Even though he was just a hired expert, not an accused or accuser, his technical knowledge had become the focus of the case. Closing arguments had literally come down to the other side claiming that Gavin's testimony was biased and couldn't be trusted, while the lead attorney on Gavin's side told the jury that Gavin is "a good man." Gavin's side won in the end, and relief had busted out of him in tears when he phoned me.

There had been literally twelve attorneys on his side, and he's grateful to each one, emotionally so. That's the biggest plus to me, that Gavin now understands that bond. I feel the same for my team, for Bill and Dan and Aprill and Evan and Kevin and honestly anyone else who shows up in court and is kind to me. They mean the world to me.

Before the prosecution, I would have listed "affectionate," "brilliant," and "kind" as Gavin's most attractive attributes, but "confident" has emerged as the most significant and relevant of his virtues this year. He supports my many friendships with both men and women. He's grateful for John's kindness and attention to me. He understands that we can't do this by ourselves.

He was unruffled when I went away to the hearing alone, though the situation could have been viewed awkwardly, my getting emotionally attached to a team that's mostly men, our bonding over a sex crime. I'm grateful that I didn't have to persuade or coddle him. He just trusted me. If he had any discomfort from my choices, he set it aside.

Now, though, he doesn't have to overlook any nagging unease, should it exist; he can just understand. He's felt it himself. We're attached now, me and Bill and Dan and Aprill and Evan and Kevin. We're part of each other, something I feel more than they do, much more; but it's real, however skewed its balance may be.

I think about what I wrote twenty-two years ago: "New memories. Wouldn't that be nice? To think of, say, my hands, and think of someone nice instead of him. But wouldn't it be even better to look at my hands and see my hands, to think of my body and think of myself? Must my hands, my body, always make me think of a man, even if someday a nice one?"

I'd wanted to see myself as just my own, and felt that Fryar had taken that possibility away from me, that the best that I was left with afterward was to cover his touch with someone else's, someone good. All I could do was add; nothing could take him away. I would never be "just me" again.

Now I wonder. I don't think that I ever really had that option of being just myself, even before. Life isn't like that. I look at myself and I see touches from everywhere. Not just sex and giving birth, though those are obvious highlights. I feel tangled up with everyone around me. It's a good tangle; it's life; it's everyone I've ever known. The detectives and attorneys are in there now, part of who I see when I look at myself, with my family and my friends, from then and now, and my lean, handsome, brilliant, gentle Cambridge man, with *that accent,* lying next to me. There's room for all of them, and for many more. I was a virgin when Fryar got to me, but I was never untouched. I'd been mixed up with other people's lives from the day I was born.

With the hope of allocution lost, I have to accept that no one is ever going to tell me about Fryar. Aprill hardly knows anything, just that Fryar's girlfriend has broken up with him. I noticed at the hearing, when discussion turned to bail, that Fryar claimed to be living off government benefits as a disabled veteran. That's all I have.

I've always been mystified by people who want to climb already conquered mountains or dive deep into well-known seas; that sort of thing just seems dangerous and uncomfortable to me. But I have complete sympathy for anyone who wants to discover something. Pushing deep into a jungle seeking the ruins of a rumored legendary city seems perfectly sensible to me; in fact, necessary. Wanting to figure out what's really there and how I fit in with it is a primal urge. Fryar's name is my crumpled treasure map.

I Google. There's not much there. He hasn't owned property. He hasn't worked, at least not the kind of work that ends up on LinkedIn. Most of his life predated the Internet, so there isn't much from his youth except for a list of high school classmates on a reunion site.

I'm tempted. I bet I could find a few of those people on Facebook. I ultimately decide, though, that for my own sake I need to be hands-off. I'll window-shop the facts of his life, but not actually interact with anyone.

That leaves terribly little. I can't see what he's posted to Facebook, but, even if it weren't set to "friends only," I doubt that there's much there. He'd joined various other sites, sometimes with a photo or birth date or graduation year, but seems to have not done much with any of them beyond registering.

Noticing the user names hidden in the URLs of his generic, uninformative reunion-site pages, I'm able to find a little more, like dating-site profiles.

He hasn't filled out much information on those either, just age, photo, and that he lived in Brooklyn. On one, he wrote "lets get to fuckin . . ." On another, he was slightly less direct, but still succinct: "fun lighthearted and ready for action. I'm here to meet not chat for ever, if you don't want to meet don't hit my profile."

It makes me queasy to see his past attempts at trawling for sex. I wonder if he's the kind of person who rapes to get the sex he wants, not caring if the woman struggles, or if the struggle is part of the attraction for him, part of the satisfaction. In Bill's notes, I can see that Fryar treated me like a pickup at first.

After he caught the door behind me, my hope had been that he lived in my building, and that I'd just happened to never see him before. I'd wanted to be polite, not make superficial assumptions that he was unlikely to be from this neighborhood. According to the file notes, I'd asked him:

[Victim]: "Do you live here?"
[Actor]: "Yes, haven't you seen me around?"
V: "No, what's your name?"
A: "Bob."

I remember that now. I think it's weird that I never wrote about his calling himself that, or really even thought about it much. I must have never believed that it could possibly be his real name. Fryar does have a known alias, according to the original arrest reports in the news: "Butch Johnson," which I suppose could have yielded interesting information on the Internet, but there's a football player who has that name, and his career, including two Super Bowls, obscures whatever Fryar might have done while calling himself that.

V: "Mine's Emily."
A: "Is that your apartment?"

It took me a while to figure this out. I remember that this conversation took place just inside the front door, not upstairs near my door, so what was the "that" that he was asking about? I think I was stalling by fiddling with my mailbox. I didn't want to lead him upstairs. So, from the mailbox, he must have seen my apartment number. That explains how he knew where to hide upstairs, to be able to jump me. Before I discovered this in the notes, I'd wondered if he'd watched me earlier from outside, seen me through a window. I can't remember if I was careful about curtains or not, or if I even had them. Turns out that I should have been more careful about my mailbox.

V: "Yes."
A: "Do you invite friends to your apartment?"
V: "No, I'm just polite."
A: "What about a husband?"
V: "That's private."

I find it interesting that I didn't lie, which might have protected me. It's pretty obvious that anything other than "Yes, and he's upstairs waiting for me" would mean that I lived alone. But I've found that even experienced liars will balk at deviating too far from what is either true or prepared. If you take things in a direction that they haven't planned for, you'll often get the truth, or at least a lie that's red-flaggingly weird, because they're being sort of truthful.

"Bob" seemed to just want to have sex with me, seemed he would have been happy with my saying "Sure! Come on up." If I'd invited him up with me, would that have satisfied what he was after? Or was he glad that I said no, so that he would have the pleasure of overpowering me? The times he's had a girlfriend, did he still rape people? Or was it only in dry spells?

Maybe *yes* and *no* were each desirable to him in their own ways. *Yes* would have flattered him and stroked his ego, but *no* was a chance to push back against past rejections or against self-loathing in his own mind. The context in which he'd approached me was completely outside of social norms and seemingly designed to get a negative response, which I think may have been the point. I think he was already angry, and getting me to say no gave him the opportunity to hurt me.

But this wasn't a beating; this was violence via sex, and it baffled me. What could anyone possibly enjoy about it? Rape seems like it would be awful for the person doing it. It takes me years to think of one possible turn-on:

Fighting against my *no* gave him the opportunity for total control. Consensual sex is a mutual thing, an improvisation created by responding to one's partner's actions and reactions. The only way for him to have total command of the experience, to force it into his exact specifications, was to neutralize my autonomy. Saying *yes* would have made me a wild, unpredictable partner with personality and preferences influencing and maybe even surprising him. Even consensual surrender would have retained an element of control for myself, just by being offered freely. By creating a situation in which

I resisted and he conquered, he was able to direct our interaction entirely. He was able to ensure that he got exactly what he wanted.

So he got just that, utter dominance through a mechanical enactment of only exactly what he'd choreographed beforehand in his mind, which turned out to be pretty bare and pathetic. I don't mean that vanilla sex is pathetic; the basics can be delightful and satisfying without remarkable elaboration. But the machinelike lack of exchange in his ideal fantasy, the lack of communication and response and discovery, is sad. Total control is by definition pitifully narrow. One of the great joys of life is being surprised by other people's generosity and individuality, though I suppose that's easy for me to say. I have been treated kindly for most of my life.

Georgia and I aren't the only ones Fryar attacked. Besides the seventies rape, there's the University of Pittsburgh student who the police suspect he may have gone after just three days before me, and who was asked, like me, "Do you wanna die?" Later, April's told me, another woman got away from Fryar by biting him. Neither of these two women can prosecute him now, because they don't have DNA evidence with which to override the statute of limitations.

They're lucky that they didn't get to that stage. I remember once a teacher in the drama department drove me home on a rainy day, when I was a senior. She said that someone once broke into her house and she scared him away, so she knows *exactly how I feel*. I was too shocked to correct her.

Mostly the Internet just gives me years: his birth and high school graduation, and various years of incarceration.

If he is indeed a disabled veteran, his military service likely fits within the five years between graduating high school and his rape conviction in Orange County, New York, in 1977.

He was in Sing Sing from 1977 to 1984, and then I have nothing for the next three years.

Honan's told me that Fryar lived in Pittsburgh from 1987 to 2002. I have no idea why he went there, and I see no connections. None of his Facebook friends appear to be in Pittsburgh, or even anywhere in Pennsylvania. More athletes get in the way of my Googling: a baseball player for the Pittsburgh Pirates has his last name; as does a football player, who never played for the Steelers but played against them enough that he clutters my results, too. Maybe the Pittsburgh years are when Arthur Fryar was Butch Johnson.

From 2002 to 2005, he was in prison in Otisville, New York (again, upstate), for selling drugs. That's when his DNA got put in the system.

In 2005, he was released and made his way south to New York City. This is also when he appeared to discover the Internet. In 2005, he registered with a reunion site as living in Long Island City, and I find an address for him that matches a Salvation Army veterans' shelter. In 2009, he changed his location on the site to Brooklyn. Records indicate that he shared an apartment address with a woman for at least part of his years there.

The Brooklyn period was when he was on the dating sites I found, and also on Twitter to promote an unsuccessful auction business. He attempted to flirt with an *X Factor* contestant, and whined about a fake lottery scam that must have briefly taken him in. That's also probably when he put himself on the "talent" site where I found most of his photos. He didn't follow through with that either. There's no evidence on his profile of his getting any work from the site. His only film credit on IMDb is as an extra in the coming-soon indie movie *Free the Nipple,* about the right of women to go topless in public.

The Brooklyn address is where they arrested him in September, so that's his whole life, sketched. I want more: some detail, some color.

I look harder.

8

When I moved back to my parents' house in New Jersey in 1994, I spent a fair amount of time in New York City. Most of my college friends were there, too, attempting the career that we had trained for. I had abandoned acting and was in graduate school, volunteering at the Metropolitan Museum of Art as my internship, first in Rare Books and then in Egyptian. I felt embarrassed that I no longer wanted what we had all wanted, and which my former classmates still wanted and some were achieving. I worried that they would think that I was cowardly for not even trying to audition for anything, but I enjoyed my quiet, orderly work. I was assigned the task of identifying all of the paintings in the museum that had books represented in them, as references for a history of bookbinding. I was left to answer the phones one day in the Egyptian department, and took a comically furtive call from an anxious lawyer who was trying to find out if it was legal for his client to inherit a mummy.

One day while commuting into the city, I saw an article in the newspaper about a rape similar to mine. I can't recall any details now. Honestly, it was probably only superficially similar, in the way that all rapes of a certain type are, but I was desperate. I had no reason then to believe that Fryar had moved to the New York area, just the idea that, well, he could have. I had; why not him, too?

I called the police in charge of that case, and arranged to meet a detective. My friend Kali waited with me, and she brought me a single pink peony. It was the first time I'd ever seen a peony, such a delightfully alien flower. When the detective met me on the famous steps of the museum, in front of its enormous banners, he was undercover, not in a uniform or suit. He looked, I think, like a stereotype of a biker. I wasn't what he'd expected to see either. I'm not sure why. I remember at the time seeing the surprise on his face, and assuming that he thought I wasn't pretty enough for someone to have bothered raping. Nothing came of the meeting; they took my information and presumably it's noted in a file somewhere.

I kept checking in with Pittsburgh every couple of years, phoning the sex-crimes number and having to introduce myself to new detectives. It was on the call that I made from California, shortly after marrying Gavin and moving to Silicon Valley for his job in 1998, that I was told that my statute of limitations had passed. No one had ever told me that there even was a limit.

After that, I began to research statutes of limitations. They're state laws, all different, so there's no simple way to make countrywide change. I e-mailed a Pennsylvania politician; no reply. I contacted a national rape organization, asking what was being done about statutes of limitations, in terms of lobbying or even just collecting information, and the answer I got was that nothing was being done. I volunteered to be part of an effort, but it didn't get off the ground.

Later, from my new home in England, I called Pittsburgh sex crimes again. That's when I got Dan Honan. I told him that I just wanted to know who it was. I knew that the district attorney couldn't prosecute, that too much time had passed, but please could he just get my evidence kit tested, and the results plugged into CODIS, the FBI's database of criminal DNA? I offered to pay for it, which it turns out isn't allowed. I brought up the recently convicted East End rapist, but he didn't think that my crime was similar enough. I bothered him several times. He finally asked the district attorney's office, and they said they'd authorize it if I'd promise to testify, traveling at my own expense, if a match was made. I didn't understand then, and I'm not sure if Dan did either, that the new law to override the statute of limitations was already in place. I assumed that they meant for me to testify in support of someone else's charges against him, perhaps to show a pattern, or to get a longer sentence.

I waited. This is what kills me with Aprill thinking that I'm not patient. I was patient, mostly because I found phoning the sex-crimes office to be really stressful. No one at that point had given me an e-mail address.

Later, much later, after a span measured in months at least and possibly over a year, I called back, to see if my evidence had made it to the lab. Dan was surprised to hear from me. He'd assumed that I was dealing with the DA's office. I have no idea why he thought that. At any rate, his contact who had agreed to authorize testing my kit had left. I was back to begging again. At least he gave me his e-mail this time around; I find writing to be easier.

It was shortly after that that Arthur Fryar was arrested for Georgia's rape and Dan told me of the likely connection to mine. I clicked links. I found the news stories.

I'm convinced that the Internet still has more to tell me.

I Google "serial rapists psychology." Apparently there are several types, as coined by Dr. Nicholas Groth in the seventies and ex-

panded upon today. My kind, the "power reassurance rapist," is inse-
cure and feels powerless. Rape gives him a moment of the authority
that he craves. These men only use force as much as is necessary to
control the victim, not beyond. They're not sadists; threat, pain, and
actual harm are tools, not ends. Some sources prefer to override the
clunky "power reassurance" title and substitute instead the ridiculous and inflammatory phrase "gentleman rapist." I remember one
of the detectives at the hospital, I think Bill, calling him that right
in front of me.

Another feature of power reassurance rapists is that they sometimes fantasize, as best they can, that there is a form of relationship,
a sort of kindness at play that the victim may resist now but will appreciate later. I remember when Fryar was done he told me, gently,
to rest. He didn't do anything to prevent me from being able to call
the police as he must have known I would as soon as he left. He
asked me not to, but didn't threaten me or take my phone (I mean
unplug my landline from the wall; cell phones had just barely been
invented). He didn't restrain me; he'd gotten what he wanted; he
was done with me. He left me on the floor.

I wonder where he went. How did he hide from the prowling
police? There were a lot of busy restaurants just a block away, but I
have trouble picturing him dining out. He must have been awfully
keyed up, maybe even hyper, high on his victory.

Maybe he was sad, though. Maybe after it's done, all the urgent
feelings used up, it doesn't seem worth it.

Maybe he was scared. Maybe he saw the police looking, and didn't
have the money to get a restaurant table. Maybe he hid between
houses or in the aisles of a drugstore, trying hard to look small and
uninteresting but sweating under his clothes and unable to focus.

No one's ever going to tell me, so I pick the one I like: I pick
scared. I hope he's been scared, for twenty-two years, of what's finally happening now.

I explain the sentencing possibilities to a friend, and what can affect the number, like the Offense Gravity Score, the Prior Record Score, all of that. She latches on to something I hadn't thought of, something that the justice system doesn't use but should: how long he's gotten away with it. She says that he should have to serve, at minimum, the number of years that he's had free after committing the crime. Those are years he never should have had at all. He owes them. We should start with twenty-two and add from there.

Evan's told me that they're ordering only the "disposition" of the old rape from New York, meaning the summarized result, not the full court transcript. I try to order the transcript for myself.

The only information I've found online is meager and contradictory. One New York database lists his arrest year as 1984, while another lists that as his year of release from prison. One implies a town called Orange as the place of arrest, the other Orange County. I phone both. The woman at the Orange County Clerk's Office seems at first officious and bored with me, reciting instructions on how to request a search: in writing, $2.50 per search year. I decide to search through a decade, 1975 to 1985.

If I'm lucky, this search will get me the number of the case, which I can then use to request a transcript from the court. I hastily scribble notes in my terrible handwriting, trying to get everything right, to think of everything I need to ask. Can they send me the result by e-mail? No? Oh. Well, I can enclose a self-addressed envelope, and I can use the U.S. address of a friend, but I don't have any U.S. stamps for it. I do have an American checkbook; maybe we could add the cost of postage to the check I'll be writing anyway? "I'm calling," I explain, "from England."

The words are magic. Just as saying "DNA sample" to the police had automatically triggered their cautious, calming, sex-crimes mode, saying that I'm calling from England now mobilizes the newly friendly woman on the other end of the phone. There will be none of this in-writing request making. She puts me on hold and goes to find the crime for me then and there.

I don't know if she trawls through a database or through file cabinets, but after a little while she returns, having hurried, to save me money on long-distance charges. She's victorious: Arthur Fryar, aka Frank Fryar (so that's what his middle initial *F* stands for), arrested in 1976, which fits with his 1977 entrance to Sing Sing and with 1984 as his year of release. She gives me the case's number and transfers me to criminal court.

The bureaucrat at Orange County's criminal court is snappish and annoyed. She finds no such case. I suggest that perhaps the database in front of her doesn't go back that far, and she shuts me down. I call the county clerk's office again. She, the nice lady, calls criminal court herself.

I hold for ages. When she comes back, she tells me that she got nowhere with the court lady either. So, she promises to find me the case file herself. "It may be just the disposition. There might not be any minutes. Is the disposition okay? What do you want it for?"

"I'd really like the minutes, the transcript, if you can," I answer. "It's—it's personal." I'd already decided not to explain who I am in relationship to the case, and had toyed with the idea of saying I'm a journalist, which is sort of true. In the end, "personal" is what pops out. That explanation is truthful, suggestive, and effective. She knows that it's a rape case.

She says that I should call back in a week, on Good Friday. They'll be open. Her name is Mary. She'll find me whatever she can.

This same day that Mary is kind to me, I submit my Freedom of Information Act request to the U.S. military's National Personnel Records Center in St. Louis. I use Gavin's name and his work address in Massachusetts, in case there may be some policy of letting those being researched know who requested their information.

I'm not hopeful of getting a result. Most of the information they require in the request, like "branch of service," is the information I'm trying to find. All I have is his name and birthday, and some good guesses, like that he probably enlisted in his high school graduation year, 1972, somewhere near his high school town, and that he must have returned home from service sometime before the rape four years later.

1976. I've always liked that year, because of the Bicentennial, which marked two hundred years since America declared itself a country, no longer a colony. I remember the specially minted quarters, that Fourth-of-July feeling all year long. My mom gave my sister and me each a silk scarf with an image of the Declaration of Independence on it, and showed us where to find our ancestor's signature. For most of that year I was six years old.

I don't know how old Fryar's then-victim was. He pleaded to second-degree rape, which now means a victim under fourteen, but it might not have meant that then. I don't think he's a pedophile; he wouldn't have wanted twenty-two-year-old me if he was.

Fryar would have been twenty-four in 1976, presumably recently returned from military service. Strong. Trained to fight.

I realize that perhaps Fryar didn't enlist. He might have been drafted. It took me this long to consider that possibility because no one in my family, immediate or extended, had been the right age for Vietnam, which had left me oblivious. My father's father had been en route to serve in France when World War I ended; my mother had been born into Nazi Germany. There had been war in my family tree, but that was all before I was born. We were unaffected by Vietnam.

If Fryar had been drafted, he would have been assigned his number on August 5, 1971, just before the start of his senior year of high school. That was when the government randomly matched

the numbers 1 through 366 (365 + 1 for the leap year) with all of
the birth dates for men born in 1952, for possible draft in 1972.
Fryar's birthdate, March 19, was assigned the number 53. The draft
would start with the men whose birth date had matched with the
number 1 and go up from there. It wasn't clear each year how many
numbers would be gotten through, just that the low numbers were
likely to be called up and that numbers in triple digits were safer.
Of 1972's potential draft groups, President Nixon called through
number 95, more than 49,000 young men.

Of the seven infantry training centers I see listed for draftees,
the nearest to Fryar would have been Fort Dix, New Jersey, just a
little over an hour down the Turnpike from my hometown. I would
have been two years old when a drafted Fryar was in basic training.
For all Fort Dix's nearness, I can't recall ever knowing even one
active military person while I was growing up, not even any friend's
sibling. My dad had been in the navy before I was born, before he
met my mom, but not as a career, just as a rite of passage, like his
Ivy League undergrad years and law school. He'd asked for combat
duty during the Korean War but had been kept stateside.

The draft lottery was suspended in 1973. If the draft is how Fryar
ended up in the military, he was among the last of those forced.

I'd been completely protected from all of this. I wasn't just shel-
tered by the fact that I was a toddler; the margin around me was
bigger than that. The news about it was never on in our house.
None of my friends' moms were widows, at least that I knew of.
There's nothing that I noticed then, or can recall now with hind-
sight, that was in any way touched by that war. I remember being
surprised, when I got older and learned about Vietnam as history, to
discover that it had happened while I was alive.

I feel like I should hide that I'm looking for information about
Fryar. I'm not sure people will understand.

Gavin answered the downstairs phone when I got a call back from a librarian in Fryar's hometown. He asked me later, perfectly reasonably, "So, what was that about?"

The librarian had checked Fryar's high school yearbook for me. I wanted to see what had been written beside his picture, but it turns out that he's not even in the yearbook. Two other Fryars, also black men, but not him.

I tell Gavin that I'm "doing research." That's become my go-to answer to strangers, too. This is all public information that I have a right to look at without explanation, but people ask. I say it cheerfully and a bit harried, using a tone of voice that's kind of smiley, and kind of "Don't get me started on how crazy complicated the whole story is!" The general response is commiseration and helpfulness.

Gavin's reaction to my researching Arthur Fryar is carefully neutral, as it had been when I first found out about the arrest and was Googling photos of him. I remember sitting in bed with my laptop and being like "Hey, honey! I found another one!" and making Gavin look at him.

For more than twenty years, this person who had impacted my life so hugely had been a blank to me. Getting his name, getting his picture, was a gift. I'm just opening it.

I tell my kids about life before the Internet. I remember encyclopedias, book indexes, card catalogs. When I was a teenager, my state had a phone number that linked to a late-night reference library where someone would look things up by request. It was a fantastical indulgence. Information then was almost exclusively written or printed, limited to the place where it was physically kept. Being able to acquire it by phone at, say, 11 P.M., had felt luxurious and even subversive, as if it were a naughty shortcut.

Now I can search for anything I want all night long. It's a disappointment to discover that the Internet doesn't have all of the answers.

Just because something is a public fact doesn't mean that it's findable, especially facts from before the Internet age. Newspapers, court records, yearbooks: they're still mostly in the physical realm, not digital. I'm still ultimately dependent on kind people with written records on the other end of a phone.

Some people are bored and annoyed with my requests, but most are delightful, kind, and tenacious. They chat and brainstorm. People in three different New York State County Clerk's Offices are checking things out for me. I keep track of their names and thank them effusively. Some records aren't where they should be; some have been destroyed. The supreme court offices suggest I talk to criminal court and vice versa, around and around. I can rattle off Fryar's date of birth by heart now, and the places he's lived, his milestone years. I feel like his life in upstate New York is coming into focus.

I make no phone calls to Pennsylvania, because I have nothing to even start with. His years there are opaque. Then the Internet surprises me and pops up what I'm looking for. My suspicion that the Pittsburgh years are the ones when he called himself Butch Johnson appears to be correct.

There are sites devoted to aggregating technically public information into tidy little background checks: demographic info, a lifetime's worth of addresses, even arrests and convictions.

Unsurprisingly, these facts aren't completely dependable. People with the same name get mistakenly linked, while single lives get fragmented into multiple listings. Even when the information is correct, it's out of context and garbled. But, it's a start.

Fryar's assumed name, Butch Johnson, was clearly a ridiculous amount of overcompensation: "manly" followed by a slang term for "penis." Amazingly, he's one of many using this combination of words for a name, so without more information it's difficult to narrow down the possibilities.

It's the middle initial that grabs me: F, which is Fryar's middle initial, too. It makes sense that someone changing his name, presumably changing his life, will still allow some old reality to seep through. You can't change literally everything. Generating fiction involves significant, tiring work. I had been taught in connoisseurship class that, when evaluating a portrait to figure out if it's a fake, look at the ears. Someone copying someone else's style will put effort into controlling the look of the eyes and mouth; but the seemingly unimportant details tend to be filled in on autopilot, and so reveal the unthinking assumptions of their creator.

The birth date is the other hint, the month correct and the year off by just one: this Butch F. Johnson is sixty-one, close enough to Fryar's sixty-two. Everything else fits so well that I wonder if Fryar is vain about his age, and lied somewhere about being thirty-nine instead of forty back when he lived in Pittsburgh. Forty is how old he turned two months after raping me.

I find four Pittsburgh addresses for this Butch F. Johnson, this Manly-F-Penis, and plot them on a map. Two of them are a half-hour walk to my college apartment. One is forty-five minutes' walk, the last an hour and fifteen. A fifth address, for the name without a middle initial, is forty minutes. The dotted-line routes on the screen stick out east and west from my old neighborhood, like spider legs.

Butch F. Johnson's closest address, twenty-seven minutes' walk from me, is on the same street where a Pitt student was attacked three days before me.

While confirming that I have the correct street for the attack, I find an old news report that mentions a detail I'd previously missed: she'd been thrown down steps. Her attacker's mistake that day had been to try to assault her in the apartment building hallway. Three days later, Fryar made the more effective choice to get me inside of my apartment. Struggling and screaming didn't matter in there.

Dan Honan has told me that Fryar lived in Penn Hills, near Wilkinsburg, when he was in Pittsburgh. Wilkinsburg is familiar to me, a predominantly black part of the city that I used to take a bus to on Sundays to attend a lively church. Perhaps he did live there, too, but these addresses that I've found closer to my apartment ring true to me.

There's no hint of dates in the websites I'm using, no sense of the order of these addresses, or even if they fall into the "Pittsburgh" range of Fryar's life at all. It's only a guess that the street where the Pitt student was attacked is the one a Butch Johnson lived on in 1992, though perhaps not for long after, if he didn't want his victim to run into him around the area.

If this Butch, at these addresses, was even him.

I've e-mailed that kind reference librarian in Beacon, Fryar's hometown, to ask if he has any ideas for further research into Fryar's early life now that I know that the yearbooks have nothing. He'd told me, in passing while we talked on the phone, that he'd been a freshman at Fryar's high school in 1972, Fryar's supposed graduation year. I've asked him to brainstorm with me, with the caveat that I don't want to contact or disturb the Fryar family in any way.

I think that I come across, in my more chatty communications, like an adult child looking for a birth parent, because of words like "personal" and "significant" coupled with a wariness of making actual contact with anyone related. I bet that the librarian will figure me out. Even a superficial Google of Arthur Fryar brings up our current case, and my Jane Doe is described as "a woman who now lives in the United Kingdom." The librarian knows where I've contacted him from.

He's not the only person I'm being cagey with.

Our printer is being weird. I had asked Gavin to shake the failing ink cartridge, as we always do before giving in to replacing it, and now my printouts are gray and splotched. I show him the results so he can try to fix it, but that means that he sees the letters I'm writing: to county clerks, and to a couple who may have been Fryar's landlords a long time ago. I don't actively hide things from Gavin, but I wouldn't have shared these if it weren't for the ink problem. Only results will justify my efforts; as things are now, my scattershot requests to America about Arthur Fryar must look obsessive and odd, even to the person who sees me the most generously.

9

Trial, or the formal plea, is seven weeks away.

I check on what specific news reports rise to the top in search results. One article opens, "He chose them for their legs." That, combined with the protection against describing us victims as we testify in court, must create a wrong picture in people's minds, of younger me, lovely then.

I worry about what to pack for court. I don't fuss much about clothes at the best of times, and the June date will make it even harder for me to look nice. It's easier to flatter myself with cold-weather clothes: good boots, well-cut jackets. I'm aiming to wear middle-season clothes, hoping that it won't be hot yet. I want to wear tights; I want to wear sleeves.

I need new shoes, but no place is selling the style that I can't get out of my head: black leather with a strong arch, a chunky heel, maybe a buckle. After weeks of idly shopping, in spare moments when I happen to pass stores that look promising, I realize that I'm literally looking for the shoes I was wearing the night that it happened, the shoes that he roughly pulled off my feet.

Whether I need to prep testimony or an impact statement, Evan's caution about profanity on the stand has made me nervous. It's not that I want to swear; it just feels like a difficult thing, needing to let emotion run wild so that the jury will be moved by my upset, but at the same time needing to control my emotions tightly so that I don't offend them with my indignation.

I know that Evan didn't personally mind what I'd said; he'd prefaced his advice to me by pointing out that the defense attorney from the hearing had behaved like "an ass" and certainly deserved my response.

Kevin hadn't minded what I'd said either. I think it was okay because we'd been only in front of a judge. It's the same reason why Fryar could appear in a prison outfit and handcuffs at the hearing, but will probably be in a suit at trial. Judges are trusted to overlook superficial things. Juries aren't.

Bill told me that he'd been worried during my hearing testimony that I might faint, but that when I got angry he knew that I'd be okay.

That's the difference: Bill saw that being angry helped. Being angry was appropriate. A jury, though, or a more formal judge, is more likely to reward sadness in a victim and disapprove of anger.

I like not having to be angry, so long as others are angry for me. It's just that being in the same room with Fryar will make it difficult to not be angry myself. They need me to go powerless and soft for the jury and judge, with him *right there.*

It could be that there are deep cultural norms at work, about the way that women are expected to behave. It could also be this way because of how the court system assigns roles. The victim is hurt;

the judge and jury avenge. If I take on anger, that robs them of their assigned part. They're the ones who get to say "guilty," not me.

It's easier to take on the gentle part if I see it as a job. It's right for justice to be meted out by persuaded, uninvolved parties. My job is to do the persuading, not the avenging.

I have to trust that Evan has my back. I know that the others do, I know Bill does, but they don't have any authority in the courtroom.

I think that Evan will look out for me. He seems like a nice guy. Perhaps more to the point, he seems like an ambitious attorney. He'll want to do this job, which is partly to be my anger, right.

The two most relevant leads to Fryar's history are still dangling without resolution. I've found out that the drug crime that got his DNA into the system, and that put him in Otisville prison from 2002 to 2005, happened in Staten Island, but it isn't coming up in the court records there.

I find it interesting that Fryar had this drug case there in 2002, and that back in 1985 he had a driving-without-a-license fine there. Staten Island appears to bookend his Pittsburgh years.

The file for the 1976 rape case, in New York's Orange County, is being looked for by that enthusiastic, friendly woman in the county clerk's office, Mary. Today's the day that she asked me to call her back.

It turns out that she has found reference to the file, and requested it to be sent over to her. That was a week ago. What with Easter being this weekend and all, she asks me to call back in six days. She should have it by then. She doesn't know how many pages it is. It's disappointing to have to wait, but heartening that the file apparently still exists. I will get it, eventually.

I'm collecting all of these documents in a little folder on my iPad. I have two editions of Pennsylvania's "Sexual Violence Benchbook," which describe the prosecution process; minutes from New York's extradition hearings; guideline sentence forms from Evan; transcripts of similar cases from Kevin; Bill's notes from 1992, scanned by Dan. I also have the transcript of our hearing from January.

I recognize most of it. One surprising line to me is when I answered a question with a clear "yes" followed by a trailing "yeah, yeah, yeah," as my patience waned. I think that's probably when I felt faint. A few questions later, what should have been a polite, alert confirmation of my name came out as a weary, almost sarcastic-seeming "sure."

I notice a small discrepancy. In the transcript, when the defense asked Dan if the old detective from the case was even still alive, it says that Dan replied, "He's here in the courtroom as a matter of fact." But I remember him saying, "He's here in the courtroom. In fact, he's right behind me!" with a head toss over his shoulder, back toward where Bill and I were sitting. (Remember, in the municipal court, those testifying stand facing the judge, their backs to the room.) I remember, because he said it with almost a little laugh. The defense attorney was being skeptical and persistent, and Bill was *right there*.

I check for how I'm quoted. The court reporter didn't redact "fucking," which I appreciate, but she's mixed up my word order, I'm sure of it. Then I look above, and the way she's written the defense attorney's words seem off, too. She has him state his question positively, "You were able to see this man's face who did this crime; am I correct?" That's not how it went at all. He had phrased it incredulously, words as well as tone. He'd implied that my claim of clearly seeing his face was inherently ridiculous. That's what had upset me.

Those quotes aren't drastically different, but they remind me of how absolute the past isn't. The court reporter wrote her transcript from an audio recording; I was actually there. We should both be right. We should match. Maybe I'm interpreting, using the whole experience, not just the words. She might have been simplifying and summarizing, or might have genuinely misheard.

I wonder if transcripts are assumed to be literally verbatim, or if it's understood that there's some insignificant leeway in them, in the way that statistics are considered to have an inherent but hopefully minor margin of error. From what I can see online, court transcripts are treated as definitive once they exist. But I also see a thriving business of errors and omissions insurance aimed at court reporters. More than one company's website reminds potential customers that "Mistakes happen."

Another piece of the transcript that stands out to me is the judge's warning to Fryar to "Look forward. Continue to look forward for the duration of this court hearing, okay?" This happened while I was testifying. The judge suddenly interrupted, to tell Fryar off, commanding him to keep his eyes front, presumably off me. This admonition was reported in the *Pittsburgh Post-Gazette:* "The suspect . . . stood about 10 feet away, staring at the first victim until [the judge] asked him to look straight ahead . . . for the remainder of the proceeding."

But Bill had told me, over tea afterward, that Fryar hadn't been looking at me at all. The judge had had his attention on me, and Bill and Dan had each been keeping an eye on Fryar, watching him while he listened to me. Bill thinks that he and Dan, right next to me, must have shot a glance to Fryar at the same time, and that the judge, noticing their eyes, had assumed that Fryar had done something to engage them. But he hadn't, Bill told me. According to him, it was a coincidence that he and Dan had both looked at that moment, triggering the judge to act. Anyone reading the transcript or the newspaper, though, even the judge himself, would see it otherwise, reasonably so.

My novels are all narrated in first person, by multiple characters. In one book, two of the narrators cover the same conversation, and in my draft their versions had had slight variations from one another. Those variations were just little things, interpretations and transitions that worked better for the voice of each character relating it. In the copy-edit stage, when every word and punctuation mark comes under scrutiny, that had been flagged, and I'd "corrected" the versions to match exactly. My reasoning was that it wasn't worth distracting a careful reader when the differences in the conversations weren't a plot point. But, I still miss those contrasting tellings, which to me represent a larger theme in the way I structure my stories: everything is interpreted. It's natural for readers to trust that each narrator is giving them the plain and whole truth, and I like playing with that trust, showing how, despite each narrator being honest from their limited point of view, what they tell is not the plain and whole truth of what actually happened after all. It's the truth through their hearing and seeing and remembering. That's not exactly the same thing.

Which is all a long way of saying that while official documents appear to be neutral and precise, they may not be completely so. All memories, even official ones, are vulnerable to imprecision, error, imitation of error, and the filter of assumptions.

Aprill didn't stand with me at the hearing because she's not my detective; she's attached to Georgia. Even so, while Bill is the most important person on this case to me personally, Aprill is the most important objectively. She's the engine to the machine that's getting Fryar and others like him identified, arrested, and prosecuted. She's the star.

She started looking at cold cases in 2007 and since then has pursued about two a year, on top of her load of current cases. According to the 2004 law, only rapes for which the DNA analysis now indicates a previously unsuspected person—that is, stranger rapes—can be reopened in this way.

I've often thought how lucky I am that I didn't know the man, not only because of the help that fact has been with the police and the prosecution, but also because it meant that my rape wasn't any kind of betrayal. I never had to question my relationships, or wonder about the men who are my friends. Rape was done by "the bad man" out there somewhere, not by someone normal in my intimate inner circle, or even in the larger circles of my life. I didn't know him the least bit, not at all. He might as well have been a movie monster, not a person.

Even knowing how lucky I am, and how easily my situation could have been otherwise and is otherwise for many, I cringe when articles about acquaintance-rape swing to the other extreme and make stranger-rape out to be so rare as to be irrelevant. Compared to, say, date rape or too-drunk-to-consent rape, stranger-rape is admittedly far less frequent. But, though we may be rare like platinum, we're not rare like unicorns. We exist.

The nationwide backlog of unprocessed evidence kits exists for a lot of reasons: new backlog continually created as current demand exceeds resources; the accumulation of that backlog; and old cases from the eighties and nineties. Back then, the potential for DNA evidence was recognized before the technology and costs were practical. Most pertinent, before the FBI created their CODIS database (authorized in 1994 and activated in 1998), and then over time populated it, there was nothing to compare processed stranger-rape evidence to. In 1992, my then-useless evidence was collected anyway, and stored and looked after, when there was no present use for it, only future hope. I'm grateful to Pittsburgh for that.

Even though CODIS now offers a menu of over ten million criminal DNA profiles, Pittsburgh's old evidence is not automatically put in line for testing. The current workload in the lab is too great to allow for that. The problem is not limited to Pittsburgh; the overall number of untested rape kits in America is unknown, but statistics from a sampling of cities add up to tens of thousands.

Besides the criminal profiles, CODIS also holds on to the unknown evidence profiles once they're submitted. Even if they don't hit a match right away, these unknown profiles get compared to the rest of the database weekly, in hope of matching someone newly added or of linking up with a new evidence profile from another case. I'd been desperate to get mine in there.

To get chosen, I'd had to nag. Even my persistence with Dan hadn't been enough, until Georgia's evidence was put through to the lab by Aprill and hit Fryar.

Bill wasn't told. He heard it from me, after I found him through LinkedIn, based on lucky remembrance of only his last name. As far as I can tell, Georgia's old detective hasn't been told at all. Well, perhaps he or she has been told now, in a request to testify at trial, but he or she wasn't at the hearing, and everyone was surprised that Bill was.

These old detectives are cut off from their cases. It was like that back in 1992, even when Bill was still on the force, just moved to a different department. I was told that my case wasn't his anymore, and that all contact from then on should go to the next person it had been handed to.

I don't remember if I ever spoke to that new guy even a second time. After he moved on, as far as I can tell, the case wasn't even handed off, just filed. Until CODIS and, really, until Fryar's DNA got added to it, there had been nothing for anyone to do.

I must decline an invitation to a summer party that's scheduled for the day that I'll be testifying, so in the RSVP I mention why, explaining succinctly both the crime and the prosecution. It's a practical fact to me now, not a secret, not a grand admission. I'll be in court. The trial itself is a public proceeding, after all, even if my role in it is anonymous. The anonymity just means that the trial is mine to tell about, no one else's.

I probably make people uncomfortable.

Small things reassure me. One old friend from home wishes me luck for trial, and refers to Fryar as "this 'person,'" putting "person" in quotes. I appreciate the dehumanizing. Going up against a stranger, particularly a serially violent stranger, is easier than going up against one's peer. It's like those sci-fi movies that make it comfortable to cheer violence because the enemies aren't like us: they're aliens who want to destroy the world.

Fryar's Staten Island years continue to elude me. I can't find any address for him there, or any obvious family connections. But he must have lived there, at least some nights, with a friend or girlfriend maybe. Geographically, Staten Island isn't someplace you wander into or pass through without a reason.

His 2002–2005 prison time for his drug conviction there is confirmed by the New York Department of Corrections, but the crime itself has no record in the Richmond County court system. I pester them. They mention other charges attached to Fryar: a 1985 driving citation, a 1985 disorderly conduct, and a 1986 sealed case. *Sealed?* I'm not sure if the guy on the phone was supposed to say that out loud. The sealed case at first sounds intriguing, but it turns out that only juvenile, insignificant, or dismissed cases are likely to be sealed. Fryar wasn't a juvenile, so the sealed charge, whatever it is, must be simply unimportant or even not true.

My last effort to confirm the details of the conviction for which he was imprisoned in 2002, a quickie online "background check" for criminal history, turns up an arrest and guilty plea that matches the county and the drug charge I'm looking for, but with surprising dates: August 1986 arrest, and a guilty plea in June 1987. Why would there be a fifteen-year gap between plea and serving his sentence?

I suppose it could be that this happened twice, in the same place, sixteen years apart; but why would the 2002 case not be showing up, either in the county clerk's records, or in whatever records are used in the background check? And why would the incarceration for the 1987 guilty plea, which carried a sentence of three to six years, not be in the department of corrections database? That database has Fryar's rape incarceration from 1977 to 1984, so it's not a matter of the data not going back far enough.

If the 2002 date in the department of corrections source is just wrong, and this all refers to one case in the late eighties, that doesn't fit either. CODIS wasn't started until 1994, and New York didn't start collecting offender DNA to put into it until 1996. Even then, New York only put in the DNA of convicted murderers and rapists, not dealers. It took years for New York's net of qualifying offenses to widen enough to catch Fryar in it. So, the 2002 incarceration must be right, or at least more right than not. There simply has to be some conviction around that time to have gotten him into CODIS.

Then what about the thing in the eighties? Is this the sealed case? Why on earth would an adult's guilty plea to a felony be sealed?

Weirder, the "disposition date," which is supposed to be the date that the case was decided, and which is listed right under the 1987 guilty plea, is Halloween 1996, nine years later. Then there's a further gap of six years before the consequent imprisonment. Something odd had happened in Staten Island.

I e-mail Evan to ask if he has any solid knowledge of Fryar's legal past. This is all public information, so it's no betrayal for him to share it with me if he knows it; but I'm acutely aware that it looks strange for me to ask. I'm afraid that he'll ask in return, "Why do you want to know?" I worry, when he doesn't ask, that he's thinking it.

All of this could be simple if someone just asked Fryar directly for his basic life facts. It's impossible for me to do, both in that it's not allowed for me to communicate with him, and in that I couldn't bear to even if it were. No one else is going to ask him for me; no one else cares. The police and the district attorney have everything they need: they know what he did to me and to Georgia, and they know where he is now. That 1976 rape only matters because it changes his sentencing range. Everything else, literally everything, is irrelevant, to everyone except me. And, I suppose, to Fryar.

His arrest this past September was much more than just finally catching him. They'd finally *identified* him. For more than twenty years, I hadn't known who he was. The possibility of now learning what urged him on, what directed him to me, and what he got out of it, is electrifying.

I keep myself in check. My methods don't even involve leaving my house, which is already an ocean away from him. I treat this investigation as if he were dead, or even deeply in the past, like an academic speculating on the life of an ancient using only chipped paintings from the wall of a tomb.

I find his sister.

At first I hadn't noticed her among his Facebook friends, because he doesn't publicly identify family and she doesn't have the same last name anymore. Something else she doesn't have: any privacy settings. All of her posts, photos, and information are entirely open.

Up until now, everything I've found has been distant-feeling: addresses, arrests, numerous abandoned attempts at social media. This spareness fit how I remember him: he appeared, then he disappeared. He only exists in my experience as the thing that he did, nothing else.

But his sister seems to love him.

When she first joined Facebook, in 2009, she did what many do: posted a flattering photo of herself (nine years out-of-date) then a flurry of pictures of special moments, such as her high school re-union, and family highlights. They make me catch my breath.

There's adult-but-very-young Arthur in a tuxedo with a lapel flower, with smiling friends, seeming to be on his way to a prom, or maybe a wedding, some formal event.

There's older-than-that-but-younger-than-now Arthur playing guitar with the Drifters. His suit doesn't go with their matching outfits, so it wasn't official; but he's onstage with them, enjoying himself hugely, probably as a let-someone-from-the-audience-give-it-a-go sort of thing.

It makes me angry. How can someone who has friends and family, how can someone who has music, claim the desperation that is the only excuse I can imagine for what he did? I write characters who do bad things, and they do them because their worlds are so small that they think they *must* do what they do. They *need* something, desperately. I look at him playing a guitar, I look at him happy, and I think: *How dare you?*

The formal portrait photo of their parents has only Arthur's sister in it with them, so she's likely the oldest. According to various Mother's Day and Father's Day posts of hers over the years, their dad died in 1977, at age fifty-two, when Fryar would have been on his way to prison for second-degree rape if not in prison already, and their mom died in 1983, at age fifty-six, the year before he got out. Those ages are awfully young for death.

Arthur's sister didn't post anything about him when he was ar-rested this past September. To be fair, neither did I. Both of us just kept posting in our usual way: I continued on about kid stuff, book stuff, and cats; she posted more all-caps religious encouragement with multiple exclamation points.

I stopped posting entirely after the January hearing, though plenty has happened that I could have noted: Easter celebrations; W.'s new and awesome shark pajamas; S.'s first paintball battle for his thirteenth birthday. But it feels like lying now to write about anything that isn't the upcoming trial. I can talk about other things, and successfully do things that have nothing to do with Pittsburgh, but writing is different. Writing is where I'm most honest and most selfish. Right now, all I want to write is this.

Googling the death years of Fryar's parents, I discover that his dad's name is the same as my dad's.

Now that I'm a generation back, the genealogical sites can help. Besides the many Fryars from Beacon, there are a bunch from nearby Newburgh, just across the Hudson River. Newburgh is where Arthur was arrested in 1976.

I can't stop looking at the tuxedo and guitar pictures. Now I think that the formalwear photo is likely the four siblings, two brothers and two sisters, rather than two couples. Comparing it to a more recent photo of the four, there are confirming similarities. Given the age differences between them, a thirteen-year spread from oldest to youngest, Arthur must be at least midtwenties in that pic. He went into prison at age twenty-five, so if the picture was snapped just before then the younger sister would be at most a grown-up-looking fourteen, which I suppose is possible. I'm pretty terrible at guessing ages. The other option is that Arthur was out of prison there, in his thirties, with the younger two in their early twenties, but it seems like the kind of photo that a parent would take. By the time Arthur got out of prison, both of their parents were dead.

I stare at the candid pictures, of Arthur joking around in black tie, Arthur in a suit with a guitar. That's what his side will try to show in court, that version of him: Arthur dressed up, Arthur who has family to pose with or snap his picture. I wonder if any of them will be at trial. I'll recognize them if they come.

I've been worrying about what he'll wear in court, and these photos help me to adjust in advance to what it will be like to see him like that, in clothes that one would wear to an important meeting or a special event. Gavin wears a suit to visit customers in Asia. S. wears black tie for performances. That's the point of putting male defendants in suits: suits make someone look responsible, respectable-until-proven-guilty; they're for people with good jobs or special skills, with places to go. It's been panicking me, thinking about having to see Arthur Fryar like that, and to see other people seeing him like that. I suppose that's what my testimony is for: to make everyone see what he's capable of, however he tries to show them otherwise with his clothes and controlled manner.

I know that it was stupid to think that his playing guitar was shocking, that "music" is supposed to be enough to keep someone from doing awful things. I just couldn't help it. Art to me—any art—is such an obvious outlet that it's difficult for me to think of someone having an ability to express themselves, an ability to pour out what they feel and make something good out of it, yet not using it to divert their difficult emotions and thwarted desires. But just being able to play an instrument isn't that. It's a step toward that ability, but only a step. Knowing a few chords isn't the same as being creative, and even being genuinely creative can go badly wrong. Maybe if someone is that broken, creativity doesn't use up the bad feelings and desires, but legitimizes them and urges them on.

"Using up" difficult or confusing feelings is exactly what writing does for me. Once I've put something down in a logical, expressive way, it's out of my head. Then someone reads it, and understands, and I feel connected. After that, there's more to discover past those expressed feelings, things that I wouldn't be conscious of if I'd left myself stuck, keeping the first things to myself.

It wasn't always this way. I was originally secretive about the poetry I wrote in college. I was honest in it about struggle and weakness and wanting things I couldn't have, and was embarrassed by all of that, even as I was proud of the way the words fit together. I only let strangers read my writing, specifically contest judges. When I started winning, I felt I had to show my work to one person who was alluded to in one of the poems, someone I admired tremendously. I didn't identify her by name, but anyone who knew us would recognize her. It wasn't fair for me to pursue publication including that one poem without her permission.

At the time, I'd honestly believed that anyone who read my poems would hate me afterward. I'd thought, *Well, this is it,* that that was the last day that she was going to want to be my friend, the last day that I would be able to fool her into thinking that I was the person I wished to be, the person I worked hard to come across as. I grieved in advance, but giving her the chance to veto my use of the poem was the right thing to do. I gave her the whole collection so that she'd know the context.

She read them all, overnight. The next morning, she said something that became the most significant fulcrum of my life: she told me that I'd described how she feels, too.

There's life before that revelation, and life after, as different as black-and-white Kansas and colorful Oz. Up until that moment, I'd thought that other people, she in particular but so many others, too, really were as they presented themselves, really were that good and that special, and so easily, too, and that I was the one who didn't match. When she admitted to being a little bit like me, I grasped the possibility that perhaps I was a little like her, and, instead of seeing the admirable people around me as massively important and myself as very, very small, I saw us all as suddenly medium-sized and far more complicated than I'd previously allowed.

As for what I'll wear in court, opposite Fryar's presumed suit, it has to be trousers and blazers for me. No dresses. I've got to cover my legs. I know that Fryar likes them, or at least that he did twenty-two years ago, so I don't want him to be able to see them. And I don't want anyone else to think about them, when Aprill testifies about his saying that it's our legs that he remembers. I don't want anyone to peek at them and judge.

He hasn't pleaded guilty yet. That makes me wonder if he wants this confrontation as much as I do, and if he thinks about seeing me.

10

As cathartic as testifying will be, catharsis is not its purpose. There's a goal, and I have to keep that firmly in mind. Only a part of me will be useful at trial: the part that's soft, sad, and invites being defended by others. The rest of me, while useful elsewhere, is not required.

I make myself a little list of rules:

1. Don't faint.

Really this just means eat breakfast, bring water, and focus.

2. Don't swear.

Not even to use the swear words' literal meanings, no matter how stupid and textbookish the alternative words sound.

Those two rules are a start, from my experience at the hearing and from talking to Evan. I look up advice online for more, and write down the ones that surprise me:

3. Review your past statements.

I'd thought that this would be a kind of cheating, but I suppose that after twenty-two years it's reasonable to refresh myself by looking over Bill's notes and my pages and pages of college poetry. The recent hearing transcript is what the defense is likely to be building their case on, so I should be careful to clearly match up with however I described things then. I don't want to give the defense any superficial confusion to work with.

4. Look at the jury.

Wow, I do not want to do that. I think that that advice is for a different kind of witness. Besides, I doubt that they'll want eye contact with me when I'm saying the things that I'm going to say. The other listed option is to look at the attorney asking the questions and I like that one much better.

5. Be polite to everyone, even the opposing attorney.

That will be difficult. I resent her already, even though I know that she's performing an essential role. Plus, even while I'm being polite, it will be desperately important for me not to trust her. She's not on my side. She'll likely be trying to trip me up. So, the politeness I'm to give her isn't like the openness I'm to give to Evan, where I'll answer anything he asks with detail and emotion, and let him lead me around. No, she works on behalf of the enemy, so I must be wary, but equally I must not harden myself in advance; if she then responds to my gentle civility by attacking with ugly implications or sneakily phrased questions, let the jury see me be hurt by it, on the spot. That can only help.

From there, it's easy to be reminded of this, from Evan:

6. If anything's worth getting angry over, Evan will deal with
it for me.

If he doesn't object, then it must be okay. I have to trust him. And, lastly, from my own thoughts:

7. Remember that the jury can see me whenever I'm in the courtroom, not just when I'm on the stand.

They'll watch me watching, watch me listening. I must remain aware of how I come across. They'll be judging me, too, not just him.

The trial is a month away. Leaving for the choir trip to Switzerland, with my trial bags packed, is just three weeks away.

I can barely wait. Basel, the choir's destination, is supposed to be gorgeous, all river and charm, but what I really want to see is Pittsburgh's courthouse. From descriptions online, it's beautiful, with a grand staircase and a courtyard fountain. It's comforting to think of the effort of design, construction, and cost that went into it. It makes the process of justice seem important to the city.

Special buildings make those who get to use them feel special. Even those who work there so often that they take the ambience for granted are affected, even if they don't realize it. They absorb the setting and the value that it confers on them. They know, even if only unconsciously: *This is the kind of place where I belong.*

That's what living in Cambridge feels like. I started writing my first novel because I was trying to express my wonder at my new home in England. I love buildings, and the human choices that make buildings. As much as I appreciate nature, it's the deliberateness of architecture that excites me.

The choral festival will be a welcome buffer between home and court. Chaperoning is much less emotional than parenting, even chaperoning that includes one's own. The schedule will be tightly organized by others, and I will have distracting and cheerful obligations. The other adults who will be in the group all know about what's ahead for me, all except for the accompanying organ scholar, who graduated last year and so won't have been around the college recently.

I plan and prepack. I put Fryar's tuxedo photo on my iPad, so I can practice looking at him. The dating- and casting-site photos freak me out a little; he looks a bit "bedroom eyes" in the way he's leaning. The youthful tuxedo snapshot, with, I think, his siblings, is unnerving, too, in that it shows him as a whole person with a silly side, someone with whom I should perhaps feel sympathy as a fellow human being, but it's at least more distant from when he was in my apartment.

I look ahead and protect the rest of June, the month I'll come home to, by scheduling extra meetings with John, and withdrawing from the lists of people who read the Bible in service and of parents who serve cookies and juice to the choirboys. I remember that, for a few services after January's hearing, I preferred to sit out in the nave, just listening, not inside the inner chapel participating in the recitations and hymn. I won't have that luxury of distance this time around. W. is being promoted from probationer to chorister, and will start wearing his white surplice while I'm in Pittsburgh. When I get back, he'll be keen for me to sit close, where he can see me seeing him.

My absolute favorite Bible verse is two words from the Old Testament: "Choose life." It's from Deuteronomy, and in context is specifically about choosing to obey God or not, asserting that the former leads to life and the latter to death. It says, "I have set before you life and death . . . Choose life."

I'm not a fan of the minutiae of Old Testament law, but I aspire to the compassion and goodness implied by the command to follow God. Sometimes the "life" option in a situation is easy to recognize, even if it may be hard to follow; sometimes there's no clearly right thing to do, just several muddled options. But I look for life, and try to choose it when I see it, or at least to choose the most life-ish way.

I'm the kind of person who always wants to finish, who wants to get on the other side of whatever I'm in the middle of: I wanted to graduate, to marry, to get my babies born; I want to finish the next book and see it on the shelf. I resist and resent being in the middle of things; I do the doing only because it's the means to the end, and the end is what I want. I want it, I think, because only when something is finished do I really know if it was a success. While anything is still happening, still coming into being, it can fail or go wrong or just not become what I'm so hoping it will.

It finally occurred to me, though, that always wanting to be past things, to be finished, looking back, is like wanting to be dead. So I remind myself, often, to "choose life" instead: embrace being in the middle of things, not knowing the ending.

There's a lot that I'm waiting for, that I'm fantasizing about being past so that I can bask in their completion: I want confirmation from my publisher that my recent revision is acceptable. I want my sons' concerts and exams to go as well as they should. I want to get to trial, want it more than anything, but I mustn't rush through these weeks, rush past life.

On the Richmond County/Staten Island paperwork about Fryar's drug case, I find some index numbers that I haven't tried yet, so I call, again, just to be thorough.

I can't tell the difference between any of the men at Staten Island's county clerk or court offices. They all sound alike to me, harried and with strong, twangy accents. I bounce from county clerk to criminal court to supreme court, seeming to talk to the same man over and over again. The one at the supreme court tells me where to write a letter to request photocopies, and I pepper him with questions about the file in front of him, while he keeps trying to get off the phone. He blurts out, in passing, that this case covers "years" and I pounce on that. "Well," he explains. "The guy warranted."

The word "warranted" confuses me, but his tone and the context explain it: Fryar jumped bail. He pleaded guilty in 1987, then never showed up to court for sentencing. I'm not sure if he lost his own money, or if he'd used a bail bondsman. If it was a bondsman, bounty hunters might have been dispatched.

That's probably why he went to Pittsburgh. That would explain why he changed his name.

It still doesn't explain why he was sentenced in 1996 but only started serving his time in 2002. Could he have escaped Richmond County courts twice?

He'd been in prison before, for the seventies rape, and must have been scared of going back in, scared enough that he gave up his name and family relationships to go on the run. During his Pittsburgh years, Fryar was, at best, lying low, unable to use his real name and so perhaps unable to get legitimate documents, to work jobs that require legitimate documents, or to collect veterans' benefits. At worst, he was being pursued by armed bounty hunters sent by his bail bondsman. He was, in any case, stressed, and separated from family support and any familiar places.

I'm glad he hates prison that much. I hope he's hating it right now.

The years bounce around in my head:

Because of when New York lowered the bar for the standard of submitting DNA to CODIS to include drug offenses, if he'd gone into prison in 1996, his DNA would likely not have been added. We might have never found him. I should be glad for whatever caused the delay before he served his time, for whatever reason.

But if he'd gotten his sentence over with without ever running

away, starting in 1987, he likely would never have come to Pittsburgh at all.

Goddamn Staten Island. Why couldn't they keep track of him?
Either hold on to him or let him free. Why did they have to drive
him on the run toward me?

As far as I can tell, no one in Cambridge thinks I'm lying, which I
find really interesting. Shouldn't they? My stories are getting out-
landish now, with armed bounty hunters added in. If you Google
my name, nothing comes up about the case, because of victim anonymity. Yet no one has questioned my version of events, at least not
to my face. I'm glad.

It's weird from the other direction, too. Over all of these years,
whenever I phoned the Pittsburgh police with changes of address,
no detective ever asked me to prove who I was. I called them, and
they, always total strangers to me and to my case, just updated my
contact information with whatever I said. When Honan told me
about Fryar's arrest last September, he e-mailed me at an address
I'd given him just weeks before. No one's ever asked me to prove
that I really am Emily Winslow, that student from 1992. No one's
asked to see a driver's license, a passport, anything, not even in
court.

They do know for sure now that I'm me, because I submitted
fresh DNA to be used to tease out the "me" from the "him" in the
evidence. But if that hadn't been needed, if they'd still had a good
1992 sample of just me (as opposed to the combined-with-Fryar
evidence), then really I could have been faking who I am entirely. I
could have fooled even Bill. He could have fooled me, too. Twenty-
two years is a long time. I wonder if Fryar would have noticed if
someone pretending to be me testified.

My mind wanders. Lying and trusting interest me. *It's time to start
another book,* I think, happy to have the urge to write fiction again.

—

We're waiting on the lab again.

They need to confirm that the evidence's DNA matches Fryar himself, from a swab taken at the hearing, not just his entry in CODIS. When that confirmation comes through, the defense has the option to delay the trial by requesting an expert to examine and dispute the results.

Evan and I have another Skype call scheduled so he can let me know what they decide. He's eager to push the defense to commit to or waive a delay. Fryar's choice; Fryar's power.

I continue to mentally practice what I should and shouldn't do in court, and prepare to be open and vulnerable in front of the jury. Over and over, I snap back to remembering, always, that I will also be in front of him. They're asking me to be soft and hurt in the same room with him, which can only flatter him, even after all these years. *You big, strong man. Look what you did to me.*

Evan has to delay our call because he'll be in court too late to make our scheduled time. I know that that's fine, good even; I'll want him to delay calls about future cases when he's in court for me.

But it hurts and shocks me anyway. It's like when the kids were really small and Gavin had to travel. I would pace myself for his return date, and be just fine, only a little more weary, a little more wired as the day approached. Then the day would come and, the few times that he had to reschedule a flight, it was like a sudden drop, an extra step under my feet when I had expected to find floor. I'd meted out my energy to last till exactly then, and had had nothing left to stretch.

That's how I am with milestones in the prosecution, with scheduled points of contact. I plan to last exactly until the next one. As the day approaches—such as the extradition hearings, the DNA results, the pretrial conference—my body reacts. I feel overcaffeinated and sensitive, waiting for news. But these things that mean so much to me are just items on the to-do list to those on the other end.

I have three siblings, but come from a pretty small extended family. My mother is an only child and my father has just one sibling, a sister. She's my only aunt and her much-missed, now-deceased husband was my only uncle. Their three children are my only cousins. I treasure them. To them, though, I'm just one of many cousins, because they have heaps on their father's side. They mean a lot to me; I mean much less to them.

That's how it is with Evan and the detectives, understandably. I must remember that. This is my once-in-a-lifetime trial. But, to them, it's just their normal work. They deal with far worse than what happened to me; they even deal with kids. I work myself up until I assume the worst, that they're secretly annoyed and impatient, and only kind to my face. I'm surprised that they don't throw their hands up and say, "It was just sex. You were an adult. Deal with it."

Evan has sent me the DNA results to tide me over until we can talk. I appreciate that he knows that I like to have the paperwork. The first page says CONFIDENTIAL at the top, has fancy logos in the letterhead, and mentions that the test cost the county four thousand dollars.

DNA testing doesn't compare entire genetic sequences; that would make an already lengthy process completely impractical. Instead, the lab compares just a few pieces of genetic code, fifteen to be exact, pieces that are known for being highly individual as opposed to generically human. Matching just those few provides a likelihood well beyond reasonable doubt. For example, the likelihood that the sperm sample they swabbed out of me would match a randomly selected black man are 1 in 2,600,000,000,000,000,000,000. (The listed odds are separated out by race and the chance of finding a white or Hispanic man to match are even farther out there.)

Evan's also given me the revised sentencing forms. Now that

Pennsylvania has the certified conviction for Fryar's 1976 rape in New York, his Prior Record Score has jumped from zero to three. Evan had hoped that it would hit four, and on the page I can see that the automatic calculation of "4" has been whited out and replaced with a handwritten "3." That's one of the things I need to ask him about. In any case, the improvement in sentences from a PRS of zero to three doesn't seem terribly much, at most eighteen months extra per charge, even for the top counts.

Looking at these forms, I can understand why I can barely make sense of Fryar's official past. The system wouldn't accept the true "date of offense" in all charges, as the crime was so long ago, so some of the boxes say that this happened last August (a date that Dan had chosen because it's when I'd started badgering him again, just before the arrest). Other charges, which have the correct offense date of January 1992 in a different database, mysteriously say on this form June 1997, which I suppose could be the early limit in this particular database, though the change of month from January to June is inexplicable. Both of these incorrect dates contribute to automatically generated and incorrect "age at offense" numbers for Fryar. Anyone looking at this twenty years from now would not get any kind of accurate picture at all. It would even look like he'd attacked me more than once, years apart.

Even more significantly to me, one of the "indecent assault" charges, which is supposed to be of the subtype "forcible compulsion," is coming up in some databases incorrectly as subtype "mental disease or defect," meant to be used when the victim is too mentally disabled to consent. I've been after Dan to correct it, assuming it to have been caused by a typo in the charge number. Turns out that it is the right number, just linking someplace to the wrong charge, perhaps to an older version of the laws. The wording is as it should be on Evan's paperwork, but I hate seeing it wrong elsewhere, especially publicly accessible elsewheres.

Other things confuse me, too, I think because the page automatically generates sentence information based on current standards,
but we're limited to using the standards as they were in 1992, when
the crime was committed. For the first four charges, for example, the handwritten "guideline range" maximum is well below the
generated "statutory limit" minimum.

I'm learning new acronyms. For every charge, the option for
"IP eligible" is checked off. Google tells me that IP stands for
"Intermediate Punishment," which allows for house arrest, elec-
tronic monitoring, or probation instead of prison. Another is
"RS," which is what's listed as a possible sentence for the misdemeanor charges. These are "Restorative Sanctions," also meaning
no prison time.

I'm horrified to discover these, and I'm relieved that the delay of
our call gives me the chance to review these documents thoroughly
before we talk. I send Evan an e-mail that says, in part, "No, no, no,
no, no."

Now in the headspace of poring over paperwork, I look carefully at
all of my collected documents.

Just after returning from the hearing in January, I'd finally received
minutes from two of the extradition hearings in New York, which
had been a struggle to get. I'd only glanced at them when they arrived. I'd wanted them desperately before the Pittsburgh hearing,
but they seemed insignificant when they arrived after. Fryar hadn't
appeared at either of these New York hearings, but rather had just
been represented by attorneys (different ones, both Legal Aid). One
report is only a single page. The other, just a few. I look at them now.

He did fight extradition, by not waiving it. He made Pennsylvania go through the rigmarole of getting a Governor's Warrant. I
wonder why he was happier on Rikers Island. Is he a connoisseur of
prisons, fearing Pennsylvania's more? Or was it the official charges

that would be attached to him once he got to Pennsylvania that he feared? Anecdotally, it's more difficult to be in prison as a rapist than as, say, a drug dealer or fugitive. He would know this firsthand.

I hadn't noticed before that the Staten Island warrant from the eighties was mentioned at the first extradition hearing in Manhattan. Interestingly, the warrant appears to have been still outstanding, though I don't know how this can be, considering that he finally served time in Otisville. At the end of the hearing, the judge specifically adjourned the Staten Island case back to them for the next day, with a token bail of one dollar.

I need to call Richmond County, again, and talk once more to that sounds-like-just-one guy.

There's a day to go before my Skype call with Evan.

In the short term, he replies to my e-mail to quickly clarify that the check box next to the "IP eligible" phrase is actually in a column that's headed "no" farther above. That X actually means Fryar's *not* up for punishment outside of prison. Relief. And annoyance—these forms are more difficult to read than even tax returns.

There's an hour to go before our call.

So I call Staten Island, this time the court reporter office. Instead of getting "that guy," I get a shrill, awful woman. Before she's even found the case, she wants to know who I am that I want her to look, and demands that I explain to her why I want to order court minutes if I'm not an attorney. I say simply that I'm a member of the public and I'd like to order the minutes of a public proceeding. She says, slyly, "Oh, are you one of those court watchers? You sit in courtrooms all day, huh?" Her voice is full of disgust, as if she thinks I get off on it. I say again that I'm a member of the public and I have the right to order minutes of a public proceeding. She insists that I explain myself. I tell her, carefully but firmly, that I don't have to. I don't, not any more than I would have to explain why I want to buy something in a shop or order lunch in a restaurant. It's not her business why.

She yells at me and hangs up. I'm shaking. I call the Richmond county clerk again, and get one of the interchangeable guys. I babble, upset, about the horrible woman at the court reporter office. The guy's voice is soothing and friendly over the tapping of his fingers on the keyboard. He finds a reference to what happened this recent September 13, when the extradition judge sent Fryar's old warrant case back to Staten Island. There, it was "dismissed in the interests of justice." It's also sealed.

I suspect that this dismissal was a kindness to our case, deferring to Pennsylvania's greater claim rather than competing with it. Because New York already had him in custody then, if they'd tried to keep him over Pennsylvania's request they probably would have succeeded. Thank you, Staten Island, for letting us have him.

I'd been wondering why Fryar had a sealed case in 1986. I'd assumed, from the law, that the sealed case had to have been something minor or unproven. Maybe, though, it is the drugs and warranting case that was referred to, and the sealing happened as recently as this past fall, because the case had been dismissed, for Pennsylvania's sake. For my sake, mine and Georgia's.

I'm still rattled by the vicious woman who answered the court reporter line. People must have all kinds of reasons to want information about a case. Family, right? Family of the defendant, or of the victim. Really, anyone who's been affected by things that are so awful that they get all the way to court might want to know more. Why should those people have to parade their reasons to her satisfaction? Why should I?

I can't be the only nonlawyer who orders minutes. That's simply not possible. I want to know everything. Doesn't everyone?

It's almost time for Evan to call.

11

Evan looks older on this call, and more tired. Maybe it's only be-cause I turned the brightness of the screen to max, but this time he has a bit of five o'clock shadow. That's appropriate, I suppose, as for him it will be five o'clock in about an hour. For me, it's after nine.

He clarifies the sentencing forms for me.

The Prior Record Score is a handwritten three instead of an automatic four because that's what it would have been in 1992. He points out that the results of a PRS of three when applied to the 1992 guidelines are very similar to the way a current PRS of four interacts with the current guidelines, so that makes sense.

The sentencing Guideline Ranges, which come in "mitigated," "standard," and "aggravated" versions, have no concrete rules about which column certain kinds of cases must be put into. It will be the defense's job at sentencing to argue for mitigated, our job to try for aggravated, and the judge's job to choose.

I assume that the Guideline Ranges are what's recommended, and that the Statutory Limits are the absolute extremes to which sentences can be pushed outside of those recommended ranges. I'm not quite right. Instead of the Statutory Limits being the absolute lowest and highest that sentences can go, meaning the lowest that the minimum can be and the highest that the maximum can be, they're actually both highests: the highest that the maximum sentence can be, yes, and also the highest that the minimum can be. They're there to protect from draconian sentences.

Evan tells me that, in the case of a negotiated plea, he'll likely start with an offer of thirty to sixty years, for all charges in both of our cases combined, and go no lower than accepting twenty to forty.

He asks me not to worry about the minimum being too low. He says that Fryar is unlikely to be given parole, and that he, Evan, will speak against Fryar at any future parole hearings. Evan's youth suddenly becomes valuable. He'll still be working then, after I'm old.

If it comes to a jury conviction, Evan will present to the judge how the low ends of the mitigated, standard, and aggravated sentence ranges add up if served consecutively, and argue for standard and consecutive at least, really for aggravated and consecutive. For my half of the case alone, the minimums in the standard range add up to almost nineteen years, and the minimums in the aggravated range add up to over thirty-one. Georgia's charges, which are slightly fewer, would probably come in at about three quarters of that, so together the standard would start at something over thirty years, and, within guidelines, could hit an aggravated maximum around seventy. Eschewing the guidelines, which the judge has the right to do, and obeying only the absolute Statutory Limits, the sentence could break a hundred years.

Serial stranger-rape cases in Pittsburgh, of which there are more than I expected, routinely do get sentences that high—dramatic, reassuringly punitive sentences—but not from this judge.

———

The larger point of the call, the potential delay of the trial, is itself put off. Monday is when the defense will at last meet with Fryar to discuss the confirmatory DNA results. Evan has insisted to Fryar's assigned attorney that they must decide then whether Fryar will plead guilty, or, if going to trial, whether they'll delay for an expert. If the defense chooses trial without first delaying to find a DNA expert, that could leave any eventual conviction open for appeal under the Post Conviction Relief Act. If Fryar wants to go to trial as scheduled, without an expert, Evan will insist on a signed waiver of Fryar's right to one.

We'll Skype again Monday night, three days away, to discuss whatever the news may be.

If it's a plea, Evan will give me a to-do list to start prepping my impact statement for sentencing, which he promises we'll work on together, back and forth.

If it's a trial coming up, he'll give me a to-do list for readying my testimony. We'll schedule more Skype calls, with Dan sitting in. Evan has to have someone with him when he and I discuss my testimony, in case I mention anything that's not already written in a police report. If Evan's alone when he hears any new information from me, that can force him to become a witness in his own case and therefore prevent him from continuing as the prosecutor. If there's a second person there, then he or she can be the witness to the new information, and it might as well be a police officer, because any new information will require an official supplemental police report.

I ask if I can see the courtroom before whatever official thing, whether plea or trial, starts. My plane will land late-ish the day before, so he says that we can meet at seven the next morning, when the building opens, and get a sheriff (again with the sheriffs!) to open the room for us. Then he promises me a conference room to wait in, between the early look-see and the official start of court, presumably a couple of hours later. It'll be an upgrade from waiting in the busy, bare municipal court hallway for the hearing.

He tries to prepare me, gently, for a plea, and assures me that it would be a good thing, a guaranteed thing. That's what he thinks is going to happen on Monday. He lists the pros of such an outcome, tripping over the benefit of the victim being spared giving their testimony. "I know that skipping that isn't what you want," he corrects himself, "but most victims do."

I accept "most," but surely that leaves, oh, I don't know, maybe 30 percent who do want to testify, right? The way that I feel can't be completely oddball, surely.

He agrees that there are those few who are eager to testify, but says that they usually fall more toward the extreme, prioritizing their day in court and the official expression of their anger over their effect on the jury or sentencing outcome. I want that, too; testifying is important to me. But apparently, in his experience, my interest in the process details and my cool focus on nailing Fryar to the wall is indeed unusual.

Georgia doesn't want to testify again. The hearing was hard enough for her. If I get what I want, that will hurt her, and vice versa.

Oh, and Fryar's apparently "found Jesus" in jail.

Evan cracks a joke about that. I laugh, and just think, *Bullshit*. Fryar's had twenty-two years to feel guilty, and it hasn't motivated him before now.

Mother's Day (the American one, two months after Britain's "Mothering Sunday") comes in handy. Fryar's sister posts an old photo on Facebook, and relatives comment. Now I know their mother's name, and from that find her maiden name and where she grew up. Newburgh, New York, where Fryar's first convicted rape took place, was her hometown.

I feel better now, knowing both of his parents' names, especially his mother's. This makes him less mysterious to me, less symbolic. He's just one limited man, with one limited life, not a force. He keeps getting smaller to me, piece by piece.

According to my religion, I'm supposed to pray for my enemies.

As with forgiveness, I'm not sure what this actually means. Pray for what, exactly? Not pray for them to get what they want, which is to hurt me. That doesn't make sense, even in the turning-everything-on-its-head way that Jesus tended to talk. After all, one of the biggest commandments is to "love your neighbor as yourself," which assumes self-care as the foundational, appropriate, and natural way of things. If I treat myself poorly, then treating others the same way wouldn't really help anyone. The commandment only works if I'm kind to me.

I think that praying for my enemies means something along the lines of praying for their general well-being, in ways apart from whatever they're trying to take from me. Maybe in this case it means to pray that Fryar makes a place for himself in prison that is safe and perhaps in some ways satisfying; that he is able to keep connected to his family and to have friends.

But that feels condescending and almost comical. I'm working to put him in prison, a place he desperately fears, for so long that he'll die there, yet I'm to pray that he'll have some peace, distraction, and satisfaction while inside? It's a pathetic scrap to drop onto the floor for him. Let's not pretend that it's generous.

It reminds me of the laughable "gentlemanliness" that he showed me afterward, telling me in a soft voice as he zipped up: "You'll feel better if you lie here." I think, from my memory, that he gestured toward my futon bed in the corner while he said it. We'd never gotten as far as the mattress. Everything had happened on the floor between the door and the back of the couch.

"You'll feel better if you lie here" is from Bill's notes. I remembered the sentiment without the cue of the notes, but not the exact
words, just the command, in that sweet voice, that meant "rest." It
was a bizarro-world generosity, a gallant "oh, it sometimes hurts
your first time, sweetheart, give yourself a break" kind of thing. I
read into it something else, too: *Don't stand up.* He needed to get
away. I needed to show him that I wouldn't do anything to prevent
that. I had to present as obedient, so that he wouldn't have to do
anything to make me unable to get up once he was gone.

Bill's notes tell me that I said, "Good night, Bob." I was nice. I had
one goal: *Don't get killed.*

I don't want to pray for him, but, if I do, being motivated by this
verse makes it a backhanded kindness: it defines him as my enemy.
It feels satisfying to call him that. I can't think of any other person
in the world who is personally "my enemy."

I'm probably supposed to pray that he realizes the extent of his
guilt and accepts the forgiveness of Jesus's sacrifice, which is supposedly what he's already done, and about which I'm utterly cynical.

One of the things that John has been plain about from the start is that
the goal is not some touching scene of my forgiving Fryar in person
and our having a new relationship as siblings in Christ, which is the
hero-ending that lots of religious stories work toward. John knows—
it's probably pretty obvious to anyone near me—that I'm idealistic and
ambitious, and so susceptible to aiming for such things, or at least to
feeling guilty if I don't. One of the early things he'd said to me was that
Fryar forced himself on me once, and that any religiously motivated
scenario that shoves him up against me again is not okay.

Just as Fryar must ask God for forgiveness if he wants it, and stay
away from me, if I want to forgive Fryar (should I ever figure out
what that means), that's between me and God. It's not necessary or
desirable for the two of us, me and the bad man, to interact again,
ever.

John agrees to pray for Fryar for me when I ask him to, but it's plain that the request takes him by surprise. He cares about me, not Fryar.

I do wonder if, as a priest, he's supposed to care about everybody, which would include Fryar. But I suppose that, as a priest (and just as a person), he's supposed to be disgusted by what Fryar has done, so I guess it all evens out. Besides, Fryar has his own chaplain, in jail. Perhaps Christians aren't each meant to do all of the faith individually, but can share the duties. Just as the ideals of the legal system would fail if the prosecutor and defense attorney were the same person, perhaps religion also requires people to take on discrete roles. Fryar needs someone to care about him, but it would be a betrayal for Evan or John to do it. There are sides here.

That I get to see John today, before Evan calls with Fryar's decision, feels almost decadent. Normally I get only about two chances to talk about the prosecution in a week, on top of short, in-passing references. It's a luxury to have two chances to talk about it in a day.

I wait for Evan to call to tell me of Fryar's decision to plead, delay, or move forward. In this prosecution year so far, Fryar has had very little choice. This is his opportunity to act, which must be a thrill, or a relief, or overwhelming to him.

John's asked me to let him know what happens tonight. We can meet again this week if I need to, if the news rattles me.

I make a little list of who else I'll tell once I know what's going to happen. I now treat news about the trial like party invitations, carefully considering who are in the same social circles or at the same friendship level, and so should be included in the same way; they should hear about it at roughly the same time.

Then, an e-mail instead of a phone call. The festive feeling of "something is going to happen" evaporates. Fryar's lawyer isn't answering Evan's calls. If she doesn't answer by 5 P.M. his time, twenty minutes away, that's it until tomorrow. Evan has only her office number, not her cell phone's.

She should be the one doing the calling, I speculate. Has she not been able to meet with Fryar yet? Has she met with him, but he hasn't been able to decide? Has he decided something, but she doesn't like it and is trying to persuade him otherwise?

I wish that my e-mail would make a sound when a new message arrives. Instead, I have to stare at the mail window, to immediately catch whatever Evan might say in what is now the last eight minutes before the workday finishes in Pittsburgh. I choose a song that's eight minutes long—the choir singing Bairstow's "Blessed City, Heavenly Salem"—explicitly for its length, to remind myself of exactly when the time runs out on learning anything tonight.

The music finishes; five o'clock in Pennsylvania; no message. Evan must be on the phone with her now. I play the song again, to give him time to have the conversation I hope he's having, then I'll look at my e-mail again.

Nothing.

I play the song again. Gavin is downstairs, watching a TV show that he knows bores me, saving the shows we both like for when we can watch them together.

I check my e-mail again. I stay up here. I play the song another time. Repeat, repeat, repeat.

Morning. No e-mail from Evan has come in overnight. Even though it's not yet dawn in Pennsylvania, I continue to click hopefully on my in-box throughout the next hours, on my iPad while the kids are rock-climbing and swimming. We homeschool, which is why I'm with my kids on a day of the week that I can reasonably expect Fryar's defense attorney to be answering Evan's continued calls to her office phone. When we get home, the boys have math and programming to do, and there's new paperwork to distract me.

Thanks to the Freedom of Information Act, the bare bones of Fryar's military record have arrived, revealing him to have been in the air force starting in August 1972. My research tells me that the air force didn't take draftees, so he must have volunteered, possibly to avoid being drafted into a situation more likely to see combat, which was a common tactic. If that was his goal, he made a good choice. He never left the United States. I've been reserving some sympathy in case he'd had some traumatizing Vietnam experience, but no: he was an airman basic at Lackland in Texas and at Chanute in Illinois. He received the National Defense Service Medal for being on active duty during wartime, and was discharged in May 1974 without ever leaving the country.

Staten Island has sent me the "Appearance History" for Fryar's drug case with them. It's a several-page printout listing every time the case was put before the Richmond County Supreme Court.

One date stands out to me, at the top of the first page. It says that he was arrested (presumably the arrest for dealing) on August 27, 1986, then "INC" on December 22 that same year. "Incarcerated"? Maybe. That December date sticks out because it was also my sixteenth birthday. I'd had a bigger party than usual, "sweet sixteen," with three dozen friends over my house for soda and cake. That night was the first time I ever French-kissed. Fryar was thirty-four then, and his apartment was only a half-hour drive away from me.

The documents are full of abbreviations and acronyms that I don't understand. Only gradually, with the help of Gavin and Google, do the New York legal system hieroglyphs become words to me. I still don't understand all of it, but this is what I do get:

Fryar's Staten Island address is an apartment building that I learn is in an area that was nicknamed "Crack Hill."

The charges for that one 1986 incident include dealing, multiple counts of possession, and "criminal possession of a weapon in the third degree."

Fryar finally paid bail in June 1987, and was released until sentencing. July 23, his sentencing, is marked "BFWO," which means "Bail Forfeited, Warrant Ordered." He didn't show up. That's when he got away.

The dates then jump nine years, to 1996. Between April and October of that year, Fryar's sentencing was attempted seven times. It kept being adjourned and rescheduled, until it finally succeeded on Halloween, assigning him three to six years.

He was, understandably, held without bail during this sentencing process (the abbreviation "RE" indicates "remand"), so it's a mystery why I can't find a prison record for this crime until six years later. But there's something even more interesting to me here, given that I'm waiting for news from Fryar's public defender, who seems to be avoiding Evan.

It's a Latin phrase in the header which I had to Google: *pro se.* Just below that, there's an "attorney summary," which I had assumed at first to be a style of summary meant for attorneys to read. Gavin figured out that it's actually a summary of the attorneys defending Fryar. I can be forgiven for my confusion; Fryar himself is listed twice. Apparently, in 1996 and again in 2005, he represented himself. That's what *pro se* means.

Another Pittsburgh rapist did that last year, represented himself in court, and cross-examined his own victims. If Fryar's proposing to do that, maybe that's why his defense is stalling.

I hate possibilities. I hate not knowing. This is when I have to repeat it: *choose life, choose life.* Accept being in the middle of things. Not knowing means that there's more to happen, good things, too, things so good that I can't even think of them. This is what I struggled for on the floor of my Shadyside apartment: being alive.

Evan, on his way to a training out of state, e-mails me from the plane; he doesn't want for me to have to wait to hear: Fryar's attorney is filing for a postponement.

It's almost midnight here. I was about to go to bed, but suddenly can't sleep. My flights and hotel will have to be canceled. My passport, which is nearing expiry and which I've been holding off renewing until just after the June trial, will need to be dealt with to accommodate the new date. My expectations will need recalibrating. Friends will need to be told.

Evan sends a second e-mail only minutes after the first. He doesn't yet know much, but the delay is not, as we had supposed it would be, for bringing in a DNA expert. It's for a psychiatric evaluation. I reply with bafflement and questions.

The last thing that Evan writes to me before I go to sleep is that the evaluation likely isn't for an insanity defense; Fryar's probably just investing in a future argument for mitigation at sentencing. I think, given Fryar's avoidance of extradition back in the fall, that realistically it's just a delay tactic.

I e-mail Evan back that he should prod Fryar's defense to get a DNA expert now as well, because I don't want to have to put up with new delays later. Fryar waiting for the DNA test results—same as the results we'd already had—as a prompt for requesting this evaluation was game-playing anyway. He could have started the ball rolling weeks ago, no delay required. *Bullshit, bullshit, bullshit.*

I wake up angry.

Ever since the calendar ticked over to May, I've felt the imminence of the trial, its nearness. It's not just my emotions that had tensed up and not just my mind that got distracted; it was my body, too, taut and buzzing with readiness. I want trial, and I want to get on the other side of it, not for it to dangle forever in the distance in front of me, like a rainbow.

Changing this date is bigger than canceling a few reservations. There's a lot that we've built around this, kid things and work things. More than that, I've divided my life into *before* and *after*. Now *before* is stretching out further, perhaps much further, and the *after,* with all its plans for becoming normal again, is suddenly a long way off. I don't think I can sustain this level of intense preparedness, but neither can I just drop it, knowing that the trial is, in fact, going to come, even if only eventually.

Maybe Fryar just likes the power, just likes messing with the system. They've given him these rights and he's going to use them, just because he can. It's probably useless to read any strategy into this, practical or psychological. He has to know that the outcome is always going to be the same, eventually. Maybe he's not thinking long term at all. Maybe he's just thinking, *I can affect this,* and that feels good.

There's an addendum of "motions" in the Staten Island appearance history that began as early as November 1995. Five times, there's a motion for "reassignment of counsel" that's adjourned; the sixth one is granted. This might have been Fryar demanding the right to represent himself when the drug case caught up to him, or might have been him nitpicking the quality of his public defender. Three times he tried to withdraw his 1987 guilty plea (the motion was ultimately denied), and after it was all over he tried and failed to vacate the judgment and then the sentence.

This present request for postponement shouldn't surprise me. There will be more.

12

Just as we're about to pull out of our driveway, to take the boys to drama and yoga, our mail is delivered. I notice a large envelope in our postperson's grip and wave to her. She pulls back from the slot in our door and instead hands our mail to me through the car window. The return address on the big envelope from New York is stamped "Orange County." I've been waiting for this.

This is Fryar's first conviction, for the rape in 1976. He was twenty-four, two years out of the military, unemployed, and living in Newburgh, his mother's hometown, across the river from his hometown of Beacon. The stack of pages is half an inch thick.

Compared to Richmond County's terse summary of their case with him, the full records of which have been destroyed, the variety and detail Orange County has photocopied for me is astonishing, not least because their case is much older. Besides the many legal pages that I've only glanced over and so can't yet classify, there are the victim's medical records from that night, signed by her mother because she was only seventeen (not a preteen, as the current definition of "second-degree rape," the charge he ended up pleading to, had implied). They include a disconcerting "rape examination form" with check boxes for the state of her hymen (options for "intact," "not intact," or "traumatized") and vaginal orifice ("virginal" or "marital").

Most shocking, there's Fryar's detailed confession, apparently given to police voluntarily right after it happened, over an hour before the girl and her mother reported it at the hospital. Part of his confession includes that they had been smoking pot together, which perhaps partly contributed to his extraordinary decision to turn himself in.

He's not panicked-seeming in the typed words, nor sorry-seeming. After being officially advised of all his rights, he waives them.

His description is stilted, like mine on the stand at the hearing. Perhaps, like me, he was advised to be listlike and unambiguous in his official statement, which presumably followed a more spontaneous, and possibly more emotional, confession. Perhaps on top of that the person typing his statement exacerbated the formal tone in how he or she took it down. Fryar dictated to the officer (all spellings and style *sic*):

> Between the hours of 9:45PM and 10:30PM on 9-8-76 I picked up a young Lady on the corner of Renwick Street and William Street. We rode around looking for a friend, we rode around for a couple of hours getting high, we were just talking about a whole lot of different things. We rode around Newburgh and then we went down to Front Street. We were there about a half hour whene I made advances, trying to kiss her and feeling her all over her body. Then a struggle broke

out with me trying to force my will upon her and her trying
to ward me off. She got the door of my car open and we
struggled outside. From fear she struggled harder and I hit her
a couple of times and knocked her down. Before we struggled
out of the car I took her pantie hose and panties off. I think
I tore the pantie hose. After I knocked her down I pulled my
pants down around my thighs and then I layed on top of her.
Then I proceeded to have intercourse with her.

He's weirdly objective and fair, describing her resistance in a way
that accepts it as reasonable and to be expected. The act is unabash-
edly made clear to be forced. There's no pretense that the encounter
was consensual, deserved, or unimportant. Neither do I see any
pride or bragging; nor the opposite, guilt or shame.

Q. Arthur, when you first started to kiss this girl and feel her
   did she resist in anyway?
A. She just said Don't do that and Stop.
Q. Did the girl resist when you started to remove her pantie
   hose and panties?
A. Yes.
Q. How did she resist?
A. She started pushing me away and saying Stop and Don't.
Q. When you say that you hit her outside of the car, in what
   way did you hit her?
A. Closed hand, fist.
Q. Did you hit her hard enough to knock her unconsious?
A. Yes, but she didn't go unconsious.
Q. Did you stun her when you hit her?
A. Yes.
Q. After you hit this girl and she fell to the ground, did she
   [illegible—probably "resist"] you in any other way?

A. No.

Q. Could she resist?

A. I think if she wanted to she could have but I think she
   probably felt the safest thing to do was be cool.

What he describes feels eerily familiar to me. I wasn't in a car
with him, and he smothered me instead of punching me, but her
story feels just the same, in its essence. I, too, felt that the "safest
thing" was to "be cool." He communicated that very clearly.

Q. Do you know this girl's name or have you ever met her
   before?

A. Her name is [redacted]. I've never met her before to talk
   to but I have seen her a couple of times.

Q. Why did you pick [her] up at William Street and Ren-
   wick Street?

A. Because she was there.

So she was Mount Everest, and so was I.

He doesn't describe her at all. He doesn't seem angry at or disgusted with her, nor does he speak of her as any sort of prize. It's the
raping itself that drives him, not the particular women.

I no longer need an allocution or explanation. It's simple: he's a
machine that does this, and I was there. That's all.

At a sentencing proceeding nine months after this confession, Fryar's attorney argued for leniency. Fryar didn't get any, beyond what
the court had already allowed, which was letting him plead to a
lesser version of the charge, second degree (which back then must
have had nothing to do with the victim being a child).

The attorney argued, among other things, that Fryar's unblem-
ished record, and his behavior immediately after the crime, war-

ranted a lesser sentence (where the defense attorney's words are cut off on my photocopy, I've made my best guesses):

> The Defendant advised me that after the [inci-]
> dent occurred he sat with her, talking for a [period]
> of time and most significantly was at the Pol[ice]
> Station before she was. He did not try to ru[n away]
> to avoid any sort of responsibility. As a ma[tter]
> of fact, when he was at the Police Station th[e]
> police officers practically asked him to leav[e]
> until they had a complaint. He went there a[nd]
> gave a written statement.

I have no idea why Fryar did that. There must have been some sense of guilt, or at least some understanding that what he did is supposed to be punished. I've referred to this crime before as his first *convicted* rape, not his first rape, because who knows when he started? But, reading all of this, I'm inclined to believe that this one could well have been his first, surprising even him.

Fryar switched from confession to resistance sometime before sentencing. In hope of leniency, his defense attorney noted about the Probation Report:

> I know they refer to him being [non-]
> chalant about his prospect of incarceration b[ut]
> certainly not in this case. This defendant d[oes]
> not want to go to Jail.

He's been trying to get away with his crimes ever since.

The most surprising thing that I find in this envelope is the solution to the Richmond County mystery: How is it that he was in court in Staten Island in the middle of his Pittsburgh years, and only served the Staten Island sentence much later?

The answer is that he was in prison in Pennsylvania.

In November 1995, at the same time that he started tangling again with Richmond County over that drug sentence that he'd run away from years before, he sent a request to Orange County from inside Somerset prison, a newly built, medium-security, all-male, Pennsylvania facility, where he was serving three and a half to seven years. If he served the whole thing, that would explain why he didn't start his New York drug sentence until 2002. Petitioning from prison also explains why he was representing himself at that point. It wasn't because of an urge to stand up in court.

His typed requests from Somerset superficially look as good as the rest of the legal paperwork in this little stack of his history, even though, according to the declaration at the top of his 1976 confession, he'd had only eleven years of education (which explains his absence as a grade-twelve senior in the Beacon High School yearbook).

I don't understand why he was involving Orange County, where he'd already served his time for the '76 rape long ago. His request was that Orange County send him copies of all of his records, for free, because he couldn't afford to pay for them and required them for a Post-Conviction Hearing Act petition. He appears to have been appealing the old rape conviction, possibly in an effort to apply those years already served to his upcoming drug sentence? That's the only reason I can think of to make it worth his while, though I'm not sure that that's even possible.

My interest in the minutiae of his life is waning. I've now fit all of the big pieces together: his youth in Beacon up to age twenty; the air force for two years; rape in Newburgh and seven years in Sing Sing; drug dealing in Staten Island leading to the life of a fugitive in Pittsburgh; up to seven years' prison in Somerset, Pennsylvania; three years' prison in Otisville, New York; Long Island City; Brooklyn; now.

With all of those stepping-stones now solid enough and close enough together for me to cross the whole distance, I feel like I've at last arrived at the present. Onward.

Dan tells me—but only when I specifically ask, using the information that I'd found for myself—that Fryar's Somerset prison sentence was for a 1994 burglary, and confirms that Fryar indeed did serve the maximum sentence, from July 1995. That must have been some creepy burglary to get seven years.

I've always assumed that "burglary" has to do with theft, but it doesn't; it's entering a private or secured place with the intent to commit a crime, with higher charges for the place being a home and/or for someone being present. For example, one of Fryar's charges for me is burglary. I suppose that this 1994 burglary could have been the prelude to a rape, but the woman turned it around. I can't even picture that. I don't know what it would look like, not in a situation like mine. Aprill confirms to me that this is the case she had mentioned where the woman bit him, which I hadn't dared to do. I was already trapped and it would only have made him angry. Maybe she wasn't in as small a space with him as I was, or was closer to an escape route or other people. Maybe she was just stronger and faster than me; good for her.

It must have been this Pennsylvania incarceration that triggered Staten Island's finding him in the midnineties. It also explains why it wasn't until June 2002, when he got out of Pennsylvania's Somerset prison, that he began his Staten Island drug sentence in New York's Otisville.

Dan and Aprill knew this all along, the Pennsylvania part, but I didn't. Pennsylvania doesn't have searchable online databases for incarceration and criminal histories like New York does, not that I was able to find, not open to the anonymous public. But there had been an even bigger wall between me and what I'd wanted to know.

The detectives had only ever offered me generalities, and I'd had to be careful about seeming too persistent. People worry when I show too much of an interest. I didn't want them to think of me as neurotic or unbalanced. When I asked anything, I had to inquire carefully, with subterfuge or a flurry of explanations. It reminds me of when my brother counts cards in Vegas. Whenever he's going to do something that goes against the superficially expected, he justifies it with a joke about "lucky numbers" or something, so that the dealer won't be left with the only other explanation: counting, which is against house rules. Then, after he's won a little, he leaves the table, even switches casinos, to win a little more.

That's what it feels like I have to do: never ask too much of any one person, act blasé, distract. I'm not supposed to want to know these things.

Now I know enough:

Beacon, New York, 1952–1972
Air force, Lackland and Chanute, 1972–1974
Newburgh, New York, 1974–1977 (September 1976—his
    first rape?)
Incarcerated (Sing Sing) 1977–1984
Staten Island, New York, 1984–1987
Pittsburgh, Pennsylvania, 1987–1995
Incarcerated (Somerset) 1995–2002
Incarcerated (Otisville) 2002–2005
Long Island City and Brooklyn, New York, 2005–2013

I feel like I did the day after W. was born. All my life I'd wanted kids. When we got engaged, I warned Gavin that, two years from then when I turned thirty, it would be "baby time." After we had S., I didn't want him to be an "only"; I needed another. Then, four years later, while I was lounging in the hospital bed with one-day-old W., the urge evaporated. I was satisfied. For literally the first time in my life, I didn't want future children. I had literally never before been without the desire for as-yet-unknown-babies; but, suddenly, I had what I wanted and was done.

Little, interesting details about Fryar's life may continue to pop up. I'll notice them, sure, and continue to think about the ones that I already have, but the urge to quest for more and more seems to be now satisfied.

Now with my head out of the past, I continue to obsess about the present and immediate future. I haven't yet canceled anything. Evan had told me only that the defense intends to request postponement. I'm still waiting to hear if that request has been officially granted, and what the new date will be.

No word from Evan at all yesterday or yet today. I assume that he's working to get more information and that he'll tell me as soon as he has any. I trust him.

E-mailing me from the plane had been a simple gesture that has earned him a great deal of leeway from me. I also appreciate that he e-mailed when he had only partial information. Too many people use waiting for complete knowledge as an excuse for putting off contact; I'd always rather be told part of something than nothing at all.

I wonder if he knows that I'm hopeful of an e-mail from him literally every minute. Fryar and his defense attorney have a plan, or at least hopes and contingencies. I want to know what they are.

S. is now as tall as me. Up until this week, I've been able to beat him at arm wrestling at least half the time, and always put up a good fight; now he conquers me easily, both of us laughing in astonishment, and he asks to try again every day. He's proud to have become stronger than me. It's amazing how naturally it happened, without his even trying. With very little effort, just by growing, boys become powerful.

———

I meet John at a pâtisserie for breakfast, and we have toast with jam and expensive coffees. I tell him about the Orange County papers, tempering my words whenever the waitress passes by too close. He reads the 1976 confession right there in front of me, and I get to reread it in the expressions on his face. It's a relief to share it.

Afterward, I write a letter to the policeman who took Fryar's statement in 1976, to ask if he remembers Fryar's state of mind. He's the same age as Fryar; both were just twenty-four then. Ten years after Fryar's confession, this officer was a captain and Newburgh's chief of detectives. That night in 1976, he was a sergeant working the desk. I assume that Fryar's eagerness would have been memorable.

I'm still waiting for Evan. I force myself to act patient, not by refraining from e-mailing him, but by e-mailing him politely and, at least on the surface, undemandingly. Demand, of course, is inherent in making repeated contact. Two e-mails in three days, today's asking to schedule a Skype call, may be too much, but it's the best that I can do.

I find it funny that I ever worried that I had played it too cool with Evan, and that he might not realize how invested I am. That's not a problem now.

Going by the original date, trial is supposed to begin in eighteen days; I'm meant to leave home for it (and the choir trip first) in eleven days. There's no word yet about the proposed delay.

There's nothing that Fryar could want that couldn't have been asked for weeks ago, without requiring any delay at all. They're letting him play with me.

Days pass busily. Sometimes being a parent means rushing out to get new shoes for suddenly bigger feet. Other times it means that, having gotten those new shoes, and having thrown together a cheap tuxedo out of school-uniform basics, and having packed up his score and timpani sticks, I get to spend a sunny afternoon in the ruins of a Benedictine priory while S. rehearses Beethoven's Mass in C inside. He's the only minor in the orchestra, and so requires a parent nearby. W., hours away at home, finishes painting a model of a fighter jet with Gavin, who'll be leaving tomorrow morning on one of his monthly workweeks away.

It's Sunday. I can't expect to hear from Evan; he seems to stick to office hours. I'm trusting him less. I feel anxious. He's given me no hint of what's happening since Tuesday, not even if the postponement request has gone before the judge, or if he, Evan, is going to ask for any limits on the request at all. I've tried my best not to prod him again, but I must.

Because the priory is out of data range, my message doesn't go out until after midnight, on the orchestra bus home. Evan's reply is then waiting for me when I wake up. I'm alone in bed because Gavin had to disappear at dawn.

Postponement is set to be approved by a judge today, Monday. Refusal would give grounds for appeal of a future conviction, so there's no hope of the trial going ahead as scheduled. I scramble to organize a list of dates for Evan to work around to schedule the new trial. I list all of the details that I have to jump on, like rescheduling flights and canceling the hotel. Evan gives me his cell-phone number. I hoard it, saving it for a more desperate occasion. Just his extending it makes me feel a little bit protected again, a little bit looked after.

He explains in his e-mail that the three main reasons for a psych eval are insanity defense, which wouldn't make sense in our case because an evaluation now wouldn't prove insanity twenty-two years ago; competence to stand trial, which I hope we'll fight if Fryar tries to use it; and mitigation at sentencing, which, if it's true, will piss me the hell off. Sentencing for a June 3 trial would be more than three months away, ninety days after conviction, so postponement to prepare for that would be complete bullshit.

I hate Abigail the defense attorney now. I respect the adversarial system, and the way that defense attorneys, even for obviously guilty defendants, check the power of the prosecution and force them to earn their convictions. But I don't respect her lazy decision to do nothing for Fryar until the DNA report came in, a report that matches the previous reports and so imparts no new information. It's not as though anyone expected it to say anything different. If she ever thought that Fryar needed a psychiatric evaluation, she could have asked for one months ago when she was assigned the case. She waited till now either because she's lazy, or because she's letting Fryar manipulate her and use her to gum up the system and to hurt me. I would cross the street to get away from her. I would walk out of a room that had her in it.

I wish that there were some women on my side. I like all of the men who have been put around me, but it's sad that all of the powerful women involved are either for the other victim, like Aprill, or neutral, like the judge, or defending Fryar. Back in 1992, my doctor at the hospital was a woman. My college department head, who gave me time off without academic consequences, was a woman. I liked that. I don't need to be protected from men and I'm glad that that's not happening; I wouldn't want to replace Evan or Bill or Dan. I just wish that there were one or two women also on my side for the prosecution, just so that I wouldn't have to be wary of all of the women involved: wary of Abigail, who works for the enemy; wary of the judge, who doesn't punish near harshly enough; wary of Aprill, whose time I shouldn't be taking up.

The postponement is distressing because of more than just the wait. The worse thing will be the thinning out of my support. I can't expect people to keep caring for too long. After a while, instead of being news, the prosecution will become an eye-rolling annoyance to the people around me. I have to be careful of how much I let myself depend on anyone, or even mention it.

I'm overwhelmed.

Various friends have kindly offered to take my boys whenever I may need help, but the trouble is that when I'm in the middle of needing help, I find it difficult to ask. I can ask for help in advance, which is a lot of what I'd done to prepare for the now-delayed trial (and which I now have to unschedule), but it's harder to reach out from inside all of the feelings when they take me by surprise. Besides, if I tell the boys that they're suddenly being looked after today, they'll wonder why. I'm trying to protect them from knowing about my upset. Instead I tell them that I'm exhausted from the concert weekend, which is probably also true, and we hang out quietly together. The only time I cry is in the front seat of the taxi bringing us home from a music lesson and the park. Just tears, no shoulder hunching, no throat noises. The boys are in the back. They don't know. I don't think they know.

I miscarried between them, ten years ago. That day, Gavin had been out of the country, and S.'s part-time nanny was off taking a class. She sent her brother and boyfriend to swoop in while I went to the hospital. By the time I got home a few hours later, she was there, too. The three of them distracted toddler S. for literally days while Gavin journeyed home and I bled upstairs on hopeful, tearful bedrest.

For more than a year afterward, S. would frequently and spontaneously say, "Hey, Mom, remember that time when Delya and Olin and Chris all came over to play with me together? That was the best day of my life!" I would wince, but also feel proud. I'd wanted to protect him. Mission accomplished.

I have to constantly go back into whatever I've just written, e-mails and my diary, to correct some of my pronouns to "Fryar." I don't like to write his name, so habitually deflect it with "he" and "him" and "his." Then those words get tangled up with Evan and other men, so I have to go back in, adding "Fryar" all over the place, just to make things make sense.

First drafts reveal things. I remember sending an e-mail three years ago, when I was taking my turn tending my brother through cancer treatments. I was writing to our parents and siblings to keep everyone updated on his slow progress and wrote about his doctors, his feeding tube, his pain management. Before I hit send, I glanced the message over, and realized that I had literally skipped every instance of the word "pain." I just didn't write it at all, the absence of which left sentences jumbled and dangling. I had to go back to force the word in, in each place that I'd so hopefully pretended that it didn't exist.

Evan would make a really good customer-service person if he ever finds being a lawyer too stressful. He's good at defusing complaints. Everything I say that I'm upset about, he agrees that I should feel that way and that he would, too, if he were me. It's calming to hear. He also tells me that I'm no bother. He's either genuinely kind, or at least kind enough to lie.

This is Skype call number three. Our first one had lasted an hour and fifteen minutes; the second forty-five minutes; this one just thirty-five. We're getting to know each other. We don't need to establish backstory anymore; we can focus on the present action, which in the case of the legal profession is achingly slow.

As expected, the judge has officially granted the postponement. Evan further clarifies that denying the request for psychiatric evaluation would have been a "reversible error," meaning that everything that would have come after such a denial, even a whole trial, could have then been made as if it had never happened if the defense were to appeal that original denial. The judge had had to say yes. "Psychiatric evaluation" are magic words for postponement.

I've given Evan windows of dates for the rest of the year, only dates that Bill is available, too. I'm not going into court without him.

If I were geographically closer, Evan says, they wouldn't have canceled June 3 yet, not until a week before. After all, maybe the psych eval will happen fast. Maybe it'll get done in time. But, because of my distance, they're canceling now, so that I have time to change my plans.

I ask if we'll be countering whatever the results of the evaluation are with an expert of our own, but it turns out that the doctor won't be hired by the defense. The evaluation will be neutral, performed by the jail's own psychiatrist, who will put Fryar at the end of his or her list once the court order is given. Then the doctor will work down the list and get to Fryar eventually. Evan has no sense of when that might actually happen.

The defense has not yet shown their hand regarding the purpose of this. If it's in the hope of declaring incompetence, Evan says that everything could get postponed again while Fryar gets put into a mental hospital until competence is declared. In cases where defendants respond to meds, trial is usually back on the table in some thirty-day increment, after the defendant has spent thirty, sixty, or ninety days inside. If it's bigger than a meds issue, Fryar could stay in for years. I could get a call a decade from now saying, "Hey, trial's back on."

If the evaluation is to establish mitigation for sentencing, we should expect a plea to be forthcoming. That's what both Evan and Bill think will happen.

Evan promises that he'll press for a new court date tomorrow, working around a death-penalty case that the judge has coming up. I didn't realize that Pennsylvania still executes.

I wonder if Evan talks much to Georgia. I bet that she's doing what's expected: recoiling from the case, trying to avoid anything more to do with it. I feel like she's the kind of victim that the system is designed around. Evan's adapting to my intensity and need for interaction, but I assume that the other kind of victim is a lot easier to deal with.

Evan keeps offering up on my behalf the excuse that it must be hard for me to be so far away, across an ocean, in a very different time zone, and so out of the loop. He understands how that could make a person anxious for facts to hold on to. I correct him that I would be just the same if I were in New Jersey or Philadelphia or even Pittsburgh itself. This is just the way I am. I want to know all that he's got.

I accept that I don't fit expectations, and didn't even back then. The stereotype is that victims scrub themselves raw under hot water, but I remember that I refused to shower afterward, for at least a day and maybe a few. I couldn't bear to take my clothes off. I wanted to stay dressed forever.

I remember an oversized black cardigan handed down from a friend. I cuddled up in it every day for months. I think I've found one thing that I can definitively attribute to after the rape and not before: ever since then, I like to wrap myself up. Even now, it's such a sad time of year to me when it gets too warm to wear my woolen capelike serape. I like to be inside of it.

Evan apologizes for how the legal system is slanted toward the defendant, and for the "revictimization" that the trial process can cause. I don't feel revictimized, though. This is an entirely new sense of helplessness, not a familiar one. The crime against me wasn't committed by a heaving bureaucracy.

It takes three phone calls with Gavin over the course of the day, one he makes from Heathrow, one from layover in Chicago, and one I make to his U.S. cell phone at my midnight, for me to finally tell him that the postponement is happening. I hadn't wanted to mention it earlier, in passing and while the kids were around. Then, just after I say it, his phone runs out of charge and we're cut off.

Morning now. I haven't told John yet, even though I said I would. I feel frozen. I don't want to say "June third is canceled" until I can also say "The new date is . . . " Evan will try to tell me that today.

He does, at the end of it: October 21, five months away.

PART III

Summer

13

Summer is difficult.

It always is. In America, it's the heat and humidity that's painful. In England, it's the light.

We're far enough north that sunset and sunrise times swing wildly with the change of seasons. The summer's late sunsets keep me up too long and the dawns wake me too early, giving me migraines. Most of all, the lack of waking darkness makes me feel too exposed. The bright times reveal the world to be overwhelmingly large. I prefer winter, when daylight starts to fade in late afternoon, and the night lingers past breakfast. Then there are hours to live in little pools of artificial light, into which I invite only a special few. It's much more manageable. Winter is comforting.

But this is summer.

———

Switzerland distracts. The choirboys are joyfully, relentlessly physical, always kicking a ball around and jostling each other. They flirt with the teenage girls from the Czech choir, and dance "Hava Nagila" with the Israeli choir. They play improvised Pictionary on a chalkboard, making rebuses for words like "Higgs boson" and "Boudicca." They sing sweetly.

I take dozens of pictures and e-mail anecdotes home to all of the parents each day. Then, after return, I organize a Flickr site for all of the photos, mine first and then adding in others'. The images are inevitably similar: the boys in grass-stained black trousers and untucked white dress shirts playing soccer in the park between performances; the boys lounging in half-buttoned red cassocks, polishing their shoes and hunching over smartphones in various dressing rooms. It's only when I get the photos from one of our Swiss guides that I see something different. She's included pictures of the nonperformers, too: of me and the other chaperones, of herself and the other guides. These pictures make me feel suddenly present, suddenly existent. I was there, too. I'd been so focused on looking after the kids that I hadn't really thought about it as my trip, only theirs.

One of the youngest boys had asked me why my festival ID was white, like the children's, instead of black, like the Director's. I'd half joked to him that it's because I'm terribly, terribly unimportant. (Though I understand my intrinsic human value, it was only half a joke because we chaperones were musically irrelevant on a musical trip.) He'd responded earnestly, with big eyes, that I am important. *Very, very* important, he'd insisted, convincingly.

Afterward, I feel refreshed. Home feels new. The trip has cheered me to the point that I'm no longer angry with Fryar's defense attorney, but now fascinated. What madcap delay tactic will she try next? I imagine facing her from the stand and feel curiosity instead of fear.

I outline my new novel, the one that will have a lying character in it. I've already started it, fifty draft pages written last summer, just weeks before Fryar was arrested. If I'd realized that all of this was going to happen this year, I wouldn't have made the central crime a decades-old sex murder. The killer smothered my book-victim so hard that he broke her nose.

I'm permitted to buy a ticket to a sold-out May Ball, for research purposes. (The college May Balls take place in June, after exams, instead of in May, before exams, when they used to happen and for which they were named.) I've already written a scene in which a character chooses a dress for her college's ball, so I've got to go ahead and have the ball itself happen on paper. I've never been to one, so I need to see for myself.

I'm too old for this sort of thing, which I assume, despite the inclusion of graduate students and faculty, will be mostly tipsy undergraduates posing and flirting, so I plan to observe more than participate. From the preparations and mornings-after that I've seen in previous years, these parties are on a grand scale, each having the whole of their walled college grounds to make use of. It's the elaborate, creative details that I'm interested in. At this college, this year's theme is "Lost in the Woods."

A friend generously agrees to babysit for the night so that I'll be able to decide on the fly how late I'd like to come home. The balls go straight through till morning.

I organize a middle-aged version of dressing up: heels and dark trousers, bright top and sparkly earrings, and a velvet cape for when it gets cold after sunset. I got to wear plenty of fussy princess dresses and elegant gowns years ago (theater, high school choir solos, and a formal wedding in my twenties to thank for that), so I don't mind too much that I'm past wearing the summery, pretty things that the young women will have on. It's all right getting older so long as one has lived one's own youth thoroughly.

In the end, it turns out to be a chilly evening, so a lot of the gracefully bared shoulders are covered by incongruous cardigans and borrowed tuxedo jackets. The women sparkle nonetheless, as do colored lights, fireworks, and a spinning Ferris wheel. The men are all identical in black tie. Gavin is in California for the week; I miss him.

While I'm there, an e-mail from my publisher comes through, accepting the latest version of the finished novel that I've been salvaging so very slowly, all year. The feeling is relief, never triumph. First accomplishments are a thrill; subsequent ones just feel like catching up with fading promise.

I listen to passing snippets of conversation. Exams are over, adventures ahead. There's laughing, kissing, posturing. It's genuinely sweet. I remember being in college. I remember wanting all of the things that I have now.

Without prompting, in a friendly e-mail, a pastor from our Sunday church finally offers to talk. This is more than eight months after I told him about Fryar's out-of-the-blue arrest. He's a little late. We're already visiting other churches.

I'm not happy with the sermon at the first new one we've visited. There was nothing "red flag" in it, nothing political or offensive or overly controlling; I just hate the simplistic, self-helpy systems that are encouraged in evangelical culture. This one was about supposedly "sinful" responses to stressors, and next week is going to be about making better choices. What I found troubling was the focus on feelings not just actions, as if emotions are themselves choices. I've been feeling just about everything on their sin list, and I don't think I've done a thing wrong. Feelings are fascinating to me. I put them in the same category as physical and cultural settings, something you find yourself inside of and that you should explore, acknowledge, and understand. Actual decisions come after that. Sins have to be committed, don't they? Something that washes over you isn't the same. It's what you do that matters.

I reply to the pastor from our old church, the one who only now offered to talk. Yes, I want to meet, but one of the things we'll need to talk about is how long it took to get to this point. It took me a few days to decide to bother to answer at all, but now I'm glad that I did. Having said my part, I'm actually interested in the conversation that might come after.

I think that some people use the stereotype of victims not wanting to talk as a free pass for their own desire to flee the topic, as if their silence were for my sake. People said that they didn't want to "pressure" me to talk by bringing it up; they didn't mind at all, though, pressuring me to keep quiet, by their silence. There's no true "doing nothing" here. Ignoring the situation is as much an act as saying or doing something.

Back when I was having flashbacks in college, I remember that I was terrible at asking for anything. All I could easily do was agree, say "yes" or "it's fine," even if things weren't fine. I didn't have the strength to correct or even mildly argue or formulate specific requests; I could only accept from what was made explicitly available. My classmates were expert at this. They offered and offered and offered a full menu: company or solitude, distraction or dealing with it, food or a walk or going out or going home. There was always something good to nod at, something I actually needed. Each bad day, they would ask again, and I could nod at something different then if I wanted to.

A breezy "Let me know if you need anything!" would not have been enough. At my most desperate, I couldn't respond to that. Specific offers and invitations were necessary, especially making explicit a willingness to talk.

While my friends at the time were superb, my church back then was similar in response to my church now: total panic over it being a sex crime. The leaders couldn't cope. I was not spoken to. My Pittsburgh pastors literally didn't make eye contact with me for weeks.

There was no accusation in their avoidance, no blame. It was just ordinary discomfort and embarrassment. Deflecting those was apparently far more important to them than I was.

Cambridge is a very small city. All of the priests, pastors, and chaplains know, or at least know of, one another. I shouldn't pit two against each another, but I can't help but compare. My church's bare "I'll pray for you" with no other action to support it was bullshit, just bullshit. John listens to everything; John doesn't fling up a wall of God and Scripture to protect his worldview and sensitivities from my complications; John understands that talking about a sex crime isn't the same as talking about sex, so there's nothing to be flustered or coy or worried about. I asked him for help with this difficult year, and he took it on. That's how you be a goddamn priest.

Six days with no reply from my old Sunday pastor. I had been glad in the first few days that he was taking his time responding to me, and understood that weekends are the busiest days for clergy and that they often take Monday off, but by Thursday I give up hope and write again: "I find it really heartbreaking that you've decided to not respond at all. I don't know what to make of the silence."

He does respond to that, with a flutter of explanations over any real apology. Also with a reiterated offer to talk, but only with my husband present. I'm horrified at what that implies, about either what he thinks of my intentions for the meeting or what he thinks of rape, as if I'm asking him for sex talk. He blusters in response to my concern that such hadn't crossed his mind, but he won't back down on requiring a chaperone for me; actually, he says, for any woman in the congregation who wants to talk with him for any reason. It's insulting, infantilizing, and creepily sexualizing to demand that. I'd not experienced anything like it under the previous vicar.

Later, the senior pastor, this pastor's boss, will meet with the first pastor and me—pointedly unchaperoned—to insist that no such policy exists, that I must have misunderstood, and that I had been at fault for their inaction because I only ever talked about the situation in person in the busyness after services instead of phoning or e-mailing during office hours. They'll "good cop, bad cop" me, with the pastor I'd tried to talk to seemingly sincerely apologizing, and the senior pastor undercutting that sincerity by interjecting, over and over, explanations why the apologizing pastor actually hadn't done anything wrong.

Back in the present, I write this pastor back, insisting that I won't be chaperoned, then I vent to John. We were part of that church for years, and it hurts that they don't appear to care. I don't want to be advised or comforted by them at this point; I just want to leave with some understanding between us, and an acknowledgment that things could have been done better. They deny me even that.

I tell John, "Honestly, I'm not trying to burn bridges, but, then again, I don't think I'm the one tossing the match."

Ten days later, John is dead.

His car crashed. Bystanders helped his passengers out, but he was unconscious and the car on fire. They couldn't rescue him.

My first thought, once I comprehend the news, is anger that he never had the chance to marry and have children. He wanted that. He was sweet, hopeful. He was only thirty-five. He should have had years ahead for that.

But perhaps it's that lack of a family as a focal point for condolences (he had no siblings, and his parents live hours away in Devon) that allows for the mourning to be so widely shared. John was part of an enormous "us," really several linked but distinct usses: the chapel, the choir, the college fellows, his students, the Faculty of Divinity, the city churches. Grief is everywhere. The college flag flies at half-mast. He's the top headline of the city newspaper.

Walking toward the college gate, I see what appear to be lights on, in his rooms across the courtyard. I'm indignant. How dare someone move around in there, touch things, inhabit his space? I speed up my footsteps.

Once through, I can see that actually it's the rooms next to his that are lit. His are dark. That hurts, too. Everything hurts.

The feelings are awful, and the worst is that these are the very feelings I would have brought to John. I don't know what to do with them now. I'm selfish, angry, and lonely, even with all of these good friends who are sad, too. I'm lonely for this one good friend. Everyone else is not enough.

I try to make a list of everything he did for me. There's so much that I don't know if I can even remember it all:

He listened to everything, without ever complaining that it was too much, so that there would always be one person I could turn to who knew all of it.

He offered to tell people for me, anyone I couldn't bear to tell myself. He offered to accompany me anywhere short of America, so that I wouldn't have to do difficult things alone. He came to our house to be with Gavin while I testified far away.

He protected me from being pushed into any glib kind of grand forgiveness. He accepted, as if they were admirable, whatever small forgivenesses I could genuinely manage.

He made me laugh. When I worried about having to pray for my enemies, he cheerfully offered that I might enjoy the Psalms, which have quite a few vivid verses about revenge and judgment.

He prayed for Fryar for me, even though he hated him, too. He did it for me, because I couldn't and felt that I should and asked him to.

Tears everywhere, blurring my vision, flying when I move my head, bouncing and splashing on my chest and shoulders.

Once, I was worrying that some people might be indignant about the swear words in my writing about this. John shook his head, mouthed "no," and looked a little sad. He said that it was all right, he promised me that it was all right. Then, later in the same conversation, he casually referred to someplace he'd recently been as "a shithole," which made me laugh. I think he did it on purpose so that I wouldn't be alone in swearing. He didn't want me to feel alone.

Words are my favorite things, so I try to think of any words that John had ever said about me, but I keep remembering instead how he would light up whenever he saw me, how, when I'd ask if I was a bother, he would smile and shake his head slowly. I remember him always leaning, legs crossed, relaxed and patient, pretending, when-ever he was with me, to have all the time in the world. It's pictures in my head, not words. I don't know what to do with that.

I receive condolences. Choir parents who loved John's happy, gentle presence but didn't know him outside of evensongs bring me hugs and chocolate.

I try, desperately, to think of anything I'd done for John. My de-pending on him and trusting him feels pathetic, a take not a give, no matter how much I thanked him; I think, though, that he might have been happy to be trusted and needed, so perhaps that counts.

Once at a dinner party at our house—this was before the pros-ecution, so it wasn't out of pity—he stayed past midnight even though he had services to lead early the next day. We were all just too happy to stop talking. He's the one who got me my May Ball ticket after it was sold out. We were friends.

Alice the choir admin worries about Mark, the Director of Music; we all do. As with John, the college is in some ways Mark's family, and, like family, we feel protective. He prefers to protect all of us, especially the students and choristers. We push through recording the new CD as scheduled, as an excuse to be together and to honor John. Mark is fine when he's working. Between takes, though, his posture drops, and his bereavement is evident. He leans. He looks like he may fall.

The recording party is already booked. Mark insists that it go on, for the sake of the leaving boys whose voices have recently changed (including S.) and the sake of the leaving choral scholars who have just graduated. Alice takes me aside and urges that Mark needs for this to be *happy*.

I steel myself and stick ribbons onto a bottle of champagne. I stuff gift certificates into cards for Mark, Alice, and the organ scholars from all of the parents. Mark's card is the special one: a pop-up paper organ that Gavin bought years ago and had been saving. All of the boys have signed it, in different colored pencils, in their sweet, messy, young handwriting.

I remember one thing I did do as a friend to John: I put him in two scenes of a book (which I'd written well before he and I started meeting about the prosecution) and he loved that. This is the novel I've been revising this past year, which I've at last gotten right. I told him a few weeks ago that it's to be published this coming February, and a mutual friend says that John was excited and pleased. I don't usually put real people in my books, but this one is set at this college and I'd needed the chaplain. I'd been mindful to present him carefully and to protect his character from the ambiguity and danger that, per crime novel convention, most of my other characters suffer. He'd joked to me in return that he was disappointed that his character wasn't a victim or suspect.

I pack the champagne and cards for handing off to another mother when I get to college. Another parent is picking up the cheerful bouquets. The presentations are someone else's responsibility. Alice and others are looking out for me; no one will be allowed to turn to me for answers or instructions today. I'm no longer in charge of anything except for my own children, and even they'll be among friends who'll take up any slack I might leave. I'm given a protective circle of grief to carry with me and walk around in.

John is mourned all over the city. Besides his official funeral next week, which requires a cathedral to even attempt to hold all of the people who loved him, various churches hold their own services. For the college chapel's service, at which the boys will sing, I choose my clothes carefully: not black, which would be presumptuous; just something modest enough and dressy enough to match the men, who'll all default to suits. I unwrap an outfit that I'd had dry-cleaned for trial when I still thought it was going to be in June.

At the chapel service, Gavin and I sit with the architect who had designed the chapel's lighting and the new vestry. He shakes his head and says that John was "just a boy, just a boy" because John had always looked young, even at thirty-five, and had had a manner that was sweet and enthusiastic, despite his being a formidable scholar. When I had first asked John about forgiveness, all those months ago, he had brightened and said, with cheerful eagerness, "I once wrote an article about forgiveness! I'm an *expert* on that!" He'd been artlessly delighted to have something relevant to offer.

At home, Gavin asks me to get references to John out of our calendar because the pop-up reminders grieve him. I assure him that we're past the last one today, but I refuse to delete past events, even the two that were supposed to happen with John this week. Our calendar is more than a record of what we've done; it's a record of what we'd intended. Our expectations and hopes and planning did happen, even if they weren't fulfilled. I leave John in there. I left the canceled June trial week in there, too.

Things that didn't happen still matter, in that we wanted them to. The wanting happened.

I'm grateful for the way bodies work, how they insist on being fed and washed and touched. Having a body is like having an extra child, a young one. It makes demands. It keeps me moving forward, whether I feel able to or not.

There are a few duties left: organizing rides to the upcoming cathedral-funeral; organizing a gift from the choir parents to John's parents; organizing a schedule of choir parents to visit Alice's office while Mark is away in August so that she, whose only other boss was John, won't be alone. By then, the bouquets in front of John's rooms, and the memory book in the cloister, and the candles in the chapel will be gone. As things are now, the college is a gauntlet of communal mourning. Even just two days ago, it had been good to share the grief. Now I want to hide from it.

Even just two days ago, when I'd considered someday talking to anyone else about the things that I used to talk about with John, I'd felt certain that I could only ever turn to someone who'd known him, someone like Liz, the chaplain at St. John's College, or Cindy, from Wesley House. Now I want the opposite: someone who didn't know John, who I can then tell about him; someone who'll be surprised and amazed.

I don't need to find someone to talk to quickly. There's not much new to say about Pittsburgh yet, just that Fryar's attorney has suddenly left the public defender's office, though it's not clear whether she'll be allowed to drop this case or forced to see it through. I don't think that I'll ever get to know why she left, but in my imagination it's because Fryar disgusts her. I think: *High-five, fist-bump, join the club.*

The police sergeant (later captain, now retired) who took Fryar's confession of the 1976 rape gets back to me, even though the address I'd written to turned out to be his ex-wife's house, not his. It's another reminder that what I find on the Internet is usually, probably, only sort-of right.

His name is Santo Centamore; his ex calls him Sam. He took so long to reply because he was trying to dig up old police records on the case, which he was unable to do. The Orange County Clerk's papers are probably all that's left.

There was one local newspaper record I'd finally found, which gave all of two sentences to Fryar's rape indictment, and communicated only his name, street of residence, and the date of the then-alleged crime. I appreciate the privacy given to victims, but our facelessness makes history look strange. There are gaps.

I wish I could see us in a lineup and figure out what we have in common. I was surprised to read in the medical report that the victim from 1976 is black; we two Shadyside Jane Does are white. Like I had looked to Vietnam for some explanatory trauma, I had also wondered if resentment of racism might have been motivating, or if, like Ted Bundy, he had a physical type. These options aren't neatly fitting.

Centamore had typed the confession himself, he says. He recalls that the crime was "brutal," which comforts me. I'm glad of his respect for the seriousness of it.

I'd included a printout of the confession with my letter, and he asks if I have anything else, to help jog his memory. I promise him more.

I've told him only that I'm a writer researching the case, which is true, if not complete. His ex, before forwarding my letter, had asked me what my interest was; I'd said that I'd "lived in Pittsburgh" when the currently-being-prosecuted Shadyside crimes had happened, which is also true, also incomplete. At some point, I'm going to have to admit my involvement. I don't know if now should be that time. I would have tried to figure that out with John.

Everyone I can imagine asking for help is in mourning themselves. John will have kept all of our talking from this past year confidential, which is the right thing to have done, but it leaves me feeling lost. I wish that he'd told someone to look after me if he ever couldn't. I wish that someone would say to me, "John would have wanted me to check on you." Then I remember that people have already offered me variations of that, and I've been too ashamed to interfere with their own sadness by saying yes. I wish that someone would insist. I'm quite falling apart.

We're in the center of town, forcing the boys to enjoy the Cambridge leg of the Tour de France despite their whining and the heat. Afterward, I feel once again able to face the makeshift memorials in college, if only to get away from pretending to be cheerful. The city streets are decorated with colorful bunting and crowded with smiling people. Gavin takes the boys home and I go to the chapel.

I'm inside only a short while when an American tour group wanders in, with a boisterous leader who heartily points out chapel highlights. They file past me, tactfully ignoring my tears, perhaps not even seeing them, but they have to notice my solemnity. The tour guide points out the flowers and candles, and stammers that the chapel suffered a great loss a week ago. The visitors murmur sympathetically. I suspect that he's explaining me, my posture and mood, more than the flowers. I slip out as soon as they turn their backs.

The choristers are done for the summer and the students of the choir are on tour until the funeral, so there's no chance of seeing anyone I know, which feels lonely. Except for the funeral, we won't see any of them again until autumn.

I'm lucky to have W., who will still sing treble then; other families have finished choir forever this term. In S.'s former place in the stalls, I'd found the penciled graffiti he'd recently left of his name and choir years: *2010–2014*. It echoes in form the birth and death years that Alice had had to type on John's service sheet.

I send more paperwork from the seventies to Centamore, to help him remember: arrest warrants with Centamore's name on them, court minutes, the official sentence. I tell him about Fryar's ridiculous appeal of the conviction years later, long after he'd served the time. I don't know how far that ever got or if Centamore had known about it.

Happy memories of John continue to sneak up on me. He'd thought I was joking when I'd told him that the Pittsburgh sex-crimes police chipperly answer their phone with a singsongish "Sex Assault, may I help you?" But they really do; at least, one of them really does, and she answers often. John and I had had a good laugh.

At the funeral, everything is perfect—the music from Duruflé's requiem, the thoughtful prayers—except for the slim, black-clad undertaker who accompanies the coffin down the aisle, looking ominous and frightening, like the child-catcher from *Chitty Chitty Bang Bang*. Perhaps, though, that's perfect, too. Death is terrible, especially early death. It should look it.

The men and women of the choir sing here, but the boys don't. We chorister families sit together, our sons wearing ties striped in thick bands of black and red, the college colors, with a thin gold line to represent the choir. The cathedral is full, its high, high ceiling painted with angels, and its long, long aisle filled with procession. My two worlds are growing wider apart. My American life has become ridiculously hard-boiled, starring detectives and set in courtrooms, as if it comes bound in paperback with a titillating but painterly cover illustration. My Cambridge life, in contrast, has taken on the formal tone of an illuminated manuscript: profound medieval scenes touched with gold.

While chaperoning the last day of recording the new CD last week, I'd gotten to sit in the vestry with the record company's producer and engineer.

After the final take of the final song, and the announcement that the tally of all takes that week had been in the hundreds, the last act had been to record a minute of the ambient noise of the chapel, the unique sound of that room with the choir, just sitting still and voiceless, in it. It's a kind of silence, but not complete. The presence of people buzzes, and the walls of the chapel make that buzzing bounce, just under what we consciously notice. That sound will be used as filler as the best bits are matched together for the final cut.

I love the idea of unique silence, that they can't use just any nothing, and certainly not actual nothing. Apparently, silences have character, depending on where you are and who it is that's not making any noise.

John's silence is particular. It's in between the hymns and prayers and eulogy.

After the hearing in January, when I was in agony at the lack of response from supposed friends, I'd started sharing the diary I'd been keeping, to try to get people to understand. And they did understand, at last: what I'd been through long ago, what I was going through this year, and about all of the people who were helping me. John's kindness had stood out to them. One of the first Cambridge friends to read it had replied to me with lots of love, and a fitting observation that rings in my mind now at the cathedral:

"Hats off to young John. What a very wise young man."

14

Gavin is wrecked by John's death. He's fixing things all over the house: plumbing leaks and dodgy electricals. We'd had the place built new and have lived in it for eight years. It's gotten to that age that things are falling apart. He gets angry at the house, and tears of frustration pop out. I'm glad that he has something to do, and an object for his emotions.

It's worrisome that the best of what we can give each other right now is time alone. I need to write; he needs to do things with his hands. We take turns being with the kids, playing with them and supporting them, to make that happen for each other. We guard each other's solitude.

The prosecution is stretching on far too long. This added grief is too much. Gavin needs to be taken care of, too, but won't let anyone do that for him. It just makes him feel weak, which he hates. I don't know what men like this want. Being helped makes me feel powerful. Shouldn't it feel strong to have allies?

He wants to quit his stressful job, but S. is starting school soon and expensive tuition fees loom. I don't make much money from my books. We have good savings, but spending them down too far is a worry.

Double grief is isolating. If I were more sad than Gavin, he could comfort me; if he were more sad than me, I could comfort him. But we're both doubled over from it, both of us missing John.

Gavin doesn't like putting pain into words. I can't fathom that. Turning emotion into words is alchemy. It's the best power I have.

I get back to work. A retired forensic investigator, now a porter at St. John's College, meets me to talk about his old job, for research for my next novel. It's a hottish, sunny day, so we sit on a low wall in front of the wealthiest college, Trinity. Tourists waft past in dreamy groups, looking up and around. We talk about DNA analysis and fingerprint dust, in a distant, happens-to-other-people sort of way.

The university finished classes and exams weeks ago. Kids' schools are finishing now. Everyone's about to travel; us, too. The anchors of normal academic-year life are being hauled up. It feels disorienting, to suddenly lack patterns and schedules. Of course we can order life at home however we like, but the weekly cycle of private lessons, group classes, and rehearsals has come to a close. It's freeing and re-laxing and a little bit lonely. There'll be no bumping into anyone for the next six weeks. Everyone I'm going to see I have to specifically ask for, and they have to say yes.

Even when people do meet up, I worry that it's out of duty, that they're secretly storing up resentment of my seemingly endless neediness.

There are two kinds of caring: selfish and selfless. They're both important.

Selfless caring is when you wish good for the other person above your own desires. It's the more generous kind of love, but without selfish love, too, it's just disinterested. Selfish caring is the love that wants something. It's the love that sees something valuable in the other. Selfish love alone is a terrible thing; but selfless love without selfish love is bland and uninvolved. Selfless love alone is more about the lover wanting to be a good person than about the object of their love being an adored person. I like being adored.

Cambridge is full of good people, caring apparently selflessly. I'm not sure if selfish caring is in there, too, perhaps just well hidden for propriety's sake. I hope it is. I hope that people are kind at least in part because they like being close to me, not only because I need it.

People are using the word "brave" again. It drives me crazy.

I just want all of us to live in the same world. If I'm full of secrets, and always wondering how people might react if they knew, then there are too many worlds: my world, in which the prosecution is acutely important, and the world that they live in, in which it isn't happening at all. Also, there are all of the possible worlds that might come into being if they were told, worlds in which they might be disgusted or emotional or practical or angry or apathetic or freaked out, all of them different.

Telling people what's going on not only puts us all in the same world, all of us knowing; also all of those possible reactions, all those possible worlds, become just the reactions that are happening for real, just the one world that is. One shared world is manageable. A kaleidoscope of worlds and possible worlds is madness.

And it's so much less work! Dealing with actual reactions is easier than generating might-be reactions in my mind. I only have to be me; they'll do the work of being them.

It's not "brave" to do that. I'm taking what for me is the easy way.

Centamore—"call me Sam"—gets back to me. The extra papers didn't jog his memory, except to highlight to him, as I had already noticed, that he's the same age as Fryar, just twenty-four then.

I wonder how much Fryar remembers. Thirty-eight years is a long time.

Centamore had, it turns out, found one piece of the old police notes after all: the arrest photo. It likely had been snapped the same day as the crime. I ask to see it.

I haven't yet told him of my involvement with Fryar's Pittsburgh cases, just that I'm writing about them. It's nice to have an alternate, influential identity to use, truthfully, to not have to be a victim to him until I want to. I'll tell him eventually, but here's the honest truth: I don't want to rock the boat until he's shared everything with me. I don't want to say anything that might stop him talking.

We fly away. My grandfather's old house in New England has become my family's summer house; we meet there every year with my parents, siblings, nieces, nephews. Gavin and my brother love to fish together. Our boys love to boat. Mom mothers us all, with bed-making and dishwashing, gin and tonics and homemade potato salad. Dad brings new board-game ideas for us to test-play, and submits to using headphones when he listens to conservative talk-radio shows.

The thing about the neighborhood of our summer house is that you can't tell which houses are lived in year-round, and which are second or third homes. Gavin and I once stayed here alone with our much smaller boys in the winter of our move to England, while our furniture slowly crossed the Atlantic by ship. It was unnerving, almost post-apocalyptic, being surrounded by so many quiet, only-maybe-occupied homes, right next to the rhythmic slap of the Atlantic against empty beach.

Summers are busier: the water is full of boats, and joggers and dog walkers pass us as we dip our toes in the surf and dig idly with plastic shovels.

I read an article once, in a magazine for middle-aged women

long before I was middle-aged; maybe a *Ladies' Home Journal* or *Psychology Today,* either my mother's or my singing teacher's. It said that how well someone recovers from rape is profoundly tied to how much money they have. Translate "money" as "choice" or "control," and that makes perfect sense. I recall—perhaps erroneously—that the final thesis was that therefore poverty is a more important thing to try to fix than sexual violence. I can't say for sure if that's what it said, but that's what stuck with me. I've never been able to find it again.

Rest helps. Choice helps. Some control, well-educated communication skills, security, and small indulgences help. Therefore, money helps; I know that that's true even without the article. Travel is a way to make a change, even a big one, without sacrificing the ordinary life to which one can later return. It's the means to run away a little distance, and to still have home waiting. But it's not just money after the fact that makes a difference: money systemically in my past, helping me to grow up secure and supported in my adventures, props me up from behind.

I'm spoiled at the summer house. Gavin is relaxed here, frying fresh-caught bluefish, and hammering and drilling new wood into the old patio. Rhode Island is far removed from Cambridge, and so jars us differently, shakes out different feelings. Every year that we come back, the kids are older but still slip into young habits: *Sesame Street* in the morning, *Jeopardy!* at night, American shows that we don't get in England and which they remember, reflexively, that they used to love. Gavin and I slip into old patterns, too, ways of being that are apart from grief. We still have to spend much of our time taking turns managing the kids while the other relaxes or works, and fixing and cooking and keeping things as tidy as my mom likes them. But Gavin runs his fingers across my shoulders when he walks past me toward the dock or the kitchen; when he's the one sitting and I pass him, I kiss the top of his head. The affectionate habits of our sixteen years assert themselves, crisscrossed into a safety net, a big, bouncing catchall underneath us: *touch, smile, listen, speak gently.*

It's a happy surprise to get an e-mail from Evan on a sunny Rhode Island morning; I'm used to having to wait till the end of the day to hear from him when I'm on British time.

I'd written to him, pointing out that, if Fryar's eventual psych eval might require some subsequent process of medication or therapy before trial, then it had better get started. I really can't cope with the trial getting pushed out any further than it already has, and there are three things that could do that, any one of them alone: a date clash with John's upcoming college memorial service next term (which the Master of the college says that he will try to avoid), a lazy defense, or a complacent prosecution. I warn Evan not to trust that Fryar will plead, no matter how sensible and seemingly predictable a plea would be. I beg him to push the defense to get on with their side, too.

He tells me that Fryar's new public defender has been assigned: her first name is Libbi with an *i* and Google tells me that she runs marathons. I think, *All right. That's fine. It's good to have someone who's organized enough and persistent enough to finish marathons.* Even though she'll be working for the other side, I need her to be good so that she'll see the case through properly. If she messes things up, that'll give Fryar grounds for appeal. If she's slow or scattered, she could give him grounds for more delays. I need for her to do this well.

Evan repeats that he can't force things to happen as scheduled, but that he's trying. He's requesting a meeting with the judge and the new attorney to make sure that all is moving forward as it should. I reassure him that I'll understand if some true surprise derails our October date; what I won't put up with is something which we should have foreseen messing things up. Everything that we can guess we might need, we should prepare. There's no excuse for not trying hard enough, all three of us: Evan, Libbi, me.

The other thing that Google tells me about Libbi is that she recently represented the losing side in a case very similar to mine: a cold-case Shadyside rape, this one from only twelve years ago. The man in that case was sentenced to serve seventy-five to a hundred years, just for one victim.

Pittsburgh seems to have a lot of rapes, but statistically it's not the worst city I've lived in or near. According to City-Data.com, Boston (where I'd worked in the years between grad school and marriage) has a higher percentage of rapes than Pittsburgh, as does the town in New Hampshire where W. was born. The suburb in California where S. was born, and my hometown in New Jersey, are each safer.

I look for data to compare if Pittsburgh is harsher on rape than other states. I'm surprised by the number of convictions over the whole country. According to the Bureau of Justice Statistics, there were more than 14,000 felony rape convictions across the United States in 2006, and more than 10,000 of those included prison time. That's encouraging. More than 500 of those rapists were sentenced to a maximum of life.

That same report also says that 84 percent of those 2006 rape convictions were resolved by guilty plea, not trial. No wonder that's what Evan assumes will happen.

A state-by-state listing of rape sentencing guidelines compiled by the American Prosecutors Research Institute shows statutory maximums for rape, and Pennsylvania's is rather moderate at twenty years. (Pittsburgh's very high sentences come from combining rape with other related offenses, each with their own sentences.)

I note other states' maximums. These highest possible sentences for the charge of first-degree rape of an adult aren't likely sentences, nor likely to be fully served if they are given, but even just the possibility is heartening. States with higher potential maximums than Pennsylvania for crimes similar to Arthur Fryar's include Alabama with ninety-nine years or "life"; Alaska with thirty years; Arkansas with forty or life; Delaware with life; Washington, DC, life; Florida, thirty years; Georgia, death. *Jesus*. I'm only up to the letter G.

Oklahoma also lists death as their maximum penalty for rape. Idaho, Iowa, Louisiana, Maryland, Michigan, Mississippi ("assault with intent to ravish"), Missouri, Nevada, New Hampshire, Rhode Island, Utah, Vermont, and Virginia each list a life sentence as their maximum. More than half a dozen other states have maximum sentences less than life but of significantly more than Pittsburgh's twenty years.

Further research tells me that death sentences for rape don't actually go through, and I wouldn't want them to, but I appreciate the value that such potential punishments place on the victim.

Dramatic, oversized sentences are wonderful to me, even if they can't actually be fully served, as in my case because of Fryar's old age. The extra years that he'll never live to give to prison are still useful, as points in the game. They say, loudly, that if the state could go back in time and make him serve from the start of his life—not just from the crime, but maybe even from his childhood or birth if that's what it takes, they would. That's what he owes: not just the years from here on out, but all of his life. All of it.

Big, dramatic feelings beg for big expressions. That's why declarations of love are often for "forever." Some things are too enormous to fit into just right now; we need to borrow from the past and future to have enough room to hold them.

15

Back in Cambridge, I have John's obituary from *The Times* on my tablet, along with a transcript Evan has sent me, of Libbi's recent, similar case, which is over four hundred pages. I carry them with me everywhere. My iPad feels figuratively heavy.

Libbi's told Evan: no plea. We're going to trial. I can use her recent case to help me prepare.

The recent case is the same as ours in that it's a cold-case stranger-rape of a college student in Shadyside; different in that the man had worn a mask, threatened with a weapon not just bare hands, and that he'd finished with his DNA on her clothes not in her body. As in our case, there are two victims in court, but in this case only one rape being tried, because the other victim is getting her own trial in her own county; she only testifies in this case in support. Libbi goes for two things: contesting DNA-test accuracy, and contesting the victims' descriptions. She doesn't touch victim credibility, or grill them unduly. That's good. I can prepare for this.

I look to the transcript to set my expectations. That trial took three days, at least the part that I'll be there for. Before then, there were pretrial motions and jury selection for the attorneys and judge. Libbi asked for a postponement (I must expect this), and was denied at least in part because the main victim had traveled. *Good.*

I settle in and read it.

In the pretrial requests, Libbi says "you know" as an interjection three times in a single paragraph. She doesn't speak like a teenager anywhere else. Maybe she was nervous at the start.

In the jury instructions, the judge is expansive. He explains everything that's going to happen, and the jury's main duty, which is to assess the credibility of witnesses. Everyone who testifies is a "witness," whether victim, police, scientist. You can be a regular witness, testifying to something you experienced, did, or saw; or an expert witness, testifying to a subject you know a lot about. The jury is also charged not to get information about the case from anywhere but the courtroom, and not to talk to anyone about it, not even each other. He tells them flat out: you can't trust what the media reports, so don't read or listen to anything about the case. He says that the typical daily schedule will be nine thirty to eleven, lunch, then one thirty to about four thirty. Not too long a day, but he promises that listening to testimony is taxing.

He also points out that it may be difficult to hear, and that the heaters will be turned off (it was January) because they're noisy. Evan had told me the same thing about the air conditioners when we'd thought our trial would be in June. Pretty, landmark building; uncomfortable to work in.

Everyone has a role. The judge isn't referred to as the judge, but as "the Court." The prosecutor is "the Commonwealth," meaning Pennsylvania. Her name is Ms. Necessary. One of the forensic scientists they mention is Mr. Askew. It feels like a Restoration comedy. Aprill testifies in this case, too, and her name is misspelled throughout, with just one *l*.

The prosecution has the burden of proof, so they go both first and last: first opening statement, first to present their case, last of the two closing arguments. They sit closer to the jury. They're given those advantages because they have more work to do. The defense already has an advantage: the presumption of innocence.

The Commonwealth's opening statement recaps the entire crime. I suppose Evan will do that, too. My testimony will be a repeat, but with feeling. They'll need to hear it from me. They'll need to hear it in my voice, not just my words.

Libbi's opening statement for the defense is dramatic: "[The accused] is somebody's son. He is somebody's brother. He also sits before you today an innocent man. He is not innocent because I tell you he is innocent or because [the judge] instructs you about the presumption of innocence, he is innocent because the Constitution of the United States of America and the Constitution of the Commonwealth of Pennsylvania says that [the accused] is cloaked in the presumption of innocence. That means that you have to presume that he is innocent unless and until Ms. Necessary, if she is able, proves to you each and every one of the elements and each and every one of those offenses beyond a reasonable doubt."

Okay, I'll expect grandstanding.

If they go chronologically, as they did at the hearing, I'll go first: Jane Doe January before Jane Doe November. Actually, we're only anonymous in the press. In the trial they'll use our names. Everyone will know them; they just won't be supposed to use them outside of the courtroom.

In this similar case that Evan sent me, the victim's account is simple and direct. It looks easy. *I can do this.* She literally just tells what happened, plainly, with occasional prompts from the prosecutor. Questions about the present come first: *Where do you live? What do you do? Are you married?* These were chosen to put her at ease, and to show her to be successful and settled; presumably they're customized for each victim. Next: all that had happened twelve years ago. Pages and pages of it.

Libbi's cross-examination seems simple at first read-through, but she's going after quality of lighting, initial descriptions of the assailant, and little details that it turns out are differences between this rape and the one that will be testified about later. She'll use all of these in her closing argument to claim that her client couldn't have done both.

Evan and I will have to prepare for this, go over my descriptions to the police carefully, establish that I did see Fryar clearly then and that I do recognize him now. I would never want to rely on eyewitness testimony alone, but, with DNA agreement, I trust my visceral recognition to seeing his picture on Google, in an impromptu lineup.

This case comes down to a battle over the accuracy of DNA identification, in part because the DNA samples here are not as robust as those from our case. The prosecution's big expert is the man whose company was employed to identify the remains of victims of 9/11. He doesn't physically analyze DNA; he takes DNA analysis results and uses statistics and patterns to fill in blanks. The key is that the computer does this neutrally, without reference to any suspected match. In isolation, his computers predicted a match of the rape evidence to this defendant that was in the quadrillions, statistically many times more precise than the human analysis. (My evidence, just from the human analysis, is rated many times more accurate than that, with six more zeroes, so we won't need an expert like this for our case.) He talks so long that there's a lunch break halfway through.

The reason that this DNA dispute is the centerpiece is because the prosecution has nothing else (as the defense will point out witheringly in closing arguments). In stranger-rape, there's no relationship, no buildup, no threats or escalating behavior. The victims here in this case can't even point to his face, because he was masked. It will be similar for us, though I'll have his face to point at. Libbi will sneer that we have "nothing else" to put him in my apartment: no witnesses, no fingerprints, no history. (Of course, if we did have history she would argue consent.) She wants DNA to be the cherry on top of traditional, low-tech evidence. In stranger-rape, though, that's often all there is.

After finishing on the high note of the 9/11 expert and his quadrillions, the prosecution rests. Before the defense even begins their response, Libbi makes a motion for acquittal, based on lack of evidence. It is denied.

Among her witnesses, Libbi calls the defendant's sister, who has photos from her baby's baptism in the same year that the rapes took place. The prosecution objects to the baby niece and the priest in the pictures as irrelevant and potentially prejudicial, but the photos go in as evidence anyway.

Libbi uses the pictures to dispute the victims' descriptions of the little bits of hair and head that they were able to see around the mask, and the color of the skin of his arm, whether "pale," as one victim said, or "tan," as in the photographs and as his landscaping job would suggest. The sister testifies to an appendix scar that neither victim noticed.

This makes me nervous. Physical descriptions are hard for me. I barely use them in my writing. I'm much more able to describe how someone makes me feel, and what they do. That's what my descriptions were about: "big" meaning powerful and husky, not tall. "Baby-faced," meaning incongruously sweet-looking. I daren't try to describe clothes or hair, which I could too easily get wrong (though the jacket Georgia described at the hearing prompted instant and deep agreement). I must review whatever I said then and stick to it. In the notes, Bill had noted "zipper" because I'd said he'd zipped up his pants, but I don't know if I actually saw that it was specifically a zipper or just assumed it, and meant only that he closed his pants. I hate this.

The third day of this recent trial starring Libbi begins with the option for the defendant to present character evidence. The judge says, "Under the laws in Pennsylvania, an individual of good character is [considered] not likely to commit a crime, and [so] evidence of good character is sufficient to raise a reasonable doubt as to whether that individual committed the crime [with] which he or she has been charged; do you understand that? . . . You have the right to present character testimony . . . Character testimony is not somebody's personal opinion, rather it is that individual's understanding of what your reputation is."

The defendant declines to speak on his own behalf or to present character witnesses. Considering that he has a weapons conviction, drug conviction, and had been arrested for involvement in a robbery plot from which he'd gone on the run for four years before he was identified by a tipster watching *America's Most Wanted*, that seems wise. The defense rests, and launches into closing arguments.

Libbi appears to be pretending not to understand why some DNA was excluded. Every bit of DNA has two parts: one from the subject's mother, and one from the subject's father. In some of the DNA bits that were deemed of insufficient strength to count in the report, only half of the pair was found. It makes perfect sense that an "insufficient" portion would be incomplete, and that the sufficient-to-report bits were whole. In all of the insufficient cases, the testable parts of the insufficient data did match the defendant;

it's just that there was also a piece missing. Libbi implies that these missing parts were potentially exonerative, and therefore deliberately excluded to strengthen the case, while the opposite is true: if the lab had been keen to rig the results, it would have been better to lower the standard and claim those matches. Libbi's tricky.

She harps on the variance in height between witness approximations versus his actual 5'7" as testified by his sister. Libbi claims that one victim had described him to be 5'8" and the other 5'10", a strange thing to focus on considering how close 5'8" is to his precise height. And, though it's partly true that the victims said those numbers, Libbi doesn't tell the whole truth. The victims had claimed those heights as the top of the possible range, but 5'6" as the bottom. The Pittsburgh victim had said that her assailant was "approximately 5'8" or so or 5'6"." The other county's victim had said, "I thought between 5'7" and 5'10", 5'6" and 5'10". He wasn't very tall." Perfectly accurate, and probably better than I would do, even to guess the height of someone I know well and regularly stand next to.

This kind of brazenly skewed quoting from Libbi makes sense of the judge's later reminder to the jury to base their decisions only on actual testimony, not on the attorneys' summations. "Their statements and arguments and questions are not evidence. The only evidence that you would use to decide this case comes from the witnesses that have come forward to testify and the exhibits that have been given to you." The jurors are to have each taken their own notes of the testimonies. That's what they should trust, and their own memories.

Libbi ends theatrically: "When Ms. Necessary started her opening statement to you she told you that she represents the Commonwealth. She does. You might take from that that for the Commonwealth to prevail in this case you have to convict my client. I would ask you to think about it a little bit differently. The

Commonwealth isn't just Ms. Necessary and Detective Campbell
and [the victim], the Commonwealth is you and I and [the judge]
and [the accused] and [his] family. So what should we be worried
about as citizens of the Commonwealth? We should be worried
about getting our verdicts right, about returning just verdicts. A just
verdict has to be consistent with the facts as you find them with the
law that [the judge] is about to instruct you and with that burden
of proof beyond a reasonable doubt. If your verdict is just, then all
of us in the Commonwealth will prevail."

Then the prosecution closes, answering all of Libbi's spurious claims.
Libbi had insisted that the two rapes were very different from one
another, very unlikely to have been committed by the same person,
because one victim had been punched and the other had only been
threatened, among other small variations. The prosecution takes
that on handily. Ms. Necessary (her name is Jan, but I adore her last
name too much to call her by anything else) says to the jury:

"On TV, rape cases are very dramatic and brutal and because it
is TV they show a woman being dragged off the street and being
kidnapped and repeatedly tortured. All those shows [show] sadistic
rapists. There are other kinds of rapists that use power to overcome
his victims. He uses just enough power. He is not interested in tor-
turing the victim, just interested in sexually assaulting her. I submit
to you [that] that is what the defendant did in each of these cases.
He used just enough power, just enough force, to get his victim to
submit to what he wanted to do.

"Now if the victim resists then he uses more power, more force.
For example, [the first victim] said she sort of panicked when he
started taking her shirt off and she was fighting him even though
he had a gun. What did he do? He punched her in the stomach and
knocked the wind out of her. He punched her in the mouth and
subdued her so she did not continue with her resistance.

"He didn't have to do that to [the second victim].You saw [her] on the stand and her reaction when she said she was awakened by the masked assailant and he said do as I say or I'm going to kill your baby. That was it for her. You saw the reaction that she had to it even now when she testified on the stand. He didn't have to hold a gun to her. He didn't have to threaten her personally at all. All he had to do was threaten her child. She did whatever he wanted. It shows you he uses whatever he needs to use to get his victim to submit."

Just enough power. She makes me want to cheer. She understands. She makes the jury understand. Then she recaps the crime and the efficient, high-standards lab work. She demolishes the defense's "so-called expert." I think, *Evan, be like that. Please.*

Then the jury is reminded that they must agree unanimously in their verdict. They begin deliberations at 11:06 A.M. that Monday morning.

There are a couple of fizzes of questions from the jury room, then a guilty verdict five hours later, at 4:15, in just before the end of the day.

I close the document. I feel ready. This is what's ahead, with a different judge, with Evan instead of "Ms. Necessary." Libbi is the constant. She's tough, and willing to stretch the plain truth, but she's safer for us than Abigail. In terms of ensuring that the trial will go forward in October, an active defense is better than Abigail's passive assumption of a plea.

Libbi will keep Evan on his toes. That's good. That's her job. Now that Evan knows it's her, now that she's flat-out told him that there will be no plea, we can get to work. I've been ready. Now she's making Evan ready. He'd assumed a plea, too, as much as Abigail had. So did Bill.

I knew better. Fryar has only confessed once in his life, back in 1976, within hours of what I believe was his first rape. (I don't count his plea in the later Staten Island drug case, because he used it to facilitate fleeing the jurisdiction.) By the time the '76 rape got to court, he was begging the court for lenience. He's been fighting ever since; fighting uselessly, but fighting nonetheless. His pattern, over years of lawbreaking, is denial and delay, and sometimes escape, no matter the evidence against him.

When Aprill had first interviewed Fryar in New York, he'd spoken freely about the legs of the two Shadyside victims. His girl-friend had explained to Aprill that he was confident of the statute of limitations. Later, though, when his situation under the new law was clear, he fought even extradition across state lines, which gained him only a few extra months on Rikers Island. He doesn't seem to have real confession in him, not anymore, not since he was twenty-four years old, thirty-eight years ago.

It might be a warped form of dignity, refusing to give in. At least he goes down swinging. It might be that fighting the prosecution makes it plausible for him to continue to claim innocence even if he's convicted; in stereotype, rapists are given a hard time in prison, so deniability could be worth it inside. I don't think he does it to try to convince himself. I think he understands that he did it, and just doesn't want to pay for it.

His previous court patterns fill pages with motions. I've collected New York records that not even Evan or Dan or Aprill have, about Fryar's drug arrests and other crimes. This is simply how he is: he resists. He resists conviction the way that I resisted him, even though we were each up against powers greater than our own.

I think I know Fryar better than anyone at this point. I'm the only one who tried to know him. I'm the only one who looked.

Like love, my needy grief feels like it will last "forever." It's that big. I have nowhere else for it to spill over.

Well, one place. It spills backward, too. I feel like I've always been this way, even though I know that I haven't.

A friend of John's helps me.

Months earlier, John had mentioned to her, Anna, that Gavin and I would be visiting the church where she's vicar. It was on our short list of new places to try, and is the oldest church in Cambridge, older than even the eight-hundred-year-old university. As soon as I tell her that John had sent me, she knows who I am, but not about the court case; just that we're choir parents, and that John was supposed to have baptized W. a week after the accident. I think she was the one John had been going to send me to from the start, if I'd preferred to talk with a woman.

She and I reminisce about John, there at the church door during after-service coffee time. She's supposed to be seeing people off as they go out, but she kindly gives me her full attention instead. I take care to try to phrase things as interesting or funny. I try to make it worth people's while to listen to me.

I mention the prosecution, in passing, to explain what John had done for me. I tell her that he'd been looking after me. Anna goes to retrieve her calendar, without making me ask.

Later that week, we meet in a tiny room above the sanctuary. On the way up the spiral staircase, we talk about cassocks, and street clothes that go with priestly collars, but not because she's a woman; I'd talked about vestments with John, too (and, once, with a sparkly, colorfully robed male bishop). Clothing is personal; even ritual clothing is; and it raises funny, sweet stories if you ask the right questions.

I have to explain the case to her from scratch, all the way back to 1992. I've practiced summing it up quickly and efficiently, hitting all of the important points. Enough people know about it now that it's no longer a release for me to tell the long-ago parts; I'm anxious to get to *now*, which I suppose is a sort of progress all by itself.

We both cry over John a little. I have less right to cry than she does, she who was part of his inner circle, so I tell, a bit possessively, about the kindness of the other choir parents and how they deferred to my grief. I was not as much a friend to John as she was, but, in the small world of the choir, people recognized that his death had hit me hard. I stake my claim to tears.

She says some of the same wise things as John; they were trained together, so that makes sense. She has a similar sense of humor; after all, they were friends. These likenesses comfort me and unnerve me and make me feel sick the rest of the day. I can't sleep that night. It feels wrong to replace him. It feels wrong to do anything less than freezing the world at the point just before he died.

I visit Anna again, a week later, up the same spiral staircase, in the same little room. I feel sick again, but that night I can sleep after all. I hate that John's fading away. Only being sad keeps him. I don't want to let him be gone. I want to fight. I want to object.

I'd had an involuntary thought after John's death: Who would I rather have died instead of him? Even in my fantasies, death is there. I can push reality around enough in my imagination that I can picture the dead one not being him, but I can't make up any version of that day without the crash, without *someone* dying in it. Death punctures through everything, even into my invented dreamworlds. I can only pretend that things are a little bit different from what really happened, not wholly changed, as if my imagination is powered by a genie with a single, limited wish, just one.

Anna invites me to her home for our next meeting. I prepare a little list, like I used to do for meeting with John, jotting notes during the week whenever I think of something I'd like to say. I have the last note of what I'd intended to tell him.

Just after the happy exhaustion of Switzerland, just after the distraction of the debacle with our previous church, I'd made a note to tell John about how the prosecution was feeling lighter to me, a lull before the eventual trial. There was the baptism coming, and the Tour de France; things to look forward to first. He died three days before I was going to tell him that I was, at that moment, happy.

I'm not actually suicidal; it's just something I think about; but if I were to say even just that, then people would try to "do something," at worst something awful with doctors, so I can't say anything at all, to John's friend Anna or anyone. Telling Gavin would only worry him.

Besides, I would only do it if I could actually disappear. My body is the worst part of me, and leaving it behind, empty, just seems disgusting and embarrassing, so it's not going to happen. It's not.

It's just that dread of the trial and grief over John are too much. I could manage one or the other. I was managing just the one, just the trial. When it was supposed to happen in June I was ready, but I haven't been able to sustain that blithe alacrity. I explained things to someone this week, just the practical facts, and listening to myself felt strange and surprising. I heard myself describe that Evan and I would have to practice so that he'd know what questions to ask to make me break down on the stand. (Evan wouldn't call it that. He'd say "elicit an emotional reaction.") I meant to sound merely pragmatic, but it sounded awful. Evan's the good guy and even he's got to make me hurt. Then, after he's through with me, Libbi gets her turn, and she's not on my side. Reporters will scribble, like they did at the hearing, more so now that it's a proper trial. My breathing speeds up. I have to tell myself off: *Just local reporters. Don't be so dramatic.*

It's been almost a year. In two weeks we'll lap the start: September 12, when Arthur Fryar was arrested. The trial is five weeks after that. I managed twelve months on adrenaline. I've run out.

Term is about to begin. The college's upcoming service of Admission and Dismissal panics me. It's scheduled for the night before

I fly for court, and John's replacement will be leading it. I'd prefer to sit out, just to listen from the nave, but S. with his now-low voice is being dismissed and will be honored; and W.'s promotion within the choir is to be recognized. They'll need me to be cheerful and happy for them, celebrating with smiles.

I practice for it, just like I practice looking at photos of Fryar in a suit. I sit in the empty chapel. Tears run all over my face. This isn't going to work.

Again, tourists come in while I'm weeping. Goddamn summer.

PART IV

———

Fall

16

I lie.

I tell people that it's all right if they don't have time to talk or to read my updates or to meet up. I suppose it is, in a sense, all right, in that I intellectually accept that there are many genuinely good reasons for anyone not to be able to do these things, and that these legitimately significant reasons don't mean that people don't care. But the implication that I'm therefore open to either answer, yes or no, is entirely a lie. I need yes.

I lie to Bill. I tell him that I would *completely understand* if he's unable to get away from work for trial week. I ask him to be there for my testimony and for the verdict, and *by the way* it would be great if he can be there for all of it but of course it makes perfect sense if he can't. It was one thing for him to be with me at the hearing in January; that was only one day. The trial will be at least three. October is right in the middle of the fall semester. He has to

teach, after all. He has to help run his department at the business
school.

He promises me all of the days, to just sit with me in court while
I listen to everyone else testify, all three days plus one extra in case
the trial goes long. He'd already put them into his calendar. He
thinks he'll be sequestered for my testimony—that is, kept out of
court so that my version doesn't affect his—but he'll be there.

Relief. Ground under my feet. Without Bill, the only person in
the courtroom who'd remember me from that night in 1992 would
be Fryar. Bill balances him out.

Everything is about to start up again for the new school year:
music, sports, clubs. Over and over, the other parents are going to
ask "How are you?" reflexively, with no real meaning, passing the
question around from person to person like a plate of cookies.

I plan: *Smile. Say "fine."* That should always be the unthinking
standard. I can vary this if a good opportunity pops up, but I mustn't
tell the truth without a good reason, without a considered decision
to do so.

I am not fine.

As things get worse in my head, I'm conscious of a careful balance: I could drive people away just when I need them most. I
will go ahead and talk about the trial one-on-one, but even then
I must choose my words with care, giving preference to interesting facts and good news developments. My personal mandate is
to be light, direct, and entertaining about the prosecution unless
specifically invited to be otherwise. I can't let myself mess this up.
Just being with people who know helps, even if we only touch
on the subject lightly. Being too much alone right now would be
a bad idea.

I fill the calendar between now and trial with small dinner parties
and chats over coffee and cake. I ask for yeses everywhere, asking
for so many that any noes will be obscured by acceptances. I lie in

every invitation: *Totally no big deal if you can't come.* I practice, in case of declines: *Don't be silly! I shouldn't have asked. It doesn't matter.*

August and September appear to be next to each other, but that's an illusion from looking at them from above. Really, one is miles below the other, and stepping off the end of summer is a fall from a cliff into a very different and new academic year. A lot is suddenly changed now, especially me.

S. starts school for the first time, with a fresh haircut, new jeans bought in haste to accommodate his growing legs, and a new red hoodie that he puts over a polo shirt every morning, even before leaving his bedroom. He likes the way it makes him look like the teenager he's trying out being. W. returns to all of his activities. Choir begins again for him, with a dense schedule of rehearsals, services, concerts, and John's memorial. I'm wary of the choir parties that I used to enjoy. I want to socialize individually, but don't trust myself to be able to chitchat and flit from person to person. I plan a short errand I must run after dropping W. off for the "welcome tea." I can come back if I want, or pretend that the errand ran long. I give myself options.

What I wanted isn't what I want anymore. My urge to share about the prosecution, which culminated in a flurry of e-mails in recent weeks, has reversed. Now there are two kinds of people in the world: those who already know and those who don't and won't, not until the trial's over. Everyone around me is now fixed in their position on one side of that line or the other. I won't resist if the subject comes up; if, in a group, one more person needs to be filled in just to keep up with the conversation. But I no longer feel the need to tell for telling's sake, or even able to. There's only moving forward from here, talking about what's happening now, right now, with people who are already caught up with what came before.

The defense is trying to change the dates. My affection for Libbi-with-an-*i*'s brisk efficiency evaporates. She's only trying to move things out by a week, so I think this is a schedule clash for either her or for a witness, not a preparation-of-her-case issue. Evan asks me to propose alternate dates, as if it's generous to let me. I push back: *no*. I've already worked around the current dates, and by doing so ensured that everything except for those dates has become a schedule clash for me. I don't want to scramble to change flights, give up the hotel I like, miss my children's events here at home, or push up January's eventual travel for sentencing to overlap with the February launch of my new book here in England. I don't, I realize, want to lose the connection with the Admission and Dismissal service the night before I fly. I've been dreading it, but now I cling to it. Choir people know what's happening. There will be proper good-byes. I want to keep that.

It's a good thing that Evan and I are communicating over e-mail and not on the phone. If I'd been actually speaking to him I would have blurted out that he should "man up," which is not something I should say to my attorney. I mean it, though. He should stand up to Libbi. If someone needs to bend here, I don't think it should be me.

Gavin observes that at least we're haggling over days, not months. That's true. But we are haggling over a bit else: over who matters. We'll find out who the judge thinks is important when she decides about dates.

The next morning I find out that it's me who matters. Me! October 21 sticks. I e-mail Evan, writing "thank you" six times, and "yay," and a smiley face. Bill e-mails me, "Whew." Relief all around.

A new public defender will be assigned to Fryar, his fourth attorney in this proceeding. That's how they kept the date: getting rid of Libbi. The timing feels much more important than anything else; I won't miss her.

Gavin is concerned that assigning a new defense attorney this close to trial may itself become grounds for delay, but I think that the public defender's office is so overburdened that Libbi had perhaps not yet begun work on Fryar's case anyway. Or, if she had, she can hand that work off. Honestly, I don't know how much work Evan's done yet on our side. There are still six weeks to go and he will have had other cases all summer.

This same day, Sam Centamore, the now-retired detective who had taken Fryar's confession in 1976, sends me Fryar's booking photos. I glance at them. Mug shots have that serious, direct gaze. It's upsetting. I close the e-mail but the images linger in my mind.

Of the few photos I've found online, only one is of Fryar close to now: around age sixty, gray-haired, and smaller than he used to be. The rest are from the middle of his life, a span of decades when he was recognizable as the man in my apartment in 1992. That Arthur Fryar was robust, with chubby cheeks, a husky build, and a friendly face. These mug shots from the seventies are palpably different. This is the young military man, fresh from two years of intense training. He looks angry. He looks strong. I feel sick.

I make myself open the e-mail again. He's not angry-looking after all. His stare is disconcerting, but a closer look reveals puppy-dog eyes, lost and worried. He's holding himself straight but he looks tired. This all went down in the middle of the night.

He was just twenty-four. That age looks young to me from where I am now, though I remember feeling adult when I was twenty-four myself. Then, I was in graduate school at night, had a job working at a tech company during the day, and was starting a freelance writing career on the side. I lived in my parents' house and had student loans, but I'd finally gotten my driver's license and Mom helped me buy a little red car. That age is young and old mixed together. An adult, yes, but the youngest kind of adult, a baby of an adult. That's what I see in his face: that fragile starting-out time, trying-on time.

When my kids are twenty-four, I think they'll still be coming home for Christmas.

In his e-mail, Sam asked me what kind of book I'm writing about this. That means he hasn't figured me out yet. I'd given him my website address in my first communication, which he may or may not have looked at; it's about my fiction, so even if he has looked it would still be reasonable for him to wonder what I'm writing about Fryar. What I'm sure he hasn't done, yet, is also look up Fryar's current case, or he would have noticed the similarities between the then-CMU-student victim now living in the UK, and the author bio on my book flaps describing an "American novelist living in Cambridge, England" who "trained as an actor at Carnegie Mellon University's prestigious drama conservatory." The connection is there to be made, easily, when he does look.

I give myself up. I send off an e-mail that, if his pattern holds, he'll see in a week or two. He's been kind to me and I owe him the truth.

The mug-shot images idle in my mind, and along with them a motherly sadness toward Fryar's younger self.

There's a lot that I need right now, a lot that I'm fighting for. Keeping the court date was important, and friends saying yes is important, and being understood is important. I know what it is to feel desperate. I know what it is to need things, and for that need to feel vast. What I don't know is what it's like to live in such a narrow space that bursts of cruelty feel like the only way to breathe. It must be terrible to be inside Fryar's head, inside his body, inside his life.

It became worth it to young Fryar, desperately worth it, to trade his future and his sense of shared humanity for a brief high-point of power. I believe that these pictures are of him just hours after that first decision. He doesn't seem proud of it. He seems resigned.

Whether in the end it turned out to satisfy him as he'd hoped, he'd done it and there was no taking it back.

The psych eval that had been requested by Abigail, defense attorney number two, was then canceled by Libbi, defense attorney number three, so I'm not likely to be handed any understanding. I have to find it myself. Wherever Fryar's urge comes from, and however different he and I are in how we act out, we're in one general way alike: there are things that we need very, very much.

I feel fragile, and I need a lot. I think he does, too, and has for a very long time.

I'm being pushed on a current. I float. In five weeks, I'll arrive at trial, bump against its shore.

From growing up in New Jersey, I know a certain look to the sky that means imminent rain. That same gray look doesn't mean rain here in England; that color can hold for days without a drop falling. I've had to learn to read it differently. I've learned to read people here differently, too. Their reticence that I would, at home, accurately read as a snub, is just kindness awaiting an invitation.

The college is now where I feel most at home outside of our little family. That's where John's loss is understood, and where there's the closest that I have to a cohesive group of friends rather than individual relationships. It's become a surprising bookend to my Pittsburgh college years back when the crime originally happened: two universities that, despite some rocky moments, rose to the occasion and became safe places for me. I'm not officially attached to this Cambridge college, just tenuously connected by motherhood of choristers and the participation that that allows, but nevertheless I feel part of it, and am recognized as part of it by those who matter. I'm grateful.

A major plot point in the novel I've been revising all this past year, the one that's been recently accepted and has a bit of John in

it, takes place here in this college. The character Imogen's happiest
childhood memories are of her older brothers singing in the choir
that my boys sing in. She and her littler brother had been tagalongs,
unable to join the choir because she was a girl, and he was too
young. I wrote about them, not the choirboys, because I had discovered that the tagalong experience is itself a primary experience
of its own thing, not just a secondary experience of the choir, or
orchestra, or whatever it's attached to. What W. and I did for years,
while S. rehearsed his drums and his singing, were their own things:
the unrelated jazz band we'd eavesdrop on, the nearby collection of
plaster casts of ancient sculpture that we'd visit, the jigsaw puzzles
from home that we'd spread out on the carpet of the concert hall
lobby. I wanted to capture that life, that nearby life, which was as
full as the life onstage.

W. is now in the choir, too, so I'm the tagalong left, just me. The
funny thing is, it wasn't until I'd finished the whole first draft that
I even realized that Imogen was, in that one sense, me. Obviously
the little brother had been inspired by W.; Imogen, the big sister,
had been to my conscious mind merely a necessary invention. But
of course there were two tagalongs there, not just one, not just the
little boy. Of course the other one was me.

I get to be in the center of other parts of my life. It's all right that,
for my kids, I stand on the edges. Edges are interesting places all on
their own. Edges can be the centers of their own circles.

I'm glad that I wrote about that for W. It turned out also to be
meaningful for me.

People are making me explain again why I want to go to Pittsburgh
alone. It's difficult to find the words to do so, because it's not a decision. How to explain a primal want?

The best I can manage is to say that while I'm there I'll need to
focus on this one thing, and be just this one slim facet of myself.

Most of my relationships use much more of me, require me to be all kinds of me: mommy me, partner me, friend me, me who cares about all of everyone else's life, too. I won't have the energy to be pulled in those many directions. Even if people deferred to my circumstances, and I'm sure they would, it's not as if I can just turn it off. With Bill and the rest of them involved in the case, I'm only this. That's exactly who I'll need to be for that week.

Also, I'm reminded of when I was single and traveled. I usually preferred to go alone, because when I went with friends we walked around in a little bubble of home that we brought with us. I don't mean that my friends were unadventurous; just that the routines of our relationships were themselves a part of home that insulated us. Going alone and being just me allowed me to make new relationships with the places themselves.

I need to give Pittsburgh my full attention.

Evan had said that the new defense attorney would be assigned the Monday after the judge upheld the court date. It's now eighteen days past that. I'm impatient. I'm wondering what this delay in attorney assignment might mean for the case.

Trial is less than a month away. At least, it had better be. I'm no longer able to feel sanguine about the silence. I feel cold, and ill, and frustrated. I've gone to an eye doctor because I'm seeing things in my peripheral vision, just out of reach. I e-mail Evan a fourth time, and let my desolation show.

I can do pretty well with almost any information, even with difficult news, but I'm terrible with nothing. Nothing is actually the opposite of nothing. Giving me nothing is giving me every possible thing in the world to worry about it, since what's really going on could be any one of them. Going from every possible thing to just one real thing, even if it's a difficult thing, helps.

Evan answers at last, with apology. He doesn't yet know of a new attorney for Fryar. I suppose Fryar might already have one and we just don't know. If one truly hasn't been assigned yet, that has me worried; delays now and appeals later seem to be the most realistic concerns and a rushed defense could contribute to both. Nothing to be done about it, though. I offer dates for us to Skype to prepare my testimony.

He replies three days later: we'll talk on Tuesday. He says that one conversation is all that he'll need from me. So, there it is: one conversation is all that I'll get.

But I suppose that more talking wouldn't actually help. Testifying is going to feel weird and scary regardless of prep. Evan's right that once will be enough. It's just strange to realize how little preparation there actually is, on both sides. We're just there to tell the truth that we already know, and getting it out of us with questions is a straightforward matter. It feels huge that we'll be doing it in a courtroom, in front of a jury and judge and some journalists, and being recorded and transcribed, but the words themselves won't be much different from words I've said before. In fact, they'll be much less. Friends care about more details and tangents than juries do.

The only thing that I need to fuss over is that this Tuesday Skype will be my one chance to ask questions "in person." I must think of everything I'll want from Evan before I travel.

At last, news: a public defender has been assigned to Fryar. Her name is Helen. She passed the bar only three years ago and Evan doesn't know of her having defended any rapes. The only newsworthy defenses of hers that I can find are two drug cases and a mother who abandoned her baby in the woods.

The thing that comes up most about Helen are references to her summer internship when she was still a law student. She worked at Legal Aid of Southeastern Pennsylvania, and her blog post about the experience reveals her to be thoughtful and canny. Fryar seems to have gotten a good one.

She'll have met with Fryar maybe this week; or will next week, surely. Time's running out. I wonder if Fryar's denying the crime to her. She has to know that he did it. I just wonder if that fact is openly on the table.

I don't reply to Evan right away. This is partly because I want first to think carefully if I have any questions to include, and also as a bit of bravado: my restraint demonstrates that I'm not desperate. With some effort, I can be as calm and blasé as he is. I'm not floating anymore; I'm rooted in one spot. It's the trial that's coming closer, doing all of the work.

I discover that I have some boundaries after all: I send out e-mails explicitly asking my Pittsburgh friends not to observe the upcoming trial, and that all of my friends avoid reading about it in the news.

It turns out that I want the prosecution to be known and talked about, but only if it's filtered through me, not observed objectively. Only my version of the trial, in my words, is comforting to me. The trial from other points of view, a reporter's or even a friend's, is wild to me. It feels unpredictable, maybe dangerous. It's supposed to be mine first, only then theirs. Mine first. I tame it.

My swings between anxiety and chipper socializing widen. The jauntiness isn't fake; I genuinely enjoy chatting with friends and staying up late and telling each other funny stories. I love waking up to the mess of our good china still spread out all over the table, and that our kids have to work around an empty bottle and motley, mismatched wine glasses to make room for their breakfast waffles and Asterix comics and gamer magazines. I wouldn't want a life that's all unrelieved panic attacks. But the distance between the two states, the length that I swing between them several times each day, is dizzying.

17

Tuesday gets here. Because of the time difference, my Skype appointment with Evan isn't until 10 P.M. my time. I feel it nearing all day.

I've become used to the whole situation, pretty much, and accept it as normal, but there are little flickers when I realize that certain things are actually extreme. Having to recite my testimony for Evan, and be judged and corrected by him, is bizarre. I've never even met him except via three previous video calls and a few e-mails. I'm reminded of Bill apologizing before he questioned me at the hospital that night. I'm reminded of Kevin questioning me in that cramped office in municipal court just before the hearing, while he flipped through the case file that he'd barely had a chance to look at beforehand. It's just a lot of men demanding that I tell them things.

I set up my computer so that I'm decently lit and have an unbusy wall behind me, showing just the edge of one of my mother's bright paintings from her abstract period in the sixties. I can see a framed print behind Evan. It's something to do with wine, so I think he's in his dining room or kitchen.

I'd already e-mailed him about the possibility of keeping my maiden name, which is also my pen name, out of court. I'm not at all well known in any way, even among people who love books, but I don't want the jury and any spectators to be able to Google me. Professionally, I've put a lot out there, in that desperate way that authors do. It's not just Facebook and blogging; it's reviews and interviews and articles, which I don't control. I've kept photos of my kids to a minimum, just one of the whole family on my public Facebook, but there's a slideshow tour of our house on a newspaper site. I don't mind people seeing it if they come via an interest in my work, but coming from the courtroom is too intimate.

Evan's not sure it can be managed. While he doesn't mind using my married name, or even just my first name, he can't force the defense to do so, and it could be confusing for witnesses on either side who will be referring to original documents that use Winslow. I give in that it will have to be mentioned. It would be more no-ticeable to make a big deal out of it. He offers that we'll mention both names at the start, then just stick with "Mrs. Stark" or "Emily" during my testimony. That way, we deemphasize Winslow, but if other people use it it won't seem like a contradiction or mistake.

Besides, we're in luck! A Pittsburgh doctor who murdered his wife with cyanide will be on trial the same week as us. That case will suck up all the press. Our small drama will be of little interest to anyone. I don't feel demoted at all; I feel relieved. I hate the thought of being written about by anyone else. That's mine to do.

There will be spectators allowed, Evan answers me. But, besides a few retired folk (who will probably attend the cyanide trial), spec-tators in this court tend not to be the general public. The judge will have more than just our case going on. We'll be her big case, her jury case, but she'll still have pleas, motions, and other business to take care of, on something like twenty other cases. During our breaks, she'll work on those, and those attorneys and others involved may well hang out and watch our case unfold. Maybe they'll be checking out how the judge or attorneys handle things, in anticipation of their own cases; maybe they'll just be bored.

Because we have a "trial start date" of Tuesday, October 21, I had assumed that the jury would be picked that Monday, the day before. But, no, Evan says that they'll be chosen Tuesday. His preferences: blue collar; empty nesters with kids in college who'll be emotional about my having been in college when it happened; no lawyers; no one with close ties to someone who's been charged with rape.

Depending how long that takes, I'll testify either late Tuesday or early Wednesday. This could push things out a bit. If testimony doesn't start until Wednesday, and the jury is therefore sent to deliberate on, say, Friday, there's no guarantee that they'll have a verdict by the end of the day. I might have to stay over the weekend for a Monday verdict. I note to make provisional hotel arrangements. The one near the courthouse tends to get full.

More significantly, Evan says that except for my testimony I'll be sequestered until closing arguments. I'll not be allowed in the courtroom for any of it. Hearing what the other witnesses say could taint my version of events. Even after I've had my turn, I have to stay unaffected by others in case Evan needs to call me to the stand again.

That's not what I was expecting.

That's not what I want.

I'd accepted that I would probably be sent out during Georgia's testimony, but the rest of it I wanted to hear. I wanted to be able to look at Fryar as he listened to other people. I wanted to understand what was happening in there. I won't be allowed in, and I won't be allowed to even ask about what's happening in there, not until it's over. What the hell am I going to do for three days? Georgia is fine with sequestration; she hasn't planned to stay for the verdict. She's just testifying and then going home. But that's not what I want.

I won't even be allowed to talk to Bill or Dan or Aprill about any of my testimony experience, or ask them about theirs, until after the verdict. I want to be with them, eat lunch with them, but what on earth are we going to talk about? I imagine, absurdly, bringing a board game or something. What else will there be to do?

Evan has no transcripts of Helen cross-examining a witness. She may have never even done it, that's how green an attorney she is. To Evan's knowledge, she's not bringing any experts in to testify, so I guess she's not going after the DNA like I'd expected Libbi would. Evan's okay with that at this point; the defense has had ample chance. He calls Helen's approach a "slow plea agreement." Fryar has nothing to lose by making his attorney pick at victim testimony and comb police reports for supposed contradictions. A single juror's reasonable doubt is all that it would take to make a mistrial.

I remember that Evan had said before that my practice testimony would need to be witnessed by a police officer, but Evan's alone today. He's says we're not doing a full practice tonight, just a warm-up using the parts leading up to the attack. We'll do the rest in person on the Monday before trial, at the courthouse, in the district attorney's conference room. After that he'll show me our courtroom, and the "witness room" where I'll wait to be called in.

But even that Monday practice won't be like the real thing. That practice will focus on all of the facts, but only the facts. During the actual questioning, he'll ask all the same things as we'll have prepared, and then also "How did that make you feel?" each step of the way. Just thinking about it, I frown and lean back, which is exactly why he's going to ask it. Those emotions that I'm protecting are the ones he'll need on display.

He reckons that I'll be on the stand for less than an hour. About twenty minutes for direct examination from him, twenty for cross-examination by the defense, then maybe five for redirect by him—that's questioning me again—if there's anything he wants to clarify. He warns me that he might be sarcastic if he needs to point out that something the defense asserted was stupid. That would delight me.

He'll do the work, both the work of controlling direct examination, and the work of defending me under cross-examination, either through objection or on redirect. My only job is to tell the truth.

We practice, just up to Fryar pushing me into my apartment. Then he role-plays as the defense in response, to let me practice that, too.

First he tries pointing out that while I described, both just now and at the hearing, seeing Fryar for the very first time when I exited my apartment that evening, the police report only mentions my seeing him (again) on my way home. Evan pushes and pushes, asking "Well, which one is true?" and I say that of course they're both true. I did see him on my way home, as the police report describes, and I'd also seen him on my way out before, which I'm saying now, and always remembered. I guess it didn't seem important enough to mention to the police or, if I did tell them, important enough to them to write it down. I'm raising my voice.

Evan and I crack up. I'm losing my temper. "No, no, no," he chides me. He says that while my tone wasn't yet over-the-top, he's pretty confident that he could have gotten me to flare up with just a few more verbal pokes. He tells me, "Don't get pissed off." He gives me magic words to say to the defense if she tries to trip me up or to pretend that there's contradiction where there isn't any: "I am telling the truth." Together, they make a good mantra, part to tell myself, and part to tell the jury and everyone who's listening: *Emily, don't get pissed off. Everyone, I am telling the truth.*

He offers a caveat: Don't let her disrespect me. Don't let her get away with raising her voice at me. I'm allowed to react to that. But I must match her tone. If she's being civil, even while twisting my words and insinuating things, then I must be civil back to her. Even one juror taking a dislike to me can scupper the case.

This is when Evan's laptop gets low on power. He carries it through to another room to plug it in. There's football on a flat screen in the background. There are curtains on two little high, square windows. It's homey. He says that he's getting married in November. He doesn't have any gray hair at all.

He tells me that his fiancée says that he gets intense once a trial starts, and that I shouldn't expect him to be chatty or social even on breaks or during lunch. He doesn't want that to hurt my feelings. He won't be able to tell me about anything I'm sequestered from or even just how it seems to be going. That's okay, though. I appreciate the heads-up. It isn't his job to look after me. It's his job to win.

He'll have a list of facts to ask me about, not a scripted list of questions. He wants the phrasing of those questions to be spontaneous in front of the jury, just like my answers should be. We'll practice the topics but not the exact things we'll say.

I ask, as I'd asked Kevin, about vocabulary. When we get to the relevant part I want to say that Fryar "fucked" me. I mean, what other word am I supposed to use? Evan says no. Again, what if a juror doesn't like that? What if that word choice makes one of them think less of me? And, amazingly, he says that he would have to then define what fucking is, in case any jurors don't know. I gape. He shrugs. He prosecutes a lot of sex crimes, and apparently he's had jurors who aren't quite sure to what specific act that word refers.

I want to use it because it has that aggressive, angry tone that the physical act had had. It's not "sex" to me; I like sex. I suppose it's intercourse, but that sounds like something in a textbook.

We agree on my saying that at that point he "raped" me, which still isn't quite right, because I think of the whole thing as rape, not just the fucking. But I agree, and we move on, him smoothly adding that he'll follow "raped" up with "Do you mean that he put his penis in your vagina?" Just in case those people who don't know what fucking is don't know what raping is either.

I think about having to be sequestered. What I want isn't going to happen, so now I have to pick different things to want.

Instead of sitting in the courtroom for the whole thing, I'll have about two days of sitting outside of it. I know that I don't have to sit there; I can go anywhere I want; but I can't imagine going any farther away than I'm forced to. Maybe in the end I will go for a walk, or back to the hotel, or out and about on some distracting day trip, but for now all I can imagine is sitting outside the room, observing who comes and goes, trying to read on their faces and in their postures what's just happened inside.

Instead of comparing impressions with Evan and the detectives, we'll have to not talk about it. How on earth are we supposed to not talk about it? They'll be as sequestered from me as I'll be from them and I won't be able to share anything.

Evan has been on the fence about Bill testifying anyway; he says that he likes to keep his cases lean. Throwing in a lot of police on top of victim testimony and DNA can make a case more confusing rather than more convincing, and gives the defense more people to bluster against.

So I ask Evan to keep Bill off the list. If Bill's not testifying, then he can talk to me about the case, and he can be in the room when it's my turn. He could in fact watch the case for me while I wait outside alone, but it feels more important to have him out in the hallway with me.

It's strange to think of Bill as expendable to the case. He was, after all, the detective. But he's been treated this way from the start of this prosecution, as has Georgia's original detective. Cases aren't intended to be personal. Once police move on, their ties are cut. He only learned about Fryar's arrest because I tracked him down and told him.

I've been thinking of myself as lucky to have him, but perhaps he's also lucky to have me. What a mixed-up way to think of things. How surprising. But maybe it's true all over: maybe I don't need to feel so hat-in-hand grateful all the time. Maybe we're all just lucky to have each other.

Having made my choice regarding Bill, I still need someone to watch the case for me. Someone will have to tell me afterward what happened besides the bare bones that will be in the transcript, give me all of those tells and tones that say as much as words do. I can't let this be a big blank, not after coming this far.

Several American friends had offered earlier to be available or even to drive or fly should I change my mind about not wanting people to watch the trial. I start asking around, to find someone to attend court for me, to be able to tell me later what I'll have missed.

I tell friends that I've had my first practice with Evan and that I must not get angry on the stand and must not swear. Everyone says, "But, Emily! You don't swear anyway." Clearly, none of them spend much time inside my head.

I think I've figured out what's so maddening about the cross-examination questions. The ones I got at the hearing, and the ones that Evan's practicing with me now, aren't logical. I'm not just reacting personally; I'm offended and insulted by their ridiculousness, by the smoke-blowing that's all their side has. I think I'll get less crazy about it if I treat each question as isolated, and answer each one without worrying about the implications of my answers linked together. Evan promises that he'll point out the holes in the defense's assertions on redirect or closing if there's need. I have to trust

him, which I do generally, but this specific trust is a new step: I have
to live only from moment to moment and let him be in charge of
the overall arc of my story. That's a particularly difficult thing to ask
of specifically me.

At soccer-called-football coaching for W., I watch from a distance, enjoying the mix of happy homeschoolers kicking the ball
around, from hippie kids to Muslims in modest dress. I don't sit
with the other mothers. My oldest and therefore my closest homeschool friends are the parents of S.'s peers, not W.'s, so none of this
specific group know about the case. Right now I can't really talk
with people who don't. That isn't to say that I always make people
talk about the case. I'm really good about talking about other things.
I just need the knowing to be in the background, to be available for
me to tap into in passing if it comes up.

Afterward, at choir, Alice takes me into John's rooms one last
time before the new chaplain moves in. Some of John's books are
still on the shelves. The clock hasn't been wound and the pendulum
is still.

That was supposed to be my last self-indulgent peek. Still, the
very next day, I continue in my grief routine and on my way to W.'s
rehearsal walk straight through the college gate to John's wisteria-
crowded window. I've been doing that every time I've entered
the college since the funeral. I'm startled to see the Director of
Music inside, presumably in a meeting with the new chaplain. I
turn quickly away, embarrassed that Mark might have seen me, that
he might have witnessed my stupid ritual, and also tearful that my
stupid ritual of looking through that window is utterly, suddenly
over. I go to East House, where the choristers play on the sports
field until they're called in for rehearsal. I stand among little siblings
and picnicking mothers at my feet. I make cheerful conversation,
but I can't join them on the ground, can't relax. I blink fast and try
not to cry visibly.

I feel jittery and breathless every day now. I think some people can tell. Sometimes I catch the way I'm looked at, or someone makes an assumption in conversation that reveals that they were reading subtext into whatever unrelated thing I was saying.

I'm relieved that people think about it. I think about it, too, now literally all the time.

I had expected that attending the trial would be a passive experience, that I would get to be its audience. Now, with being sequestered, I'll be forced to make more active use of my time. I'd like to smoothly change gears, make new plans, but because the timing is unpredictable—I don't know if I'll testify on the Tuesday or the Wednesday; I don't know if it will be one day or two or three from then to closing arguments—I can't really plan what to do and will just have to wing it when I get there. I don't like that, but, actually, I could never have expected the experience to be controlled, not really. Better to learn that clearly, in advance, than to be suddenly disappointed when the unexpected happens anyway.

I look up the witness room that Evan mentioned. From references online, it doesn't seem to be a private space for our courtroom, but rather a shared space for all of the trials going on in all of the courtrooms that day. I was joking when I wondered if Bill and I should play a board game or what, but I decide to actually bring travel Scrabble. I also decide to be on the lookout for witnesses from the cyanide murder, the way that one keeps an eye out for celebrities in Los Angeles or for Kennedys on Cape Cod. Maybe some cyanide witnesses will want to play, too.

I also look up where Fryar will be.

There are three "Bridges of Sighs" that I know of: in Venice, here in Cambridge, and in Pittsburgh. All three are beautiful, and all three have been important to me.

Venice is where my only aunt has kept an apartment for as long as I've been alive. I've visited their family there some summers, and they've let me use the apartment myself for occasional little trips during the school year while they were at home in Berkeley. Venice's much-photographed Bridge of Sighs connects the Doge's Palace and the old prison, long-ago convicts presumably sighing as they were sent from court to their cells.

Cambridge's Bridge of Sighs is named as a bit of a joke. There are several college bridges crossing the River Cam. Only this one, particularly gorgeous and belonging to St. John's College, is enclosed like the one in Venice. The joke is that students sigh on their way to or from exams.

Pittsburgh's Bridge of Sighs connects the historic jail and the courthouse, looming above a street, not a waterway. The county's new jail is a half mile away, on the edge of the Monongahela River; so the old jail, attached to the bridge, has now become an extension of the courthouse, for family and juvenile cases, and is also where prisoners about to be tried are transported to "begin their day," according to a narrated slide show called "Busted."

Photos show a room with metal tables and attached metal seats, separated from open toilets by a wall of glass cubes that presumably obscure but don't appear to provide actual privacy. The pictured defendants are either in prison uniform or casual clothes. I don't see any suits. Maybe I was wrong about what Fryar will wear. Wait—I see a couple of ties, over untucked shirts, so that's something. And, eventually, two suits, out of the dozens of pictured prisoners. They're all shackled at the legs, even the dressed-up few, and handcuffed together in pairs.

A female guard narrates cheerfully, "The fear of God I think has been put into these guys since they saw us wearing Tasers!" [chuckles] "Nobody wants to get Tased."

They're taken across the bridge in groups of eight, to the "bullpen," where they'll wait to be called to their courtrooms. It's "crowded and smelly," the narrator says. "[They're] sitting or standing, whatever they want to do." That really sums up jail for me, a place where a choice between sitting or standing is the full range of "whatever they want."

While all of this is going on, I still have to look after upcoming writing and promotion obligations, including tending my online presence, which I have not been paying enough attention to. In my monthly check to see what my name brings up on Google, I also check on Fryar's name. To my surprise, images that I haven't seen before pop up.

It's a page from a casting site, with a collage of photos. Three of them I recognize; the others are surprises, but they're all from that after-he-was-young-but-before-he-was-old midlife phase that is viscerally familiar to me. In his "further information," he claims to "sing, play Guitar and Bass, Dance, Rollerskate, Horseback ride and Bowl."

It surprises me that he does these things, both because anything that he does up off of my apartment floor surprises me, and also because he doesn't seem like the roller-skating or horseback riding type. Roller-skating seems not stereotypically masculine enough for "Butch Johnson." Horseback riding seems too expensive a pastime to be within his reach.

Mostly, though, it stirs memories of my own acting résumé from years and years ago. It was a desperate attempt to be everything, to prove useful to someone. If you could stay upright on ice, you could claim to skate. If you could do any stroke, claim to swim. You could always quickly learn more if they decide that they want you. Failing to embrace and announce every tenuous skill could lose you a commercial.

That aching desperation for validation feels terribly young and long ago, and yet terribly present. I, too, want to be good enough by some external measure, though I'm less willing to pretzel myself into some unfamiliar version of myself to get it. That's partly why I left theater; or, more precisely, why I didn't get started in it after I graduated: I was tired of readying myself to fulfill every possible role. It was enough work just trying to be myself, never mind the "everyone else" I was supposed to be able to instantly turn into if casting required it.

This talent page leads to a reference to a play that Fryar had been cast in almost exactly a year ago. He mentioned on the talent site's Facebook page on August 31, 2013, that he was cast in a show to be performed in Harlem on September 21. September 12 is when he was arrested in his home at six in the morning, maybe dreaming of future fame which was then replaced by the reality of this prosecution.

His girlfriend—well, I don't know for sure that she was his girlfriend but they shared a Brooklyn address—had shared the poster for this play on her Facebook wall on September 16. So, four days after arrest, he must have still had some hope of getting back to it, or at least she had hope for him.

Six months later, in March of this year, she posted a quote that "A relationship with God is the best relationship you can have." Perhaps that was her solace after a decision to break up with him.

Fryar's sister is still going all-caps gangbusters on Facebook, wishing friends "HAPPY BIRTHDAY" and praising God. I'm equally opaque about the trial on my Facebook wall, posting about, for example, the wild neighborhood peacocks I'd like to tame.

This is what I mean about conversation. I can speak lightly about light things. I'm just relieved that some people see through it.

I save random people's Flickr photos of Pittsburgh's courthouse to my iPad. I can show them to people as conversation starters; they're not so off-putting as photos of Fryar. I still need excuses and prompts for talking about any of it.

It's a grand building. There are many, many tourist shots to choose from, of stairs and arches and elaborate interior streetlamps; of flags and a fountain. Tourists review the place, too, but it's not just tourists doing that. A court witness reports on Yelp that "despite the solemnity of the building itself, I was surprised at how friendly the staff was to me. Advocates, guards, and prosecutors alike greeted me with smiles and pats on the shoulder." On TripAdvisor, someone at the courthouse for "work" describes it as "dated, but historical. clean, nice staff." A Foursquare user advises, presumably regarding security, "Don't wear a belt." Others add, "I hope you packed a lunch because the waiting game here is soo serious" and "Prepare to sit here all day." One of the Flickr photos is, appropriately, an artistic close-up of a bench.

I've been practicing waiting all year. I'm ready.

18

The trial is imminent, but I have to get through John's memorial service first. Thanks to the college and the Church of England, there are systems in place, duties and milestones, that channel our emotions and energy. We're being let to come down from grief gently, rather than expecting the dramatic, near-immediate funeral to have ended it all.

The service is lovely, with a tone of gratitude for having known him instead of the shocked anguish of the funeral three months ago. It's good to have one more ceremony, one more significant moment. I would hate if we'd been expected to start the new term as if everything were all right again. John being gone is going to become normal, but it's never going to be all right.

At the gathering afterward, a sweet friend asks me, amid a buffet of sandwiches and tea, a question I've been asked before. Well, it's not really a question. It's a compliment, assuming an altruism on my part that isn't true. She asks, rhetorically, if I'm going to trial to save all of the women who might have become Fryar's victims in the future.

Of course I'm pleased that he'll be stopped from having future chances to hurt anyone else. I'm glad for any women who'll never know that they were spared, and if I were faced with an opportunity that could stop any man like this, I would take it, for the sake of whoever would benefit. But that's not my first reason for doing this. My first reason is myself. Even without Georgia, even without any other victims at all, he deserves to be in court just for me. If I must justify myself by being a gift to others, perhaps setting an example and standard of valuing oneself is such a gift.

I suppose I could be accused of selfishness. That's what my friend was trying to spare me; she was framing my testimony as an act of generosity. Sometimes selfishness is part of survival, though, so I'm not sure I need saving from it. Besides that, how could anyone ever give if there were no one allowed to receive? Life would become one of those ridiculous, maddening pay-it-forward coffee chains where each person is obliged to pay not for themselves but for some random other, and no one, except the very, very last person, gets to actually accept a generosity. The corollary is that no one, except for the first, has really given.

Whenever I give, I want the gift to be embraced, not passed on thoughtlessly, automatically, as if truly accepting something were inherently crude. I want to create delight, not obligation. So, likewise, when I receive gifts, I take them with both hands. I show my gratitude by showing my pleasure. I hold tight and say, *"Mine."*

This friend tells me more, about how she's encouraging the young women in her life to listen to their instincts because of me, and to seek out public places when they don't feel safe. That's good advice, but it echoes the questions that Evan threw at me in the cross-examination role-play: *Well, were you scared or not? Why did you go into the building if he made you uncomfortable? Why did you go up to your apartment? Why didn't you go back to the shops?*

Of course, if I could live just that one night over, I would turn around, walk away, and stay on bright and busy Walnut Street. But in order to have made that choice that one night, I would have had to have been on high alert as a standard; I would have had to live like that all the time, and to be living like that now. Of course I would change that one night if I could, but I don't want to change every other night of my life, to live in a continual state of suspicion, which is what it would take. That's too high a price. Ultimately, I don't regret what I did on January 12, 1992. I'm not the one who I wish had done things differently that evening.

Gavin and I are among the last to leave the postmemorial reception. The catering staff have been tidying around us for a while already. It was too irresistible to talk and talk with John's family, with ex–choir parents whose boys are no longer trebles, with a previous organ scholar now moved to Oxford and about to get married. We exit with the chapel clerks who had been in the car with John when he died. I don't know them well, and it feels presumptuous to talk to them, but I remember how much it hurt when people thought it was too presumptuous to talk to me after the hearing. So we talk, and walk to evensong together.

I've made the decision to act as if we at the college all love each other. I could be wrong about that, but it turns out that, most of the time, people do care; they just need permission to show it, and sometimes instructions. I've figured Cambridge people out: I just have to go first.

I fly in four days.

I'm blanking. People are, exactly as I'd wished, bringing the trial up, and I'm so surprised that I just keep talking about whatever the subject was a moment ago, or whatever I'd thought they were going to say. I'm incongruously cheerful, probably manic really. I send e-mails about the trial, yes, and also e-mails about parties and social arrangements, e-mails checking on other people's troubles, practical e-mails, congratulations, thanks, apologies, everything. Partly this can be explained as automatic behavior, my habitual way of being that's so ingrained that it can carry on even when my thoughts are elsewhere. But its excess at this time is perhaps a panic reflex, like some cats that strangely and desperately purr when they're frightened.

I post photos from my long-ago college performances on Facebook. All of them are from the eighteen months between the attack and graduation, because it was then that I was performing on the main stages, with full costumes and proper cast parties, and Mom and Dad bringing their camera. These were all taken years before digital cameras, way before smartphones and selfies, and I'd sentimentally scanned them into jpegs years later when I was pregnant with my first baby.

I'd sent Evan some questions from the friend who's kindly agreed to observe the trial for me. They're just practical questions, but there are a lot of them, and Evan asks me to Skype. I figure that it's just easier for him to talk than to write out the answers.

He looks serious on my little screen. I figure that he's had a long day in court. He prosecutes terrible things and it's to be expected that he'll look wrung out by them.

The background in his home is different from before, I notice: shelves this time. The ones on the right are full and the one on the left is empty. I wonder idly what's supposed to go there, or if the shelf itself, a neat square, might be decoration. I'm not worried about anything.

He starts with an apology. I think that he's going to tell me that my friend won't be allowed to sit in court, or won't be allowed to take notes. I start to feel annoyance at whatever bureaucracy is getting in the way, but only annoyance. I'm not afraid.

Evan speaks respectfully, and regretfully, but he might as well have jumped out and said, "Boo!"

He tells me that it's over.

The defense has filed a motion regarding the statute of limitations, just dutiful make-work for Evan to answer efficiently, citing the DNA exception law and the convictions in several similar cases that have come before us. But Evan, while preparing his response, discovered a federal Supreme Court decision that changes everything, and overrides the state law on which our case depends.

Our entire prosecution hinges on an extension of the statute of limitations, allowing for an extra prosecution year because we have a new DNA match. But a 2003 U.S. Supreme Court decision, *Stogner v. California,* responding to a child-abuse case using a similar extension, declared that retroactive extension of a statute of limitations is unconstitutional. The extension laws can only be applied to crimes not yet past their limitations when the extension law itself was passed. Pennsylvania's DNA exception was made law in 2004. Any Pennsylvania crimes still within their limitations at that time can benefit from it. My statute of limitations had expired in 1997.

The defense doesn't know. Evan will be obliged to tell them.

How could this have been a surprise, when the Supreme Court decided this more than a decade ago? But it involved California, not Pennsylvania. It applied to child abuse, not rape. It applied to an exception for child victims, not an exception for DNA. So long as Pennsylvania law and Pennsylvania precedent were clear, in this area which is clearly a state's purview not a federal issue, Pittsburgh's lawyers had had no reason to go looking. But state laws, independent as they are, are not permitted to contradict the Constitution.

By making an issue of constitutionality, the Stogner case put a state law on federal trial. Now that this ruling's been noticed, and its applicability to our case recognized, Evan can't pretend that it hasn't been, tempting though that may be.

I go to Gavin. "What did Evan say?" he calls out as he hears my footsteps, expecting details of practicalities.

"What's the worst possible thing he could have said?" I ask in return. We're not even in the same room yet. I'm crossing the living room, entering the dining room, nearing the playroom where Gavin waits on the couch.

"Trial postponed again?" he asks. That's literally the worst thing he can imagine that Evan was capable of telling me, but Evan has a lot more power than that.

Gavin spends hours researching precedents. Everything he finds confirms what Evan has said. The Supreme Court vote was a close one, 5–4. Gavin says wryly, "Never thought I'd agree with Scalia," one of the four dissenters. He and Evan Skype about it. I stay off camera, in tearful shock, but joke bleakly from the background to Evan: "Y'know, if you were a shitty lawyer this would never have happened."

The first day that I wake up knowing it's over is staggering.

Did you know that the reason that carbon monoxide is poisonous is not because it actively hurts you, but because it fills the space where oxygen should go? Carbon monoxide doesn't do anything violent to the inside of your body; it doesn't burn, or eat like acid; it just squats there, keeping what you need from getting in. That's what this feels like. Not like an active attack, but as though something essential is being kept away.

This feels like I'm not breathing, not because he's pushing down on my face this time, but because there's suddenly no air at all.

Try it: Hold your breath. Longer; don't cheat.

That's what this *nothing* feels like. It feels like good air is locked out.

———

The second day improves.

I've been spending all of the daytime hours, yesterday and today, in a guest room, away from the kids, and from any obligations. Gavin takes care of everyday life for me. I e-mail friends, but can't bear to talk on the phone or to meet.

I read and reread kind replies, dozens of e-mails and even a hand-written letter. One friend had mailed a cheerful good-luck note the day before, and then, when he saw my news that the trial is off, had panicked to hand-deliver an apologetic new letter to beat the arrival of the first. I treasure both messages.

Contact from my old theater friends makes me smile. They habitually use the word "beautiful," in a noun sort of way ("Hey, beautiful!" "Hello, gorgeous!") whether it's actually true or not. To actors, it's a reassuring, comforting word more than an objective compliment of physical reality. It's just something that they say to each other out of love. It means, *You have value.*

Georgia has asked Evan for my e-mail address. Our only contact so far had been at the January hearing, and I've agreed that he can give it to her. After all, without the trial to bring us together again, it's important to have some means of connection, to use now or maybe in the future.

Aprill is devastated. This affects not just our case, but, potentially, recent convictions of hers as well. She apologizes, not just for this abrupt end but for starting it at all, fearing that she has hurt me. I realize, in contrast, how truly grateful I am for what we've had at all: for the hearing, and even just for learning Fryar's name.

At one thirty in the afternoon in Pittsburgh, evening here, Evan formally withdraws the case.

On that first day hiding out in the guest room, when I'd sent emotional e-mails letting people know what had happened, I'd specifically chosen the words "devastation" and "humiliation" to describe my state of mind. Several of the replies had quickly assured me that there was nothing to feel humiliated about, and I knew that. I was in fact puzzled that the word had seemed necessary, but it truly had.

It's only in retrospect that I think I figure it out. Humiliation is present because I was counting on the conviction and sentencing to speak for me. To say that the man has been put in prison for what he did to me would demonstrate the crime's severity, in fact define it as a crime at all. A significant sentence of, for example, several decades (which was a real possibility), would surely get an awed, low whistle. I wouldn't have had to say any longer what had specifically happened, just what it had been worth: "The crime against me was given twenty-five years."

Now I'll never have that shorthand, or that objective, assigned value to present. Without that, everyone gets to make up their own minds about how much it matters. Everyone becomes a jury that I have to face separately, over and over.

Losing the conviction also means that I might lose the right to speak freely. I might now have to tack "allegedly" onto what I claim, or not say his name. Potentially having my truth filtered frightens me.

I haven't yet canceled the flights or hotel, because it feels like doing so would make me complicit in ending things. I decide to go anyway. As always, I feel the need to do something physical with my feelings. Yesterday, the urges were melodramatic: *Run away! Take pills!* That impulse has now homed in on a practical action: I must get to Pittsburgh.

The trial being canceled means that instead of going there to fulfill what Evan and the detectives needed me to do for the case, I'm the one asking for this to happen, for me. I'm hat-in-hand again. They don't need anything from me; I have to hope that they want to see me. It's daring and exhausting to honestly and directly say "I want" and "Please?"

But they're not making me ask. *Evan has offered,* I remind myself, offered me time in the courthouse or just time with him in the city, but it can feel bold just to take the chance that he really means it and say yes.

Everything is prepared already: tickets, reservations, the ride to Heathrow, even clean clothes ready to pack. Embracing the going takes less effort than canceling would.

I remember I'd wanted to run away back in 1992. I'd wanted to live that Amtrak journey between Pittsburgh and home for days instead of hours, blasting my Walkman on full volume and subsisting on cheese and crackers from the snack bar. It's the journey I'd wanted, not the getting anywhere. I'd wanted to be in that in-between, nowhere-yet place for a while. Similarly, I'd wanted to borrow my aunt and uncle's Venice apartment, unshutter the windows, and stare at the view. Both of those fantasies were of temporary, transitory places, and had something else in common, too: in them I was alone.

Some people don't believe that I'm an introvert because I'm not shy. I'm good at public speaking and at making friends, but I need a base of solitude from which to interact. I treasure my hiding spots.

I'm attached to too many people here in Cambridge. There's no place to run away to within this city. The whole point of running away is to become out of reach, if not unfindable then at least to become in control of the finding.

I tell everyone what's going on by e-mail. I touch from a distance, now from our guest room with the door closed, and soon from another continent. It's all funneled through words on my screen.

I love words. Through e-mail, all of these huge feelings are translated into manageable little bricks. The things they together build and represent may be enormous and chaotic and overwhelming, but as pieces they're not too big, not too much, not too wild. I know what to do with words, how to face them, then how to use them to respond. I already turn my feelings into words. The distance I'm creating by going away forces others normally close to me, normally within talking and touching distance, to do the same.

The night before the flight, I force myself to dress up and attend the service of Admission and Dismissal. I see people see me; I notice them notice that I'm here, in a prominent seat in the inner chapel. They smile, relieved for me that I've left the house.

The congregation then sifts down to become a smaller group for drinks after the service, then smaller again for a dinner party hosted by the former head chorister's mother. I'm quieter than usual, but still manage some chitchat, prompted by friends tossing me softball questions about books and music as those subjects are discussed around me. The teenagers are out together, for their own celebratory dinner elsewhere. Our young one is in another room, supposed to be falling asleep in front of a DVD of *The Empire Strikes Back*—but he loves watching it too much to sleep. It's just grown-ups around the table, so we can talk freely.

They all know, and, unlike after the hearing in January, no one pretends not to. It's lovely. They say kind things. The prosecution—now the loss of the prosecution—is a big subject, but not the only one. We ebb and flow, into it and away from it again. The conversation is balanced just the same as what's inside my head: Pittsburgh is there, prominently, but so is lots else. The difference between what's in me and what's outside of me used to be horribly uneven. In January, and also at my lonely low-point at the end of this summer, I was full with thinking about it, so inflated by the subject that it seemed to be pushing my skin outward, while outside of me few spoke of it at all. Now the stopper's been pulled, and the overflow has leaked out of me. When the subject is shared among all of us, it's not nearly so overwhelming.

The dinner ends. We indulge, picking from ten different flavors of ice cream for dessert, amazed at how we're being spoiled.

The next morning, I fly.

19

I'd been in Pittsburgh nine months earlier for the hearing, but I hadn't looked around me. All I'd perceived then had been the individual insides of a few buildings, bounded by a robust winter.

I look at the city this time, compare it to home in Cambridge, and to my college years.

It's different from Cambridgeshire in being aggressively hilly instead of relentlessly flat, and in its typically colorful, northeastern-American autumn, compared to the drab browning of England's leaves.

It's different from 1992, in flashy renovations of the football stadium and Point State Park, and the addition of a massive convention center and riverside casino.

It's different from being here as a college student, in a rut around the neighborhoods of Oakland, Squirrel Hill, and Shadyside, and instead centered on life as a visitor and adult in a downtown hotel.

Maybe all of these self-consciously stylish restaurants are new, or maybe they were here before, and how would I know? I hardly came downtown at all back then.

On the taxi ride from the airport, eighteen hours since I left my house this morning, I keep my eyes open for that moment that the downtown skyline appears. You can tell Pittsburgh from other cities by the mirrored turrets of Pittsburgh Plate Glass, a childishly simple, castle-themed skyscraper. I remember, as a student in my parents' car, loving the suddenness of that view, how completely the city appears, all at once.

The newspaper outside my hotel room door Monday morning has this headline, above the fold, on the front page: LEGAL TITANS TO TUSSLE IN CYANIDE HOMICIDE TRIAL. Evan was right; that's where the attention is.

I've been e-mailing with Georgia. She canceled her Pittsburgh plans when the case was withdrawn, and I let her know that I'd kept mine. I encourage her to come to Pittsburgh, too. I'm glad to be here.

Evan meets me in the hotel's grand lobby, under sparkly chandeliers. He is, of course, in a dark suit, white shirt, power tie: lawyer uniform. I'm wearing the blazer I'd always planned to testify in, but with jeans, because there's no jury to judge the appropriateness of my clothes. I even have on red lipstick, instead of pink. It's freeing not to have to worry about how I'm coming across.

I've already told Evan that I want to see the courthouse, so he walks me straight there, just a couple of blocks away. Their security is a much less rigorous version of what I'd passed through yesterday when leaving from Heathrow and changing planes in Charlotte. I get to keep my shoes on! And my jacket! It feels positively welcoming.

Evan points out where the entrance used to be a floor higher, before the city was regraded. The whole morning, he alternates between tour-guide-ish architectural commentary, behind-the-scenes life-of-an-assistant-district-attorney details, and talking about our trial, what might have been. He knows that I like information, and he's generous with it.

I see his office, for the five "child abuse" (and related crimes) ADAs, five desks mashed together in a very small room, the tightness of which is compensated for by very large windows with good city views. His boss's desk is one of those five, and the nameplate on it tells me that she's Jan Necessary, the excellent and excellently named prosecutor from the transcript Evan had given me over the summer. Evan gestures toward a leather jacket over the back of a chair, and says, "Aprill's here."

It's partly because of Aprill that I was able to overcome embarrassment over wanting to come to Pittsburgh anyway. When she'd said that she regretted having started this prosecution, for my sake and Georgia's, I'd thought, *Don't you dare wish away what I did get.* It's bad enough that this is stopping here, but it would be worse to lose any of the rest of it. Hoping to comfort her had made me feel like I might be needed here, not just allowed.

My preparation for seeing the courthouse had consisted of photos, mostly of the grand staircase and its archways and lamps. Evan's tour takes me instead up and down the back stairs, into the busy, overflowing offices that are the stages of an attorney's progress up the ranks. Boxes and files are everywhere. I ask him if my file will be destroyed. He promises that it will be stored.

He takes me toward the courtrooms. The building's wide corridors, which in the artsy photos are solemn and empty, are full of stressed-out, waiting people, mashed together like the attorneys' desks. They're everywhere. They're bored. They're not allowed to use their phones here, on floors three or five, where all of the courtrooms are. In front of us, a leg-shackled defendant shuffles alongside an escorting officer. Behind us, Kevin, my prosecutor from January's hearing, catches up. It turns out that he's one of the two "legal titans" prosecuting the cyanide case. He's welcoming and glad to see me, but understandably distracted. The newspaper had said that he would be calling "about 60 witnesses" and "laying out evidence police obtained through more than 80 search warrants." I'm ridiculously proud of him, "my" prosecutor, even if for only one day in January.

Later, I'll tease Evan in front of his fiancée that Kevin hadn't minded me swearing on the stand. Evan will start to explain that it's different with a jury, and I'll assure him that I know, I know. It's just funny. Evan is careful in his speech, to avoid bad habits that could pop out in court. He says just "bull" not "bullshit"; he calls the defense from my hearing an "ass" not "asshole." It's sweet. He adores his job. He's not ambitious at the moment to get any higher, to judge, for example, because he likes what he gets to do now. He likes his role in court. He gets to argue against crimes that really deserve it.

The courtrooms, each one belonging to a different judge, are as chaotic inside as the corridor. No juries are in them yet, but things are already happening, in small clusters: motions and postponements and paperwork. Evan needs to find the defense for a case that's supposed to happen today, but which he thinks is going to be put off. Even with all of that going on, he points out to me the historic half-electric, half-flame chandelier in one courtroom, and other touristy details. No one even glances at us. Everyone has their own urgent business. Everyone's talking at once.

We finally get to what would have been my courtroom. Aprill's there, waiting to testify in a different case. This judge is part of the county's sex-crimes specialty court. Aprill must testify in this room a lot.

She seems surprised and nervous to see me. "You're here already?" she asks. Her mood makes me realize the power that I have over her, as the wronged victim. I'm the judge of whether attempting this prosecution was worth it. But there's no chance to talk more right now.

Evan shows me everyone's seats as they would have been: his, with either Aprill or Dan, at one table, then the defense and Fryar at the other. He brings me to the witness stand as my seat, though it would only have been my seat for less than an hour. It's next to the judge on one side and the jury on the other. Evan walks me to the jury box's other end, where he would have stood to ask the questions, in order to have forced me to look at them when I answered, just by looking at him. From there, he'd also have known if they could hear everything. He repeats something he'd said to me when we practiced, about taking care of everything else. All I would have had to do was tell the truth, one answer at a time.

The room is buzzing with other people's work. It doesn't feel formal enough. It feels out of control. I like being a writer in part because I like quiet places. Nothing is still here. I'd thought a courtroom would feel like it's made of strong, clean rectangles, but this one feels like sparks and swirls.

Out from the overwhelming courtroom, back into the overwhelming corridor. We visit the room where jurors wait, with vending machines and a sign on the inside of the door reminding them DO NOT GO INTO THE HALLWAY unless they've been specifically dismissed for lunch or for the day. Near to that room is the "bullpen" where the defendants wait. There's a special back entrance so that there's no chance of jurors seeing any of them arriving with their shackles still on.

Evan's case is postponed, as he'd thought it would be. He finds the detective who had been supposed to testify, to send him home. That detective rolls his eyes when Evan tells him that he'll have to help bring in a certain witness next time, a child. Afterward I ask what the guy's problem was, and Evan says, "I know, right? You saw that?" I think I'm lucky that my police and my lawyers like each other.

We go for a walk. The Point, where the Monongahela and Allegheny Rivers converge to make the Ohio River, is one of my favorite spots. The park has been significantly renovated since my time, and the fountain shoots up a neck-stretching 150 feet. Evan points out the new football stadium and new casino across the water, and the church up on Mount Washington where he's getting married next month. Predictably, we talk about weddings, and gambling, and sports. It's a game day, and all over town we see people in Steelers jerseys.

Evan tells me that he and his fiancée are going to watch the game on TV tonight, and get pizza. Would I like to come over to their apartment then?

I spend a lot of time with polite people, and it often takes something extra to get me to believe that I'm truly welcome, not just being treated nicely out of habit. This is that extra thing.

We go out for really good burgers, at a business-lunchy, all-of-the-customers-in-suits restaurant that Aprill later tells me Evan's colleagues got jealous about when he told them he'd taken me there.

Over sweet-potato fries, I tell him that we're okay, me and him, only because there are a lot of people in England and beyond who are really, really angry with him right now, for scuppering the case. One choir dad's leg shook when he talked about it. They're taking care of that emotion, so I don't have to be angry myself.

Evan says that he's angry, too.

Jet lag is getting to me. I droop while we wait for the waitress to take Evan's credit card. He walks me back to the hotel so that I can take a nap before the Steelers kick off.

Fryar was supposed to have been released "within forty-eight hours" of Evan dropping the case on Friday, but the jail doesn't release on weekends. So, Fryar will have been released today, Monday, maybe while I was in the courthouse, or maybe while Evan and I ate lunch, or maybe while I was resting.

The "forty-eight hours" rule is a fairly recent improvement over the previous "forthwith," meaning "immediately," which had often resulted in prisoners being set free, unprepared, in the middle of the night. There's now an effort made to allow prisoners phone calls, help with a place to stay or a bus ticket, and three days' worth of meds. It's a kindness to the prisoners, but they're understandably impatient at the time it takes, and some chafe at the delay. A captain working at the Discharge and Release Center is quoted in the newspaper saying that the about-to-be-free are "like racehorses ready to go. They have no tolerance."

Because Fryar had gone Christian in jail, he may have become part of a "pod" for prisoners interested in faith-based self-improvement. These prisoners are given mentors upon release. Fryar may actually have some support. He might be staying in Pittsburgh after all. Evan told me that he's not been taken back to New York, which I'd thought may have been required, a kind of extradition in reverse.

Whether Fryar's out and about here in Pittsburgh while I am, or later free in New York when I visit friends, family, and colleagues there, he's unlikely, Evan has pointed out, to ever cross my path. When is he going to be in the same shop as me? In the same hotel, or theater, or café? Evan's confident that class separates us almost as effectively as prison bars. He didn't say the word "class" out loud, but it was implied.

Of course, that didn't stop Fryar's life from intersecting with mine before. And what about: same church, same library, same park, same sidewalk? Still, I accept Evan's reassurance about the unlikelihood of a happenstance meeting, and I agree with him that Fryar is even less likely to purposely seek me out. There would be nothing in it for him.

Evan and his fiancée, Jessie, pick me up outside of my hotel. She's an immigration lawyer, so I presume that she, like Evan, has been in a suit most of the day. Right now, though, they're both in Steelers sweatshirts. They're ready to cheer on the home team.

We drive by a local pizza place to pick up an order on the way to their apartment. There's a salad already prepared on the kitchen counter, and in the fridge a six-pack of "seasonal" beers, from which I choose pumpkin-flavored.

I confess that I don't really watch football, and they explain the action patiently as things happen. Over commercials, we chat about my kids, and Evan and Jessie's upcoming wedding, and house hunting. Evan slips into Pittsburghese a couple of times and says "needs washed" and "needs fixed."

I ask Jessie what she knows about my case, and the answer is "not much" beyond the basics, and the overall legalities of why it fell apart. Evan doesn't reveal personal details about the cases he represents, even to her, though he will speak generally. She said that it was weird, when they were first dating, to observe how he could talk so matter-of-factly about terrible things, even child abuse. He has to; she understands that. But Jessie herself has no poker face, and shows her emotions clearly. She had to learn that he does care and is affected, despite his neutral expression. He serves his cases better by remaining at a distance. She's the reason that he'd warned me, when we still had a case, that he would be distant during trial, even on break.

She's the one who reacts now when I talk about 1992, specifically about the hospital afterward, and the kind nurses. I keep thinking about them, and this week I bring them up with everyone: their sweet sadness over me, and that I tried to cheer them up, and that Bill's arrival made them blush. They're a Greek chorus backing up my tragedy. I tell it like a happy story, that there were so many kind, empathetic people, and Jessie looks upset herself. She looks sick to hear it. Her face reminds me that it's actually a sad story. Well, it's both.

While Jessie washes our pizza plates, I confide in Evan that Georgia's reaction is stressing me out.

She's handling the case derailment very differently from me, and her upset rattles me. She's angry; she regrets testifying; she feels betrayed. Her e-mails make me realize how precarious my seemingly stable emotions actually are. Sure, I can watch football and tell jokes, but just inches away on either side is a long, long psychological drop. I need her to not jostle me. She's still considering, with rising panic, whether to join me in Pittsburgh.

The Steelers win at eleven thirty. Evan and Jessie drop me off at my hotel at midnight. Staying up late has done wonders for getting me adjusted to the time zone, but more importantly it's assured me of their care. You don't have someone to your home that you don't like. You don't keep friends over till midnight unless you're having a good time. I trust Evan. I believe him that he would have gotten distant during trial, but we never got that far. He's felt close.

Tuesday morning, I sleep in past five. This is a biological victory; the week I was here for the hearing, I never managed to sleep later than four.

In this morning's paper, the headline on the local section's front page is SUSPECT IN TWO SHADYSIDE RAPES IN 1992 RELEASED ON A TECHNICALITY. A law professor quoted in the article says that "It may be fair in the sense that this is what the law says, but it's definitely not just."

I wash my hair, and primp, and indulge in many cups of coffee; I'm sensitive to even the decaf that I've ordered and can't drink this much at home, but when I'm jet-lagged I know I'll sleep anyway. Bill's meeting me at ten, after he teaches an early class at the university.

I'm between him and Evan in life stage. Evan is just thirty, about to be married, looking to transition from renting to homeownership. Bill, in contrast, is past me, with a daughter in college and an empty nest looming when her brother catches up. He carries himself with effortless authority, smoothly holding every door open. He takes me to the Frick historic house and art collection, near his home. I see his old "commander" badge in his wallet when he opens it to pay for our tickets.

We meander in the greenhouse while waiting for the house-tour start time. I admit that I've now explicitly asked Georgia not to come, not this week. Late last night, in the face of her distraught vacillation over it, I'd rescinded my invite, backpedaling that she doesn't need to, that she shouldn't stress herself. She can come later to tell Aprill how much she hurts and beg Evan to fix things, which is what I think she most needs to do. That's not what I need. We can take our turns here in Pittsburgh.

Today would have been the start of trial. Evan would have been choosing a jury, using one of the questionnaires that he showed me. Bill and I would have been waiting in the witness room, or hanging out in that no-phones-allowed busy hallway.

Instead, we tour a pretty, pretty house, decorated not just in the latest fashions of its time but with things made from the latest technologies, such as ceiling and wall friezes made of molded paper and aluminum. The tour patter is well written and well delivered, but Bill is quick to point out that it glosses over Frick's robber-baron brutality. He buys me a favorite book of his as a souvenir, the story of Frick and Carnegie's contentious relationship and the bloody Homestead Steel Strike, to balance out the tour's rosy picture.

Besides having to take time off work right in the middle of the semester to be with me today, Bill has another significant thing that he's set aside for me. I knew that his nephew had been killed by a drunk driver earlier in the year. I didn't realize that that driver's trial is this week. I apologize profusely, but Bill tactfully insists that I'm a good excuse for him to take a breather. He smiles. We have lunch in the café. We visit the art collection. We walk in the nearby park, under autumnal trees, past lawn-bowling courts. Everyone has their own reasons to be sad, I realize, though I already knew it. It's just that sometimes I forget.

Bill points out his happy-looking yellow house, then drives me back to the hotel.

It's less than an hour before Dan's picking me up.

I check my e-mail, and Google around. The Associated Press story on the dropped charges against Fryar is appearing in newspapers all over the country, at least on their websites. One site even recycles that unflattering video still of my lower body exiting municipal court. Seeing the story fill the search-engine results feels big, but I remind myself that it isn't the same as its being in printed newspapers. In other cities, the story is filler, tucked away in back pages if it makes the hard-copy papers at all. Only in Pittsburgh is it an actual, if brief, story, credited to named staff writers.

Dan is less confident than Bill and Evan. He cautiously parks elsewhere and walks to meet me in front of the hotel, instead of swooping his car in front of the taxi stand to scoop me up. It turns out that he lives right near Bill, right near that park and the Frick house, just over the border in Squirrel Hill, one of the college neighborhoods I once lived in. We drive there to pick up his wife, Christine. I'd specifically asked for her to join us, because she'd come to the hearing. She'd acted as interpreter of Dan's aloof manner; if it weren't for her, I wouldn't have known how much Dan cares.

It turns out that all of them—Dan, Evan, Bill, April, and their assorted partners—are local; well, I'm not sure about Aprill's husband, but the rest for sure. Dan and Christine even went to the same high

school as Evan and Jessie, albeit two decades apart. I hear the accent
in Dan when he pronounces "steel mill" as "still mill."

Christine is effusive, emotional, and has a lot to say. She's desperate over the withdrawal of the case, and delighted to see me, flitting
between outrage and good cheer. Above all, she and her itty-bitty
Yorkie are friendly hosts. She's tidied the house and shows off Dan's
sports-themed "man cave" in the basement. They've been married
just six years, which is shorter than I'd thought given Dan's age, near
Bill's. She's just grown her hair back from grueling breast cancer
treatments, which she was going through last fall while I'd been
badgering Dan for DNA results and extradition news.

We get in the car together, Christine and I both insisting that
the other take the front passenger seat. I win this round, and get
in the back next to the doggie car seat (empty; the pup is staying
home).

They give me a driving tour, first to East Liberty, which is the
most changed neighborhood since I lived here, now significantly
developed and becoming fashionable. That leads us into always
fashionable Shadyside, which is where I'd lived in 1992. I tense up.
I'm not sure if we're coming here on purpose. I decide to just go
with it, and ask Dan to drive straight down the main street. Most of
the shops have changed, but they still have the same tone: currently
popular brands appealing to young professionals and to college students with parental money to spend.

We get to the end of the shops. Dan has to understand where
we are, but he shows no reaction. Again, I make it specific: turn left.

My apartment building looks exactly the same. It's lit inside. I
see the door that Fryar caught behind me as I entered. The address
number is clearly visible: 911.

Dan doesn't stop. That's probably for the best.

He drives through Carnegie Mellon's campus. I hardly recognize it. A frenzy of building has taken place over twenty years, in

overwhelmingly matchy-matchy ivory-colored brick. Then I see it: Margaret Morrison, the building where I'd taken more than half of my classes for four years, with its distinctive rotunda. Its familiarity hits me and I say, "Oh!"

We drive through Oakland, University of Pittsburgh territory. I recognize nothing. My life at Carnegie Mellon had been insular, not just within the university, but specifically within the drama department. We didn't get out much.

We cross a bridge to the South Side, seedy with bars and tattoo parlors. Dan and Christine have stories. We cross again, to the North Side. Dan parks the car at police headquarters.

Sex Assault moved into this renovation of a carpet warehouse just over ten years ago, along with Homicide, Burglary, Robbery, and Narcotics, long after 1992. Still, I want to see.

It tickles Dan that their office is bigger than Evan's. It's a huge, wide-open space, with, to be fair, a lot more than five desks. You can tell Dan's by the Steelers bumper sticker, and Aprill's by the flower trellis, put up for either decoration or privacy (besides her local caseload, she's part of an FBI child pornography task force). I can also tell it's hers by her leather jacket on the chair, just like in Evan's office. She's here.

Depressingly, there's a play area for children, and car seats of various sizes, ready for emergency call-outs. There's an evidence room, full of bags and boxes. There's an interview room. I step inside.

The walls have a strange kind of insulation that I suppose might be to muffle sound. There's no two-way mirror, like on TV. I hope that there's some kind of recording system, but I don't notice any evidence of one. It could just be that I'm not looking around enough. I'm staring at just one thing: the leg iron permanently bolted to the floor.

We bump into Aprill on our way out. We chat just enough for her to say that she has to cancel meeting with me the next day; the case she was in court for on Monday has unexpectedly dragged on. I'm sure that that's true, but I wonder if it's also a relief to her, to be able to avoid me.

Dan drops Christine and me off at a restaurant to get a table while he finds parking. While we wait to be seated, I show her photos of Gavin and the kids on my iPad. She oohs at my wedding pictures, and tells me about her and Dan's city-hall elopement. We're shouting over the vigorous thrum of conversation in this clearly popular spot, full up on a Tuesday night.

We get a table, and great meatballs, and mostly talk about how Christine and Dan met. When Dan gets uncomfortable with that, we talk about the case. Christine reminisces about how badly Dan had wanted to go with Aprill to New York to interview Fryar, to try to prove the initial link between the two cases. But he hadn't been able to be away from Christine, because of her cancer treatments. I wish I'd known then that he'd wished he could go.

Christine is distraught over the end of the case. She wants to change the law. She wants to go to the press. She wants to fix it. I tell her what I've told everyone back home: the new law does fix it. The problem is that the Supreme Court says that we aren't allowed to apply the new law backward in time. Things are fixed going forward. They're just not fixed for me.

So we joke about revenge instead, about how wouldn't it be nice, when we're all of us together at dinner tomorrow, well alibied, if Fryar were hit by a car. I don't mean it, not really. Violence is ugly and death is terrible, no matter who it happens to. But we're angry and sad and still adjusting to the bad news, so we all three high-five over it.

Again, I bring up the hospital in 1992, and the sad-but-blushing nurses. They seem important, and somehow very relevant to this week. I was chipper with them to try to make them feel better, like I'm chipper now, but not because I was kind; it's because I was desperate. I think I perceived that we were connected: them, and my friends in the waiting room, and my college, and the police, and that any rising above that was going to happen was going to happen together. That's certainly what's going on now. That's why I can't be angry at Evan or Aprill or Dan. We're the good guys, together. It would be like being angry at myself.

The cyanide case is still in the headlines the next morning, with news of jury selection. Our case is not, and won't be, I suppose, ever again.

I e-mail everyone back home, to let them know that I'm safely here, that I've seen Evan and Bill and Dan and Christine, that there's a permanent leg iron in the Sex Assault interview room and that I watched the Steelers game Monday night. Rambling, mostly. I read replies all day, giggling at "Off to buy an Arthur Fryar doll and pins" and, from a Presbyterian minister, a desire to say something that "doesn't sound like pietistic bullshit." Two very different friends both call me admirably stoic, which confounds me. I'm actually outrageously emotional. *Aren't I?* It certainly feels that way from inside myself. Perhaps I misunderstand stoicism, which I think of as suppressing one's feelings. But one friend defines it as "accepting our fate, being thankful for what we have and for those around us, and, I think most importantly, focusing on what we can control." I suppose that is what I'm trying to do. I joke to the other friend that I prefer to be thought of as a "tough broad."

Kevin e-mails, offering to save me a seat for tomorrow's "exciting" opening statements in the cyanide trial. I can't accept because of my flight, but I'm delighted by the invitation.

Bill picks me up for our group dinner. He's made a reservation for all of us, which turned out to be surprisingly difficult for a Wednesday. The Penguins have a hockey game tonight. Pittsburgh is apparently utterly at the mercy of their teams' home games in terms of traffic, parking, and restaurant tables.

He has the car valet parked, and we wait at the bar for the others: Evan and Jessie, Dan and Christine. And Aprill, I hope. I don't want to miss her completely.

I ask Bill to order a martini for me. He tells me the good news of his latest promotion. It's not public yet, but I tell everyone about it as they arrive. None of them work at the university, so the announcement is safe with all of us. We're friends, right? It feels like we're friends.

At the table, I make sure to sit next to Aprill. Her case, which was over the molestation of a twelve-year-old, finished today. The prosecution lost. She's disappointed and frustrated, and now she has to deal with me.

I tell her, too, about the sweetly emotional hospital nurses in 1992, how I made jokes to them, and how Bill was really good at his job. He wasn't always in charge of people; he was a detective then, Aprill's and Dan's job now, and just Evan's age, married but not a dad yet. I was a student then. Aprill was, too. It was a long time ago.

Aprill says that things are better organized now, that victims don't have to repeat their stories, like I'd had to do, for the uniformed police, then the medical staff, then Bill. That is probably better, but right now I can only think that it's a privilege to get to repeat it. It's a privilege to be listened to.

I tell her, because she'll understand, how funny it was that the uniformed police in my apartment had kept insisting that I sit. But I was only half clothed, holding my short, unbuttoned dress closed with my hands, and my couch was white. White! *Of course* I couldn't sit. I roll my eyes. She laughs. *Men.*

Actually, there had been a woman officer along, but she hadn't said much. I think she'd been included as a token, just in case. Aprill says that the stereotype of victims preferring female officers hasn't been generally true in her observation. I agree that I hadn't cared one way or the other. The detectives had been men; the doctor had been a woman. I'd just wanted whoever was in charge.

One thing Aprill had wondered at my hearing in January is if it's off-putting to be questioned by specifically an *attractive* man. Let's just say that she thinks highly of Kevin.

I hadn't felt attracted to anyone in the stressful context of the hearing, so instead of answering her broader question, I get stuck on whether I agree about Kevin. I look into middle distance to consider and conclude, "I think Evan's way cute."

"Evan? Nah. *Kevin,*" she insists.

"Ha! Nope. Evan. Totally."

He's right there, on the other side of the table. I hope he hasn't heard. Aprill and I crack up. Well, ice broken, I guess. It's unfair that it feels harmless and flattering to be gossiping about the attorneys' looks while it would be appalling if they gossiped about ours, but there it is.

We share photos of husbands: mine, dark-haired and dark-eyed, holding our first baby thirteen years ago; then two summers ago at our fifteenth anniversary dinner, with grayed hair and wire-framed glasses, leaning confidently on a bar table while we wait to be seated. Aprill and her husband pose together in their uniforms, in an official "police yearbook" photo. He's a former city lieutenant recently turned small-town police chief. I share kid photos, my blond boy with retro glasses and my redhead whose gorgeous hair gets him stopped by Asian tour groups begging to take his picture. Aprill shows me a picture of her horse.

Maybe I am stoic. Am I supposed to act sadder? I am sad, but I don't know how that's supposed to make me act.

Dinner's almost over. My trip's almost over. I ask Aprill about whether she can work with Brooklyn police to find more recent cases to use against Fryar. New York's statute of limitations for rape used to be a paltry five years, but in 2008 became no limit at all. Any rape he committed from then would be fair game.

She says that she'll try, but New York hasn't shown much interest. She assures me that my file is still in the active case pile. It's difficult for her to put it away.

I worry, too, about who else might get hurt by Fryar, though maybe he's too old now. Maybe he's weak. I know that sexual vigor isn't required, that his urges could be translated into some variant act, but he would still have to be strong. He'd have to be fast. He might not be those things anymore.

Evan had wondered, on Monday, if maybe Fryar has just stopped. We don't know for sure that he's gotten anyone else after 1992. Well, his convicted burglary in 1994 may have been an attempted rape, but we don't know that he's done anything since getting out of prison a decade later. New York proudly claims to have no evidence backlog anymore, so any reported, swabbed rape of his from Brooklyn should have matched in the FBI database by now.

Christine is firing questions at Evan, still hoping that this case can be salvaged. It can't. Having to defend Evan to Georgia and to Christine this week has helped me. I know, profoundly, where we stand with the law. Ethically, he'd had no choice but to withdraw the case. I can't speak for anyone who might be hurt by Fryar going forward, but for me, just me, and what I was to get out of this, I understand.

Organization is a powerful, amazing thing. That a plane can fly, that rubbing strings and blowing in tubes and hitting things with sticks combine to make music, that thousands of words in a certain order make a story, and that there's a legal system at all, is a marvel. All that cooperation. All that assertion and risk taking and leadership and agreement to create these systems, these enormous machines. That the city made their courthouse beautiful; that tells me something. I can't hate the law, not completely. It's the law that got us this far, even if it's the law that's stopped us short of the finish line.

We're the last occupied table in the restaurant, and it reminds me of Evan taking me back to the hotel at midnight on Monday. None of them had had to come tonight; certainly none of them had to stay so late now. They must mean it, all of them; they're not just going along out of embarrassment for the way it ended, or just because I traveled so far.

The waitstaff are cleaning up around us. We gather coats and jackets off the backs of our chairs, and I push forward to tell Evan that I'm glad that he's my prosecutor, even though he destroyed the case. I assure him again, in front of impatient waiters, that even though he hurt me he did the right thing.

Back home, retrieving my UK power cord from the guest room where I'd had my laptop plugged in before I traveled, I find the paper towel on which I'd scrawled Evan's news that the case was over. I suppose it was the only thing I'd had at hand. I was trying to capture the words that I didn't recognize but would need again, and didn't get them quite right: *Supreme Court vs California. Stogner. 42 section 5552c1. Violates expo facto [sic—should be "ex post"]. Null cross [sic again—should be "nolle prosequi"]. Tolled.*

"Tolling" is a legal term that has to do with statutes of limitations, but it brings to mind solemn bells.

I slip the paper towel between pages of a notebook, like pressing a flower, so that it won't get thrown away.

People in Cambridge worry because I'm not visibly falling apart. I tell entertaining stories, about the surprising and casual familiarity of watching the Steelers on TV at Evan's apartment, and about the practical, boring-looking Sex Assault office at police headquarters transformed by the unexpected leg iron in the interview room, revealing their job to be suddenly violent and frightening. I'm good at stories.

Or perhaps my friends see through the cracks, and I am falling apart behind a superficial and practical sociability. Maybe falling apart is yet to come. It took me about a month from the arrest to fall apart in John's office.

I don't think that I'm denying, repressing, or avoiding. It's just that I feel that I'm not myself solely responsible for all of the reactions to the unsatisfying end of the case. I feel like I'm part of larger groups that are taking care of a lot of that for me: us then, my old drama friends; us here, my Cambridge friends; and us in Pittsburgh: Evan, Aprill, Dan, and Bill, with me. These last two groups, Cambridge and Pittsburgh, are newly hatched usses, created these past few months. Their anger and sadness tick boxes for me. They've got those feelings in hand; I get to express them, too, if I wish but I don't have to worry that they'll go unexpressed if I play with other feelings instead.

There's a definite sense in middle age that families are inside of hard boxes; everyone inside affects everyone else inside, and everyone outside of the box, that very small box, inside of their own separate very small family boxes, are cast only as observers. My Cambridge friends had felt it when I went to the hearing, that they had no right to act as if it mattered to them. I felt it when John died, that I had no right to grieve him as I was grieving. But it did matter to them, and I did grieve. I feel like those rigid boxes have folded down their sides, and we admit now how much we affect each other.

Besides, how can you expect the people inside of the family boxes to take care of each other? It's not fair to say that because Gavin loves me most that he's the one who should have shouldered this alone. It's precisely because he loves me that he was hurt by it, too, and in need of help himself. We needed care from all sides, from people a little bit distant, a little bit farther away, people who, while they felt the shock waves, weren't knocked over by them.

I've felt close to Bill since the hearing, but it wasn't until this trip that I've felt it with Dan and Aprill and Evan, too. Evan had said, when we ate those posh burgers and sweet-potato fries, that he'd wanted to offer to pick me up from the airport the day before, but had worried that that would be too forward because we hadn't yet met. His saying that had surprised me at first, but it was true, I realized, that we hadn't before that day met in person. Yet we had talked through such intimate, important things together over Skype, looking at one another, looking beyond each other at hints of our homes. I'd felt that I had met him already, and yet now that I've been actually in his home I see that it's different, profoundly different, to have been in the same place together.

It reminds me of when Gavin and I had lived on opposite sides of America seventeen years ago, me in Massachusetts and he newly transplanted to California from England. Talking on the phone had been daily; being together in person had been rare and treasured, monthly at best. We agreed one evening on the phone that getting married would be delightful, and that we ought to be courteous of the upcoming wedding of the friend who had introduced us. We could wait until a few months after her wedding, or really go for it and get married a couple of months before. If we were to do that, we'd have to get the church and hotel function room booked quickly. With his eager agreement, I made those arrangements that very week, in my quaint little town, all the while cautioning Gavin that we weren't actually engaged yet, not until he would ask me in person when I flew out for his twenty-ninth birthday at the end of the month. Silly, ridiculous; of course we were engaged; we were actively booking our wedding. But, perhaps not actually ridiculous.

The intangibles of sharing space, not even of touching but just of sharing the same air and temperature, of absorbing all of those background perceptions of traffic and noise or of quiet, of crowds or of space, of hills or flatness, of green or brown, of dry or wet, of the color of the light, and whether it's trees that are tall there or buildings, that sync people in ways that can't be quantified but are easily perceived. To be someplace together matters.

Which is a long way of saying that I'm glad I went to Pittsburgh.

As for this fresh, just-baked, still-warm closeness here at home, I take care with it. I try to notice and congratulate triumphs, to wish luck for trying new things, and to commiserate over the sadnesses of others. Their bad news and even tragedies aren't competition for my recent cares; they provide a welcome opportunity to trample those newly fallen box walls and keep them down for good. For the most part, we talk about simple, everyday things, because such things are legion, and they do matter.

So when I tell funny stories about Pittsburgh—about Aprill and me comparing the attractiveness of the attorneys, of Christine appearing before the hearing only when Dan went to the men's room, of me being crude to the defense attorney back in January— it's not a deflection, no more than it was when I'd made those sad nurses laugh in 1992. It's those British hot and cold taps all over again: every feeling has its own faucet, and sometimes they're all open at once, side by side, not mixing. Those nurses had been sorrowful over me; and they'd smiled at my ridiculous jokes. One nurse had turned and left the examination room suddenly, I think so that I wouldn't see her cry, when I, still in shock, had asked her why I was bleeding (until then I had understood such bleeding to be a sort of medieval myth). Then they had blushed at young, handsome, authoritative-yet-empathetic Bill when he'd charged in to take over. All of the feelings were and are real, all at the same time, the good and sweet ones just as much as the terrible ones, even if sometimes the good ones seem weak in comparison.

I miss John. I wonder if I would be more free with tears if I were in his office, with my feet tucked up, teasing him about not having a proper box of tissues to offer. I can't have been his only crying visitor. Maybe that explains it; maybe someone else had used them all up.

I see that Anna has a copy of John's first book (actually his doctoral thesis, which was subsequently published). I'd been intending to get one myself. She offers for me to take it, because it's not actually her copy, which she keeps elsewhere. This was John's own copy, she tells me, which she'd cleared out of his office.

I will eventually read it, but apart from its content it's a talisman to me. I carry it everywhere. I tell people who knew him that it's John's book, and they coo; then I tell them that it's John's own copy, and they gasp. We pass it around, flipping through the pages, which make a little rush of air like breath.

When we had first moved to Cambridge, eight years ago, one of the first local news stories I'd read was about three Chinese vases in the university's Fitzwilliam Museum that were shattered by a man who had tripped, possibly intentionally. It made such an impression on me that I referenced it in my first novel. The vases have since been reassembled, and my boys and I—when they were younger and less resistant to visiting museums—made a point of trying to find the thin lines where the pieces had been glued back together. The restorers had done a wonderful job of linking those hundreds of shards back into their original forms, and we'd had to squint and put our faces right up to the vases to find any traces of the breaks at all.

This reminds me of what a friend has advised me. She asked me how often I used to think about 1992 before last year's arrest. I answered with a manageable and far-less-distracting frequency than has been the case for this prosecution year. She then said: *That's where we need to help you get back to*. It's a kind thought, and probably a wise one, motivated by generosity and concern for my happiness,

but I bristled. I don't think I'm doing anything wrong to be thinking a lot about what's happened.

Ten days after my return from Pittsburgh, I find a more comfortable goal, through a chat with a stranger. One of the entertaining
things about Cambridge is that anyone you talk to is very likely to
be an expert in whatever it is that they do. This man is a restorer,
specializing in *kintsugi,* a Japanese method of fixing broken ceram-
ics. Unlike the restorers at the Fitzwilliam, who smoothly hid the
lines where the shards were joined, practitioners of this method
highlight the repair lines with gold, admitting to the object's past
shatters, incorporating the object's experience as part of its presen-
tation, and of its changing, growing, aging beauty.

Epilogue

Bill Valenta is the assistant dean of MBA and Executive Programs at Katz Business School at the University of Pittsburgh. After numerous delays, the drunk driver who killed his nephew pleaded guilty and was sentenced to two and a quarter to four and a half years in prison.

All of Detective Aprill Campbell's cold cases except for ours have skirted the Supreme Court decision unaffected, because the statutes of limitations for those other vulnerable cases had "tolled" when their defendants left the state while the cases were still active. After Arthur Fryar was released, Aprill stopped pulling unsolved case files out from basement storage. She wrote to me, "Maybe someday I will go back down there, but right now I can't because I care about how we made you and Georgia feel. The only people I want to hurt are the 'bad guys.'" In July 2015, she finished out twenty years with the Pittsburgh police and is now an investigator with the Pennsylvania attorney general's Computer Forensics Unit, working with the Child Predator Unit.

Detective Dan Honan continues to investigate Pittsburgh sex crimes, domestic violence, and child abuse. Christine's cancer is in remission.

Assistant District Attorney Evan Lowry is now married to Jessie, and he continues to prosecute rapists and child abusers. Assistant District Attorney Kevin Chernosky won a conviction in the cyanide case, with an obligatory sentence of life in prison for the defendant. He continues to prosecute murderers. The district attorney's office has a strict media policy that was triggered by this book, so we're not allowed to talk to each other anymore. That rule took at least Kevin by surprise and the silence fell suddenly and without explanation to me. I miss them.

I thought that Sam Centamore, who arrested Fryar in 1976 and helped put him away for seven years, would be pissed off that I'd been less than candid with him at first, but he was a peach about my confession of personal involvement in the Pittsburgh case. He wrote to me: "I could never understand over my 40 years of experience in law enforcement how we as a society and our law makers have not taken a much stronger stance on the prosecution and sentencing [of rapists] . . . New York state finally got it! There is no more statute of limitations for rape by forcible compulsion . . . Please live a peaceful and happy life. My thoughts are with you."

New York has done more than lift their statute of limitations. New York City cleared their rape kit backlog in 2003, and in 2014 Manhattan's district attorney turned $38 million from an asset forfeiture into a grant pool to help other jurisdictions clear their backlogs. In 2015, the federal government added $41 million to the same purpose. It's estimated that these combined funds could back the testing of as many as seventy thousand evidence kits nationwide.

Arthur Fryar is free. His DNA profile is in the FBI's CODIS database, and will be automatically compared to the results from any new or newly processed evidence from other crimes.

AFTERWORD

My mandate for myself while I was writing this book was to be "direct, vivid, and compassionate." It's an honest record of what I felt and did, not meant to define what others should feel or do. It's not meant as advice.

I'll put some advice here instead.

IF YOU'VE BEEN SEXUALLY ASSAULTED:

This should not have happened to you. You need and deserve support. Reach out, even if it's hard. The consequences of not reaching out are harder.

Discover who helps you. You may be surprised by which friends step up and in what ways. Be open to that surprise.

Figure out how you feel. There's no template for this; your feelings are your own. Think about what you want, even if it's something you can't have, or if your desires contradict each other. Just knowing what things you wish for is useful. Perhaps you can work toward a variation of them if not the ideal things themselves. If you can't do even that, you'll at least know specifically what you're grieving. That can be valuable just on its own.

Your body is important; seek medical help. Allow evidence to be collected, if you're in time for that. The experience is unpleasant but it will leave you options in the future. If you choose to make a police report, you deserve to be treated with respect and kindness. If you choose to pursue prosecution, value each step along the way, even just the act of standing up for yourself. You may not get a satisfying ending, but there can be value in what happens along the way.

If you feel that there is any chance of self-harm, seek help. If someone you turn to is not helpful, seek help elsewhere. Help is not everywhere, but it is somewhere.

IF YOU'RE SUPPORTING A FRIEND WHO'S HURTING:

There's no generic right way to help. The right way will be something you discover from knowing your friend, from observing your friend, from asking your friend. What they want from you may be different from what they want from someone else, depending on your specific relationship. Help requires listening, and accepting things that may be different from what you expect, or from what you want.

It's a wonderful thing to protect someone physically if you find yourself in a position to do that, but you will be much more often in the position to protect someone emotionally or psychologically. Protect people when they cautiously express feelings that embarrass them. Protect people when others say cruel or mocking things to or about them. Speak up. Be kind.

IF YOU'RE ANGRY ABOUT THE WAY THE LAW APPLIED IN THIS CASE OR OTHER CASES:

Violence is always a terrible thing. Violence can't make up for violence. Being kind to wounded people is more helpful than taking revenge on the people who hurt them.

You can't go back in time and make others do right things, but you can do right things yourself from this day on. First, do no harm.

As for actively doing good: Be a friend. Listen to those who are hurting. Consider volunteering with or contributing to groups that do good work. Support legislation that makes the system work better for those who come after. Use your vote to help the vulnerable.

Lastly, whether a victim will want to forgive someone who has brutalized them, and how such forgiveness would manifest in practical terms, is something each person must consider individually for themselves. But I do have a recommendation regarding another kind of forgiveness: victims, forgive your friends.

Some of your friends will likely hurt you, in tiny ways, in biggish ways, mostly accidentally, mostly in ignorance or misunderstanding or panic or self-protection. Maybe someone will hurt you in a way that is so significant that you have to step away; do so. But most of them will be trying to be kind; some of them failing but, yes, trying; or too frozen to actively try but in their hearts thinking kind thoughts that you wish they would actually say; or saying things that come out strange but are kindly meant. Forgive stumbling. Forgive awkwardness. Forgive when they make you ask for what you wish they would offer. Treasure those relationships. You'll need their forgiveness, too. We all need each other.

ACKNOWLEDGMENTS

Being both protagonist and author makes for a long list of thanks.

I'm deeply grateful for the support of Bill and Jane Valenta, Dan and Christine Honan, and Aprill-Noelle Campbell. It was kind of you to let me get to know you, and to let me write honestly about that. I appreciate your willingness to be in my story, both in the living of it and the publishing of it. I'm equally grateful to Evan and Jessie Lowry, and Kevin Chernosky. I wish I could thank you directly. Thanks also to Sam Centamore.

When I first started sharing my thoughts, I began with friends who write or are in the writing world, because I felt that they would be most able to understand the impulse to make a record of ugly and difficult things, and to see something perhaps lovely and good in these things being written well.

In New York, this was Randall Klein. We were no longer working together officially, but he will always be "my editor." Elsewhere in America, these were Carla Buckley and Mimi Cross.

Here in Cambridge, they were Sophie Hannah, Amanda Goodman, Kate Rhodes, and Allison Pearson. Sophie treated my writings as the start of a proper book from day one. Her practicality and praise made me smile, and helped me to eventually transition from living inside the story to living past it, connected to it by a different role.

David Carter and Nick Austin were the first of the choir parents to read it, and it's thanks to Nick's urging that I began to share with friends outside of writing circles. Many thanks to those who read along as it was happening: Ysanne Austin, Victoria Goodman, Melanie Hey, Maree Richards, Marianna Fletcher Williams, and Margaret White; Gina Holland, Morag Nevay, Laura Gerlach, Hannah Bekker Diller, and Ella Kennen; Anna Matthews, Steve Midgley, and Cindy Wesley; Amy Weatherup and Sarah McQuay; Delya Stoltz, Tom Paquette; Matt Miller, Allison Metcalf Allen, and Melissa Bell Lusher. Your understanding and encouragement were meaningful, and in some ways shaped the telling.

I finished the last chapter a week after returning from Pittsburgh, on Halloween night, just home from trick-or-treating. From then, both Randall and my agent, Cameron McClure, gave concise editorial comments. By Christmas, what had started as a diary was a manuscript. I'm grateful to Cameron for putting our friendship first and making me convince her that I really wanted this published. Once she was confident of my intentions, she worked fiercely to make that happen.

For early legal guidance, thanks to Louis Smoller and Jonathan Lyons at Savur Threadgold. Also to Paula Kautt, criminologist, for corrections and comments. I have done my best with their helpful advice.

Thanks to Deb Brody at William Morrow for sensitive and wise editorial comments and to publicist Danielle Bartlett for her creativity and enthusiasm. From our first conversation onward it has been a pleasure. Thanks also to the team at Harper360 who are bringing the book to my overseas home and beyond.

Thanks to those friends who read *Jane Doe January* in the manuscript stage with such kind responses: Mark Williams, Ian White, Nick Widdows, Rebecca Fitzgerald, Mary Laven, Jason Scott-Warren, Clare Bantry Flook, and Janet Hughes; Kali Rocha, Angel Rocha, Bradley Dean, John Hollywood, and Rik Nagel; Brenda Harger, Gary Harger, Joanne Spence, and Michael Fuller; Alexander Finlayson; Helen Orr and Nick Moir; and Kate Miciak.

Thanks to talented and wise colleagues, without whom writing would be lonely: Melanie Benjamin, Lisa Gardner, Eliza Graham, Julia Heaberlin, Allison Leotta, Jamie Mason, Brad Parks, Kristina Riggle, and Amanda Kyle Williams. I needed that expanded support as I approached publishing.

There are a few who did not read the manuscript who were nonetheless very present. Thanks to Sarah Dane, Matt Wise, and Jennifer Fields for sharing grief, and to Alice Kane, not just for listening but for always asking.

Throughout all of this, Gavin's confidence, patience, generosity, and affection were my steady foundation. Thank you for going through it with me.

ABOUT THE AUTHOR

Emily Winslow is an American living in Cambridge, England. She's the author of the novels *The Whole World, The Start of Everything,* and *The Red House.*

http://www.emilywinslow.com